The Politics of the Labour Party

The Politics of the Labour Party

Edited by
DENNIS KAVANAGH
University of Nottingham

London
GEORGE ALLEN & UNWIN
Boston Sydney

George Allen & Unwin (Publishers) Ltd,
40 Museum Street, London WC1A 1LU, UK

George Allen & Unwin (Publishers) Ltd,
Park Lane, Hemel Hempstead, Herts HP2 4TE, UK

Allen & Unwin, Inc.,
9 Winchester Terrace, Winchester, Mass. 01890, USA

George Allen & Unwin Australia Pty Ltd,
8 Napier Street, North Sydney, NSW 2060, Australia

First published in 1982.

British Library Cataloguing in Publication Data

The Politics of the Labour Party.
1. Labour Party (Great Britain)
I. Kavanagh, Dennis
324.24107 JN1129.L3
ISBN 0-04-329037-X
ISBN 0-04-329038-8 Pbk

Library of Congress Cataloging in Publication Data

Main entry under title:
The Politics of the Labour Party.
"Selection from papers which were originally presented at a conference . . . at Nuffield College, Oxford, in September 1980" – Pref.
Includes index.
Contents: Introduction/by Dennis Kavanagh – The Labour Party and the electorate/by Ivor Crewe – Changing styles of Labour leadership/by Philip Williams – [etc.]
1. Labour Party (Great Britain) – Congresses.
2. Great Britain – Politics and government – 1945– – Congresses.
I. Kavanagh, Dennis.
JN1129.L33 1982 324.24107 81-22803
ISBN 0-04-329037-X AACR2
ISBN 0-04-329038-8 (pbk).

Set in 11 on 11 point Times by
Performance Typesetting Ltd, Milton Keynes
and printed in Great Britain
by Biddles Ltd, Guildford, Surrey

Dedicated to the memory of
Robert T. McKenzie
1917–1981

List of Contributors

Hugh Berrington, *Professor of Politics, University of Newcastle upon Tyne*

Ivor Crewe, *Director, Social Science Research Archive and British Election Study, University of Essex*

Colin Crouch, *Reader in Sociology, The London School of Economics and Political Science*

Dennis Kavanagh, *Professor of Politics, Nottingham University*

Robert McKenzie, *Professor of Political Sociology, London School of Economics (until his death in 1981)*

L. J. Sharpe, *Fellow of Nuffield College, Oxford University*

Philip Williams, *Fellow of Nuffield College, Oxford University*

Paul Whiteley, *Lecturer in Politics, Bristol University*

Contents

List of Contributors *page* viii
Preface xi
Introduction *by Dennis Kavanagh* 1
1 The Labour Party and the Electorate *by Ivor Crewe* 9
2 Changing Styles of Labour Leadership *by Philip Williams* 50
3 The Labour Left in Parliament: Maintenance, Erosion and Renewal *by Hugh Berrington* 69
4 Still the Workers' Party? Changing Social Trends in Elite Recruitment and Electoral Support *by Dennis Kavanagh* 95
5 The Decline of Labour's Local Party Membership and Electoral Base, 1945–79 *by Paul Whiteley* 111
6 The Labour Party and the Grography of Inequality: a Puzzle *by L. J. Shapre* 135
7 The Peculiar Relationship: the Party and the Unions *by Colin Crouch* 171
8 Power in the Labour Party: the Issue of 'Intra-Party Democracy' *by Robert McKenzie* 191
9 Representation in the Labour Party *by Dennis Kavanagh* 202
Index 223

Preface

These chapters are a selection from papers which were originally presented at a conference on *The Politics of the Labour Party* at Nuffield College, Oxford, in September 1980. The papers were then revised for publication during 1981. Other papers, presented at the conference but not published in this volume, were read by David Butler on 'Labour and Europe', Patrick Seyd on 'Labour and the left in the 1970s', David Lipsey on 'Labour's left and right' and Bernard Crick on 'Labour and the intellectuals'. A small grant from the SSRC helped to meet the costs of organising the conference. Like many other students of politics I am happy to acknowledge the generous support of the Council and the hospitality provided by Nuffield College.

This book is dedicated to the memory of Robert McKenzie, Professor of Political Sociology at the London School of Economics. He was both famous and admired as a student of British political parties and as a television broadcaster. Bob had been a lively and disputatious participant in our conference. His sudden death in October 1981 came as a great shock to his fellow-contributors. Bob faced many demands on his time and the editor had to cajole him to submit his manuscript on time. I am proud that I pursued him and delighted to carry his last published word on the Labour Party.

Dennis Kavanagh

Introduction

DENNIS KAVANAGH

It is difficult to think of any other major Western political party whose internal travails have been so closely and publicly scrutinised as have those of the British Labour Party in recent years. A split or collapse of Labour has been prognosticated too often before to permit ready acceptance of the latest post-mortems. Yet the recent spate of changes in its constitution, the formation of the SDP and the adoption of particular policies, do bid fair to transform the party. The leaders of the SDP were, until recently, major right-wing figures in the Labour Party. The ground is shifting under Labour and indeed under the British Party System. This uncertain background may or may not make it a suitable time to present a set of essays on the Labour Party.

These chapters were originally presented at a conference in September 1980 and rewritten for publication over the following three months. Contributors were not specifically asked to look at the contemporary problems of the party. With such a changing situation, whatever was written ran the risk of soon being out of date. Instead they were invited to look at certain themes, or topics, which had been and would remain of longer-term significance. The chapters are not presented as the 'last word' on contemporary disputes, whose consequences are still unfolding. But they should, it is hoped, promote an understanding of the context in which they have occurred and will develop.

No common viewpoint was suggested at the outset to the contributors, and one did not emerge out of our conference. We were not primarily concerned with the question – Whither Labour? There was and has been no shortage of published views on that subject. And we were not seeking a 'balance' between different political standpoints within and outside the Labour Party. One thing the ample literature on the party does not lack is partisanship and commitment to one view or another. The Labour Party and its leaders have, literally speaking, had their 'own' journalists, historians, biographers and political scientists, and this has had its expected strengths and weaknesses. Instead, we sought scholars who could write on such topics as leadership, factions, and electoral behaviour, in a reasonably detached scholarly manner, as they would on other subjects. No doubt some discerning readers will still label particular contributions as 'left' or 'right'. But that is a problem that faces students of the party as well as its members.

The theme underlying these essays is that of change. The charge made by those departing for the Social Democrats is that the Labour Party is no longer the party they joined twenty years ago. Whether this is progress or decline depends on one's perspective. Many of the assumptions of social democracy, eloquently stated in Anthony Crosland's *The Future of Socialism* (1956), are now in retreat. These include, particularly, the confidence that the mixed economy was working well, and the expectation of economic growth sufficient to make redistribution and the growth of public expenditure relatively painless. Instead, governments have experienced a tax resistance as income tax and insurance deductions have bitten into the average worker's pay packet. The 1970s have witnessed the development of levels of unemployment and inflation that would have been considered politically unthinkable only a few years ago. Successive Labour governments' ambitions in the fields of social reform and welfare provision have been frustrated as efforts to set an ailing economy right took priority. The Labour government's growth record between 1964 and 1970 was 'lamentable', to quote Crosland, and was even worse during the recession years after 1974. There have been growing doubts about the usefulness of many traditional Labour assumptions – about state ownership, central planning, greater public expenditure, social engineering and the consent and co-operation of the trade unions. And this against a background of growing doubt about the effectiveness of Britain's political institutions, continuous relative economic decline, and lack of confidence in the ability of government to cope with problems. Since 1964 these challenges have coincided with two other political changes. First, there have been regular periods of Labour government, making the party appear as 'the national party of government', together with an upsurge of dissatisfaction and disappointment with the record. Secondly, there has been a sharp shift to the left in the extra-parliamentary party, and a heightening of the divisions in the party.

Ivor Crewe in 'The Labour Party and the Electorate' reminds us of the scale of the party's decline in electoral support. In 1979 Labour gained 36·9 per cent of the vote (23 per cent of the total electorate), its lowest share for nearly fifty years. This was the third successive election in which the party has gained less than 40 per cent of the vote. Labour seems to be in secular electoral decline; at each election since 1951, except for 1966, a further slice of the electorate has turned away from the party. The fall-off in support has been most marked among the working class, of which only 48 per cent voted Labour in 1979. More devastating are Crewe's findings about how out of touch the party is with the electorate and with many Labour voters. Many policies favoured by the left (public ownership, extension of trade union rights, unilateralism) or by the right (incomes policy, help for racial minorities and a constructive role in the EEC) are rejected by most Labour voters. Even on many issues on which the party is more united, the electorate remains hostile. It is surprising that the party, wedded to unpopular policies, has managed to win elections. A difficulty for the party that stands for (*a*) a redistribution of power and wealth and (*b*) the interests of the working class is that most redistributive policies now favour some sections of the working class at the expense of others. Labour's problem is to find policies on which it is united and which appeal broadly to the working class. Economic success, something that has eluded so many postwar British governments, is Crewe's recommendation for recapturing voters.

Philip Williams, the author of the definitive biography of Hugh Gaitskell, is well qualified to write about the changing styles of political leadership in the party. The party ethos, a compound of egalitarianism, collective decision-making and rejection of deference and elitism, has downgraded the role of the leader and of leadership. Yet the actions and personalities of leaders (from MacDonald in 1931 to Callaghan in 1979) have created controversy and myths, and given rise to many 'if onlys'. Williams shows the persisting difficulties that leaders have found in reconciling the idea of intra-party democracy with the hard realities of parliamentary and electoral politics and the responsibility of government. Conflicting goals and the need to keep 'the broad church' intact have meant that Labour leaders have more often been 'stabilisers' than 'pathfinders'. Attlee and Callaghan fit the first type, Gaitskell fits the second.

The difficulties of Labour leaders have become more acute not only because Britain has probably become more difficult to govern over the past twenty years, but also because Labour has been in office for most of the period. A party structure and an ethos largely developed before the party assumed office have added to the strains. The tasks of party management involve bargaining with trade union leaders and faction leaders, and appeasing or countering rivals who are sheltered in the party's federal structure. The recent constitutional reforms are only likely to add to the difficulties.

The Labour Party has long been fertile ground for factions. In some other West European countries the political left is divided between socialists or social democrats, and communists. The ability of these tendencies to coexist in the Labour coalition (or 'broad church') has been a strength. But the groups have appeared to be more incompatible in recent years – both have been dissatisfied with the results, and the electorate has been deprived of the option of voting for a clearly left or a clearly social democratic alternative. For the past decade the left has dominated the extra-parliamentary arm of the party, and the right has dominated the PLP. One has to avoid oversimplification here. Many issues do not lend themselves to easy left and right divisions and many MPs rightly refuse to assign themselves to such classification. The separate centres of power have, in a way, institutionalised the factionalism. One factor that shaped the relative influence of the centres was the party's proximity to or occupancy of office. Out of government the party developed an opposition mentality, a liking for 'resolutionary socialism'. In government the restraints of the situation and exposure to other viewpoints sometimes meant that policy priorities shifted. Hence the gap between Labour promise in opposition and performance in office. The recent constitutional reforms should have the effect of ending that compromise and diminishing the autonomy of the PLP and a Labour government *vis-à-vis* Conference and the NEC. How significant the exodus of right-wingers from the party will prove to be and how it will affect the prospects for a realignment of the party system remains to be seen.

Hugh Berrington's painstaking study of Early Day Motions (motions tabled and signed by MPs) shows how the factional balance in the PLP between left and right has altered over the past twenty years. Change may occur as a result of a member's *experience* in the Commons, of *the pattern of replacements* by new MPs of those who retire or die, or of *alterations*, through differential gains and losses in the factions at general elections. Berrington shows how the left has gained disproportionately in the party's general election victories, and lost some – though less than expected – ground when Labour is defeated. The left has also gained through its replacement of a number of right-wingers in safe seats. For example, the heavy losses of Tribune MPs in the 1979 election were largely compensated by left-wing replacements for retiring right-wing MPs. The author notes: 'The flow of the tide carries the left forward, but the ebb takes the left back only a little way.' For the next few years, whether Labour wins or loses elections, the left is well entrenched and likely to profit further from the redrawing of constituency boundaries and mandatory reselection.

Kavanagh notes the smaller proportion of the working class which now votes Labour, the increasingly middle-class composition of the MPs and the NEC, and asks if Labour is 'still the workers' party' in Chapter 4. There has been an embourgeoisement of the PLP in the sense (*a*) of more MPs coming from middle-class social backgrounds and (*b*) MPs from working-class backgrounds achieving social mobility, often through attendance at university, before entering Parliament. The MPs are largely drawn from a particular segment of the graduate middle class, from the professions in the state sector, particularly education. The change may be regretted by those who think that a party's MPs should be socially representative of its voters. However, it is difficult to demonstrate – though it is often claimed – that there is a link between the change in social composition and de-radicalisation (if there has been any) among the PLP.

Although there are no reliable figures for individual membership of the Labour Party, there seems no doubt that there has been a sharp decline compared with the mid-1960s. Labour is hardly a mass party today. Paul Whiteley's statistical analysis in Chapter 5 shows how the decline in members and votes has occurred over a number of years and how it correlates with the poor economic record of Labour governments. His survey of activists shows the importance of instrumental reasons for joining the party. Such members come largely from the working class, are more concerned about the performance of Labour governments, and are the most likely to be disappointed and to leave. In contrast, members who join for more expressive and ideological motives are less likely to leave. If this analysis is accurate, then the smaller membership is likely to be more ideological, largely because of the selective pattern of withdrawals over the years. But what of the claim that the policies favoured by the activists will alienate voters and that, therefore, their influence should only be a modest one? Whiteley's view (cf. Crewe) is that if the left-wing policies (planning, public ownership, import controls, withdrawal from the EEC) were tried and succeeded, then they might become more popular with voters; after all, he claims, the revisionist policies, over the years, have been tried and failed.

Sharpe's Chapter 6, on the 'geography of inequality', tackles another puzzle. How is it that the party, so committed to combating inequality, ignores the imbalance in wealth and influence between London and the south-east on the one hand, and the periphery on the other? Historically, Labour has regarded a centralisation of power as the first step towards redressing inequalities – which are viewed in terms of social class rather than regional differences. These would be tackled by action from above and from the centre in the form of a Labour government. A striking feature is that the party's electoral strength is now so unevenly concentrated in the country; Labour holds some two-thirds of seats in Scotland, Wales and the northern region, and only a handful of seats in the south-east, outside London.

Labour's traditional view has been that a socialist central government would have no problem in guiding local authorities in the direction it chose. But Conservative governments have used the central powers to block policy developments by Labour local authorities (e.g. the 1972 Housing Finance Act, or Mr Heseltine's use of the rate support grant and local budget expenditure guidelines in 1980–81). Sharpe argues that more decentralisation might release more local socialist initiatives. Decentralisation, smaller units of decision-making and self-management are now in fashion, in part as a reaction to state-managed socialism and bureaucracy. But the author is appropriately sceptical about Labour's latter-day decentralism, as evidenced in the opportunistic handling of devolution for Scotland and Wales in 1978–9.

Sharpe then proceeds to explain the various structural and ideological considerations that have inhibited this strand of thinking in the party. Labour has certainly embraced the 'top down' model of British politics encapsulated in parliamentary supremacy, ministerial responsibility and control from Whitehall. The trade unions, as national organisations, have also been primarily concerned with making national bargains over wages and conditions of employment. These tendencies are expressed in what Sharpe calls a bourgeois model of a political party. According to this view, the main task of the party in the country and of the constituency parties is to sustain the PLP. The security of MPs and the restriction of the party leadership to MPs reflect this centralised view of party organisation. Again, the constitutional changes achieved in 1980–81, promise or threaten to overturn a long tradition of Labour politics.

The Labour 'movement' has political and industrial wings. Traditionally, the party's alliance with the unions flourished as the two kept to their respective separate spheres of interest, one political, the other industrial. In recent years, however, Labour governments have transgressed the border by trying to reform industrial relations in 1969 and, persistently, seeking incomes restraint. In office, ministers have shown their disbelief that free collective bargaining is compatible with full employment or the attack on inflation. Colin Crouch views the relationship as 'peculiar' (Chapter 7), because of the party's dependence on the unions. As an organisation (in terms of money and individual members) the party is weak. The trade unions are important on both counts, as well as in the policy-making bodies of Conference and the NEC. This dependence is a product of history, almost unique to Britain, and Crouch wonders if the security the relationship provided has removed the incentives for Labour to become a genuinely mass party.

Crouch does not doubt the necessity for a link between the party and the unions. Yet he raises a number of questions about the advantages to both sides from the relationship as presently constituted. The main growth for unions recently has been in the non-manual and public sectors and these unions have little of the older unions' historic attachment to the Labour Party. The more successful periods of Labour government have tended to coincide with a strong centre in the TUC; the decentralisation of power within the unions has strained the relationship between the party and union leadership. How do governments and trade union leaders cope with the new shop-floor power and why should governments try to negotiate with weak national union leaderships? Certainly the structure is ill-suited to the corporatist, social contract relationships favoured by Labour governments.

Dick Crossman once claimed that working the party's constitution, as it was originally intended, was 'impossible'. The late Robert McKenzie shared this view and here he discusses the potential incompatibility between intra-party democracy and parliamentary democracy. He claims that, if taken literally, the former concept would supersede Parliament. For most of its history, particularly when in office, Labour has been a 'living lie', ignoring or downgrading the constitutional claims of the party outside Parliament, simply because they are impractical under our parliamentary system. He claims, controversially, that while democracy in groups may be useful for democracy in society, its practice within political parties is dysfunctional for democracy in the political system. Recent constitutional developments have shifted the party decisively in the direction of 'activist democracy'. It will be interesting to see the extent to which McKenzie's claims, advanced in his *British Political Parties*, about the autonomy of the parliamentary system still stand in a future Labour government.

In spite of all the studies of democracy in the party and the rival claims about where power lies, there has been little examination of the theory and practice of representation in the party. Does the shift of power to the trade unions and constituency activists actually make the party more 'democratic', more 'representative', as it is so often alleged? This is the theme of the final chapter, 'Representation in the Labour Party'. Labour's steadfast rejection of the principle of one man one vote, the refusal to reform the block vote system at Conference and the commitment to delegatory democracy have led to anomalies redolent of an eighteenth-century Parliament. In his conclusion Kavanagh points to the potential tensions between greater representativeness and greater participation within an organisation. Greater influence for the participants may be a good thing, but whether or not it ensures more representative outcomes depends on the representativeness of the participants. In many respects the tensions between the two ideals and the tenuous connection which the constitutional changes actually have with democracy and representation, have been exposed during the elections for the deputy leadership in 1981.

1 The Labour Party and the Electorate

IVOR CREWE

Those are not the policies with which to win the next general election. The Labour Party needs a socialist policy, and not the tired worn-out social democratic policy that led to our defeat in 1979.

(Arthur Scargill on James Callaghan's speech to the TUC, as reported in *The Times*, 3 September 1980)

Some Yorkshire miners are ignoring their union's policy and paying £150 for hernia operations at a private clinic. They are paying for private medicine rather than wait for two years for the operation on the National Health Service.

An official of the National Union of Mineworkers at Barnsley said: 'It does not surprise me. While the union's stand would be against private medicine, obviously our members are free to choose. A man earning top money in the pits would regard the £150 as a drop in the ocean if it meant he could get back to work quickly and not lose pay.'

('Yorkshire miners choose private clinic', *The Times*, 6 September 1980)

Exactly twenty years ago, in the aftermath of Labour's decisive defeat at the 1959 general election – its third in succession – Mark Abrams, Richard Rose and Rita Hinden wrote a lengthy post-mortem called *Must Labour Lose?*[1] The answer they gave was: probably. Their pessimism was founded on three interconnected arguments. First, the sheer size of the working-class base on which Labour had traditionally relied was gradually contracting. Labour-intensive heavy industry was in decline; capital-intensive light industry and the service sector were expanding. More and more voters were changing their boiler suits for white collars. Secondly, working-class standards of living had markedly improved: a decade of economic growth, full employment, slum clearance, widening educational opportunities and mass production of cheap consumer durables (especially cars and televisions) had left its mark. With middle-class standards of living, it was inferred, went middle-class values – and voting patterns. Thirdly, as a result, Labour's traditional 'cloth-cap' image and policies, notably public ownership, were losing appeal. The only way to avoid yet another election defeat was to catch up with the times and become a cross-class party committed to maintaining, rather than abolishing, the mixed economy that had worked so well in the 1950s.

It is tempting to dismiss the book as a historical memento. Academic research has since provided strong evidence that a rise in working-class living standards does not necessarily lead to Conservative voting.[2] And anyway, the affluence of the 1950s gave way to the stagnation of the 1960s and the apparent decline of the 1970s. More compelling still, in the two decades that have elapsed since the book's publication Labour has won four of the six general elections and occupied office for longer than the Conservatives. Yet Labour's defeat in May 1979 prompts a return to the issues raised twenty years earlier. This is not simply because the defeat was a serious one – more so than is usually realised – but for two additional reasons. First, the cause of Labour's downfall was close to that predicted by Abrams and his colleagues: the party's desertion by working-class voters out of sympathy with its policies. And secondly, the 1979 election, far from being yet another swing of the electoral pendulum, marked a further stage in what has turned out to be, despite the four election 'victories' under Harold Wilson, a long-term erosion of support. It is right that one should once again ask: must Labour lose?

The last general election marked the most emphatic rejection of the Labour Party for almost half a century. Not since its débâcle of 1931 had Labour suffered such an adverse swing or seen its share of the vote (at 36·9 per cent) or of the electorate as a whole (at 28·0 per cent) fall so low. Only the malapportionment of constituency electorates and the below-average swing in Labour marginals prevented a Conservative parliamentary landslide of 1959 proportions. As it was, Labour was virtually wiped out as a parliamentary force in the south (outside London) and in rural and small-town Britain (outside mining areas).

The Labour Party also took a severe knock as the parliamentary representative of the working class. The consistent findings of three separate large-scale surveys[3] leave little doubt that the heaviest desertion from Labour occurred among manual rather than non-manual workers, especially among the younger generation and skilled workers. (This was reflected in the above-average and sometimes unprecedented anti-Labour swings in such high-wage working-class areas as the new towns, the Lancashire and Yorkshire coalfields and the car-worker suburbs.) The large majority of Labour voters were, as in all elections, manual workers; but by 1979 this ceased to be true. The large majority of manual workers

(63 per cent) did not turn out to vote Labour; indeed, even among manual workers who voted, the majority of their ballots (52 per cent) were cast for non-Labour candidates. From this perspective Labour had moved some distance from being *the* party, as opposed to *a* party, of the working class.

Although this chapter's focus will be the last two decades, it is worth dwelling initially on the main reasons for Labour's defeat in 1979. Here I must summarise drastically the results of detailed analyses to be published elsewhere.[4] First, Labour did not lose because of such 'undemocratic' factors as inferior organisation, poorer funding, or defective public relations. The survey evidence shows that the coverage and impact of convassers, advertising and television broadcasts gave only a trace of an advantage to the Conservatives. (The effect of the press is, of course, another matter; but to attribute to it major responsibility for Labour's defeat one would have to show that the press was significantly *more* anti-Labour in 1979 than in 1974.) And it did not lose through the relative appeal of the party leaders: the polls consistently showed Mr Callaghan to be more popular than Mrs Thatcher, and to be drawing further ahead as the campaign progressed. Nor did Labour lose as a result of last-minute incidents: there was nothing comparable to the Enoch Powell speeches or embarrassing statistics of the 1970 and February 1974 campaigns. On the contrary, the 1979 election was unusual for its sober uneventfulness, and for the clarity of choice offered to voters. Labour lost, in fact, for the most obvious and proper of reasons: partly on its record, but mainly on the policies and objectives of the Conservative Party.

Secondly, as already mentioned, Labour lost through the desertion of its working-class supporters: the swing was 10–11 per cent among skilled workers, and as high as 16 per cent among younger working-class men. These deserters did not stay at home, moreover, but in the main switched right over to the Conservatives. A replication for October 1974 to 1979 of the kind of calibrated vote-turnover table that was a feature of *Political Change in Britain*[5] shows that 'differential abstention' had a negligible impact. The main components of the anti-Labour swing were, in order of importance, straight conversion from Labour to Conservative, and movement to and from the Liberals (especially October 1974 Liberals reverting to their original Conservative loyalties). Thus the best summary answer to the question 'Why did Labour lose, and lose so badly?' would be: because, after a long and serious campaign, large sectors of the working class regarded Conservative policies and objectives as being more in line with their own interests and values.

One should be wary, of course, of exaggerating the significance of a single election result, however dramatic. Strictly temporary factors such as the preceding winter's strikes and the inevitable disillusion with an outgoing government explain part of the result. After all, at the previous election Conservative support had dipped to its lowest level since 1906 and to third place among young voters and in Scotland; yet the doleful prognostications of the time turned out largely to be unfounded. None the less, for reasons this chapter will reveal, the two cases are not exactly parallel. As I have argued elsewhere,[6] the Conservatives' low stock in 1974 could be attributed to the combination of an increasingly fickle electorate and short-term forces *alone*. But the placing of the 1979 results in a long-term and comparative context does suggest a more enduring basis to Labour's electoral decline.

This can be illustrated in various ways. First, as Table 1.1 shows, 1979 marks a further stage in what transpires to be a *quarter-century's* almost unremitting erosion of Labour support. At every election since 1951, with only one exception (1966), an additional slice of the electorate has stopped voting Labour; added together the slices amount to a loss of almost a third of Labour's support between 1951 and 1979. It is easy to forget that in 1964 Harold Wilson rode to power on a smaller share of the electorate than Hugh Gaitskell obtained five years earlier; and that although Labour twice won office (just) in 1974 it did so by electoral default. Labour's loss of votes in February 1974 was, I believe, particularly significant, for at the time Labour was not simply out of office but in opposition to an unpopular and unsuccessful government which was attacking the prerogatives of Labour's traditional constituencies – trade unionists and council house tenants. Analysis of the four-election vote flow from 1970 to 1979 shows that, in contrast to the Conservatives, Labour has so far failed to recapture more than a minority of its 1974 deserters to the Liberals (see Table 1.2).

Secondly, Labour's falling vote has occurred despite earlier predictions that time and demography were on its side. In the late 1960s Butler and Stokes suggested, albeit tentatively, that Labour would become the net beneficiary of three demographic processes: (1) the dying out of those who had first entered the electorate before 1918 and thus had been socialised into partisanship before Labour became a serious contender for power; (2) narrowing class differences in longevity; (3) the greater fertility of manual than non-manual women (combined with the fact that party allegiance tends to be bequeathed from parents to children). All three of these demographic processes have occurred (although class differences in fertility are narrower than originally envisaged), yet Labour's share of the vote was lower in 1979 than exactly fifty years earlier. One might also have expected Labour to profit from the near-disappearance of two purported sources of Conservative support in the 1950s and early 1960s: social deference and 'affluence' – the common experience and expectation of constantly rising living standards.

Thirdly, electoral decline for the moderate left on this scale is unique to

Britain. Among European countries since the war not even the faltering position of the Danish Social Democrats bears any resemblance to it. It is true that, with the exception of the German SDP, social democratic parties have been in retreat throughout the West in the 1970s. However, by the late 1970s there were only three European democracies – Belgium, Eire and Switzerland – with a smaller 'combined-left' vote (Social Democrat/Labour plus parties to the left) than that in Britain.[7]

Table 1.1 *Labour's Share of the Great Britain Electorate, 1950–79*

1950	39·3	1964	34·6	February 1974	30·0
1951	40·8	1966	37·2	October 1974	29·3
1955	36·4	1970	31·6	1979	28·7
1959	35·3				

Note: These figures are based on the registered electorate of Great Britain (i.e. Northern Ireland is excluded), which will have included people who died, emigrated, or moved out of their constituency by the time the elections took place. Adjustment for the age of the register at the time of the elections would raise the figures (by 4 per cent on average) but not alter the direction or magnitude of the trend. No adjustment is made for changes in the number of Liberal and other minor party candidates.

Table 1.2 *The 1979 Vote of Major Party Defectors to the Liberals between 1970 and February 1974*

1970 vote	Con.	Lab.
Feb. 1974 vote	Lib.	Lib.
Vote in 1979	%	%
Con.	55	17
Lib.	30	33
Lab.	–	39
Other/did not vote	15	11
	100	100

Source: British Election Study Feb. 1974, Oct. 1974, May 1979 panel.

And fourthly, at the risk of reading too much into the present, one cannot actively ignore the recent local elections, by-elections and polls. They suggest that, by 1980 at least, Labour had done no more than recover the ground it lost after October 1974 – if that. Except in Southend East (where the local factors were unusual), parliamentary and GLC by-elections had registered low anti-government swings of under 5 per cent. The two-party swing to Labour from the 1979 general election to the 1980 local elections was lower than that for 1970–1[8] and Labour's lead in the monthly polls of 1980 (Gallup) averaged 5·7 per cent compared with 8·3 per cent in 1971. Moreover, in 1971 the economy was in considerably better shape than in 1980 and Labour was then advancing from a higher base. At a time of raging slumpflation the evidence hardly points to a major reversal of Labour's declining fortunes.

There is one other aspect to Labour's electoral decline: the asymmetry in the two major parties' electoral vulnerability in periods of unpopularity. This manifests itself in various ways. The anti-government swing in local elections, by-elections and the opinion polls tends to be sharper in Labour than Conservative periods of office; dissatisfied Labour supporters are more prone than dissatisfied Conservatives to switch right over to the other major party (rather than voting Liberal as a 'safe' protest); Liberal voters usually see themselves as slightly closer to the Conservative than the Labour Party; Conservative voters are more hostile to the Labour Party than Labour voters are to the Conservative Party.[9] No doubt the bias of the press and the anti-socialist cast to the 'political culture' are part of the explanation; but the trend figures that appear later in this chapter will shed further light on the matter.

Enduring trends do not necessarily arise from enduring causes; Labour's persistently falling vote could be the accumulated result of a series of various temporary factors which happen always to have worked to its disadvantage. James Alt has shown that much of the two-party swing at any one election can be accounted for by the electorate's judgement of the economic record of the party in office, partially discounted by its judgement of the future economic performance of both parties.[10] But whether such a formula would successfully cope with the 1979 result is not certain; for both the BBC and British Election Study (BES) surveys suggest that it was on its record of industrial relations, and *not* prices, unemployment, living standards, or the economy in general, that Labour lost votes. Moreover, explanations of this sort, which rely on short-term forces only, leave important questions unanswered. For example, why has Labour lost support not only after a period in office, but also when in opposition, notably in February 1974, but also in the 1950s? Why has the fall in the Labour vote been sharper and more persisting than the fall in the Conservative vote? And, more important, why has the swing between the two major parties remained relatively low, given the incontrovertible failure of successive governments to halt Britain's economic and international decline? Why have postwar elections not resulted in consecutive landslides and/or sustained major breakthroughs for the Liberals and Nationalists?

The answer is that deeply held attachments to the two main parties do still exist. They sustain the loyalties of most of a party's supporters in times of doubt or disillusion, and thus protect the party from the full electoral consequences of a spell of unpopular government. They underpin the stability of the party system by breaking the amplitude of swing and placing obstacles in the path of flash parties. But as I have documented elsewhere,[11] the early 1970s witnessed a decline in such attachments – which was *not* reversed in 1979 – leaving more room for self-interested voting subject to short-term forces. (This is a probable reason for the gradual growth in the volatility and heterogeneity of electoral change in Britain.) And although the decline affected both parties I would argue that it has been more serious for the Labour Party; hence the sharper fall in its vote and its greater vulnerability in times of unpopularity.

Simplifying radically, I shall distinguish between three sources of enduring party attachments: psychological, social and ideological. By 'psychological' I refer to the attachments induced by family upbringing and neighbourhood tradition, reinforced by processes of selective perception over the elector's lifetime. By 'social' I refer to the attachment engendered by an elector's sense of belonging (or not belonging) to a social 'group' whose interests are seen as being represented by the party. And by 'ideological' I refer to the attachment produced by an affinity between the elector's opinions and values on the one hand and the party's policies and objectives on the other. I shall examine each of these in turn.

Psychological Sources Of Labour Partisanship

In this section I shall mainly refer to trends in the incidence and intensity of 'identification' with the Labour Party, as measured by the two questions 'Generally speaking, do you usually think of yourself as Conservative, Labour, Liberal, or what?', followed by 'And how strongly (Conservative/Liberal/Labour, etc.) do you generally feel?'[12] This standard measure has proved an excellent indicator of many aspects of partisan behaviour in Britain (and 'travels' well abroad); in particular, strength of party identification is a consistently reliable *predictor* of future turnout and electoral loyalty.

Table 1.3 reveals that the incidence of Labour identification has fallen by only 5 per cent since 1964; this is the same as Labour's declining share of the electorate over the same period, although less than its fall in

Table 1.3 *The Level and Strength of Labour Party Identification, 1964–79*

	1964	*1966*	*1970*	*Feb. and Oct. 1974 (average)*	*1979*	*Change, 1964–79*
% electors with Labour identification	43	46	42	40	38	−5
% electors with 'very strong' Labour identification	19	23	20	15	10	−9
% of Labour partisans whose identification is:						
very strong	45	50	47	37	27	−18
fairly strong	43	41	40	44	50	+7
not very strong	12	9	13	19	23	+11
Mean partisan strength*	2·33	2·41	2·34	2·18	2·04	−0·29

* Respondents were scored 3 for a 'very strong', 2 for a 'fairly strong' and 1 for a 'not very strong' identification.
Sources: 1964, 1966, 1970: Butler and Stokes Election surveys; Feb. 1974, Oct. 1974, 1979: British Election Study cross-section surveys.

the share of the vote (8 per cent). By 1979, for the first time since data were collected in 1963, the electorate contained a fraction more Conservative than Labour identifiers (40 to 38 per cent). The 5 per cent figure is a net loss, of course, and masks larger movements to and from Labour; moreover, as we shall see later, the net change within social classes has been larger – in both directions. None the less, the gentleness of Labour's downward slide is testimony to the glacially slow rate at which a major party in Britain is finally abandoned by the electorate. Labour has retained a sizeable base from which to recover, and prophecies of doom are clearly premature.

The trend in strength of party identification makes gloomier news for the Labour Party. One might have assumed that with the contraction of Labour identifiers would come consolidation; but the electoral forces that have led small numbers to abandon the Labour Party altogether have led larger numbers at least to distance themselves from it. In 1964 'very strong' identifiers made up 45 per cent of all Labour partisans; by 1979 they made up only 27 per cent. In the electorate as a whole their number has been halved: in 1964 one in five was an unswerving Labour loyalist; in 1979 only one in ten.

This loosening of ties has occurred, moreover, at a uniform rate throughout Labour's ranks – whatever their sex, class, education, or age.[13] The patterns within age categories and age cohorts ('generations') are worth closer attention, however, because they provide some clues about the partisan strength of Labour supporters in the future. Table 1.4 sets out the mean partisan strength of identical eight-year age categories for each election from 1964 to 1979 (the two 1974 elections are combined). Two main patterns emerge. One is the long-known tendency for partisanship to strengthen with age at any one point of time (see the columns); this is true for all the elections covered here. The other, as already mentioned, is the evenness of the rate of partisan weakening within the same age category (as opposed to cohort) across the 1964–79 period (see the rows). Thus at each election the Labour Party has been injected with a batch of young first-time supporters whose partisanship has been successively weaker.

1964	*1966*	*1970*	*Feb./Oct. 1974*	*1979*
2·22	2·18	2·04	1·97	1·91

This does *not* mean that the overall weakening of Labour partisanship can be pinned on the younger generation of Labour identifiers alone, since similar (but slightly lower) rates of weakening have occurred amongst those in their thirties, forties and fifties (but not sixties and older). But it does mean an increased probability of Labour partisanship overall *continuing* to weaken. The partisan weakening arising from the dying out of staunchly loyal older generations is now less likely than in the past to be balanced by the stiffening of attachments among younger generations. This is partly because the most recent new generation of Labour supporters simply has more catching up to do (see outside bottom row); but also because the normal processes of partisan consolidation as electors mature through their thirties and forties has been retarded in the last fifteen years by countervailing forces (see the top left to bottom right diagonals). It is of interest, incidentally, that these countervailing 'period' forces have wiped out the surplus partisan strength that the Labour Party might have expected to be an enduring feature of its 1934–5 and 1958–68 cohorts.

Analysis of this kind, however, only registers the fact of partisan weakening in Labour's ranks; it does not explain it. The concept of party identification is rooted in a more general approach to electoral behaviour which stresses the importance of parental socialisation, and it is possible that changes in the pattern of such socialisation account for the trends I have recorded. But here paucity of reliable data reduces one to mere speculation: the growth of social and residential mobility, the earlier leaving of the parental home both physically and spiritually, the rise of non-partisan television as a source of young people's values and knowledge are all plausible explanations, but cannot be investigated here. Instead I turn to two possible factors: trends in class-consciousness and trends in ideological consciousness.

'Social' Sources of Labour Partisanship

Outside Ulster occupational class remains the single most important social basis of party attachment. The assumption of the social group approach is that if the large majority of manual workers were class-conscious, and automatically regarded the Labour Party as the natural representative of working-class interests, they would overlook the occasional setbacks, uncongenial policies and disagreeable members of a Labour government and unswervingly vote Labour. No doubt the social group explanation of partisan attachments is most appropriate for those countries like the Netherlands, Austria, or Italy in which social divisions have been thoroughly institutionalised by a set of overlapping social and political organisations, rather than for Britain where, despite the formal tie between the trade union movement and the Labour Party, manual workers have not been organisationally mobilised in the same way. None the less, class attachments and the class or anti-class appeals of the parties remain an important component of party choice. In 1979, as in previous elections, the single most frequent reason given for 'liking the

Table 1.4 *Mean Partisan Strength Scores* of Eight-Year Overlapping Age-Categories of Labour Identifiers, 1964–79*

Age group	*First entered electorate in***		*1964*	*1966*	*1970*	*Feb. & Oct. 1974 (average)*	*1979*	*Age cohort difference*	*Age group differences, 1964–1979*
18–25	1958–64	(2·22)	2·24	2·18	2·04	1·97	1·91		–0·33
22–29	1954–61	(2·18)	2·20	2·16	2·07	1·97	1·91		–0·29
26–33	1950–57	(2·15)	2·16	2·15	2·13	2·02	1·92		–0·24
30–37	1946–53	(2·20)	2·17	2·17	2·18	2·08	1·95	–0·23	–0·22
34–41	1942–49	(2·29)	2·25	2·25	2·24	2·10	2·00	–0·22	–0·25
38–45	1938–45	(2·39)	2·34	2·31	2·30	2·12	2·09	–0·09	–0·30
42–49	1934–41	(2·42)	2·42	2·34	2·34	2·15	2·12	–0·06	–0·30
46–53	1930–37	(2·42)	2·44	2·36	2·38	2·21	2·14	–0·01	–0·28
50–57	1926–33	(2·45)	2·44	2·43	2·38	2·30	2·21	+0·01	–0·31
54–61	1922–29	(2·50)	2·47	2·49	2·40	2·29	2·17	–0·12	–0·33
58–65	1918–25	(2·52)	2·52	2·53	2·46	2·36	2·23	–0·16	–0·29
62–69	1914–21	(2·43)	2·49	2·54	2·55	2·40	2·29	–0·13	–0·14
66–73		(2·38)	2·41	2·58	2·59	2·40	2·34	–0·11	–0·04
70–77		(2·42)	2·38	2·57	2·57	2·41	2·39	–0·11	–0·03
74–81		(2·50)	2·42	2·56	2·55	2·42	2·42	–0·08	–0·08
	All		2·33	2·41	2·34	2·18	2·04		
Difference between 18–29 and 70–81			0·18	0·04	0·50	0·45	0·50		

* The entries in each column are smoothed from raw data by setting each cell entry equal to the average of itself and its two nearest neighbours, except for entries on the end of columns, which represent the average of self and single nearest neighbour. The overlap of age groups is for the purpose of reducing sampling error resulting from small numbers.

**The figures in parentheses should be used for 1964 if the reader wishes to follow the progress of an age cohort.

Labour Party' referred to its role as a representative of workers and the trade union movement; the single most frequent reason for 'disliking the Conservative Party' was that it stood for the middle or upper classes.

From this departure-point one can single out three possible sources of the declining Labour vote. The first is, quite simply, that it arises from the shrinking size of the manual worker category – one of the fears of Labour's embourgeoisement theorists in the 1950s. This explanation can be dismissed straightaway. It is perfectly true that, for well-known reasons, the proportion of the electorate made up of manual workers has been slowly diminishing, from 63 per cent in 1964 to 56 per cent in 1979.

But as Tables 1.5 and 1.6 show, this trend has been compounded by the declining willingness of those in the contracting category of manual workers to vote Labour, or even to identify with Labour. Between 1964 and 1979 the net movement (swing) from Labour to Conservative identification (a more cautious measure of electoral change than the vote swing) was 3·5 per cent among skilled workers, 8·0 per cent among the semi- and unskilled. Only the large compensatory swing of 10·5 per cent to Labour among the less numerous professional and managerial classes and a smaller swing among routine non-manual workers have saved Labour from even deeper trouble. It is worth noting, incidentally, that these working-class swings are the result of desertions from Labour rather than conversions to the Conservatives; much of the slack has been taken up by non-identification.

It is the erosion of Labour support within the working class that is crucial; and this in turn could have arisen *either* because manual workers have become less class-conscious, *or* because fewer of them now regard Labour as the party of the working class, or both. Table 1.7 sets out for 1964 to 1979 the proportion of manual workers who, in answer to the question 'Do you ever think of yourself as belonging to any particular social class?' said without further probing or prompting: 'working class'. As a measure of class-consciousness this is undoubtedly crude, but it is surely the minimal requirement (even if not a sufficient one) for evidence of a sense of class membership. The figures suggest that manual workers' sense of class interest has declined to an even more modest level than before. Admittedly, the fifteen-year trend encompasses an increase in the 1970s after a sharper decline in the 1960s; and the overall decline is very gentle. But among non-manual workers there was no parallel drop in the proportion 'spontaneously' labelling themselves 'middle class'; and if, in addition, the growth of trade union membership, the outbreaks of industrial militancy, the post-1973 recession and the increasingly 'third-generation' composition of the manual working class are all taken into account, the figures do point to a remarkably weak sense of class interest.

To reinforce this point let me add some evidence from the 1979 British Election Study, which attempted to tap some additional facets of class-awareness, such as a sense of deprivation or of the barriers to cross-class relationships (see Table 1.8). The questions were designed to 'encourage' respondents to reveal at least an element of a sense of class; but astonishingly little was displayed. For example, barely more than a quarter of manual workers were prepared to agree that being working class rather than middle class made life even *a little* harder; fully 60 per cent insisted it made no difference and 12 per cent perversely said it made life easier![14] Only a quarter acknowledged that they usually noticed other people's social class; a mere 8 per cent that cross-class friendships were difficult. Not surprisingly, these proportions are higher among the

Table 1.5 *Changes in Major Party Vote and Identification of Manual Workers, 1964–79*

	1964	*1966*	*1970*	*Feb. and Oct. 1974 (average)*	*1979*	*Change, 1964–79*
% of manual workers* who:						
voted Lab.	55	57	46	48	41	−15
voted Con.	24	21	26	21	28	+4
Lab. lead over Con.	+31	+36	+20	+27	+13	−18 (9% swing)
'Identified' with Lab.	58	60	55	55	51	−7
'Identified' with Con.	27	24	29	26	29	+2
Lab. lead over Con.	+31	+36	+26	+29	+22	−9 ($4\frac{1}{2}$% swing)

* That is, all manual workers in electorate, not voters only.
Sources: 1964, 1966, 1970: Butler and Stokes Election surveys; Feb. 1974, Oct. 1974, 1979: British Election Study cross-section surveys.

Table 1.6 *Social Grade of Head of Household by Party Identification, 1964 and 1979*

	Social Grade of Head of Household																	
	I			*II*			*III*			*IV*			*V*			*VI*		
	Higher managerial and professional			*Lower managerial or administrative*			*Skilled/supervisory non-manual*			*Lower non-manual*			*Skilled manual*			*Unskilled/semi-skilled manual*		
	1964	*1979*	*diff.*	*1964*	*1979*	*diff.*	*1964*	*1979*	*diff.*	*1964*	*1979*	*diff.*	*1964*	*1979*	*diff.*	*1964*	*1979*	*diff.*
Party:																		
Con.	66	53	(−13)	67	56	(−11)	57	63	(+6)	49	44	(−5)	28	29	(+1)	25	30	(+5)
Lab.	12	20	(+8)	15	25	(+10)	20	18	(−2)	26	31	(+5)	57	51	(−6)	61	50	(−11)
Lib.	14	21	(+7)	13	12	(−1)	16	12	(−4)	17	15	(−2)	9	11	(+2)	10	11	(+1)
Other/none	8	6	(−2)	6	7	(+1)	7	8	(+1)	8	10	(+2)	6	9	(+3)	3	9	(+6)
'Swing' to Con.		−10·5%			−10·5%			+4%			−5%			+3·5%			+8%	

Sources: 1964: Butler and Stokes Election survey; May 1979: British Election Study cross-section survey.

Table 1.7 *The 'Spontaneous' Class Identification of Manual and Non-Manual Workers, 1964–79*

	1964	*1966*	*1970*	*Feb. & Oct. 1974 (average)*	*1979*	*Change, 1964–79*
% of all electors giving themselves a class identity	48		42	42	47	−1
% of non-manual workers calling themselves 'middle class'	26		25	24	28	+2
% of manual workers calling themselves 'working class'	44		34	36	39	−5

Note: The figures refer to the proportion giving themselves a class identity, without further probing or prompting, in answer to the question 'Do you ever think of yourself as belonging to any particular social class?'
Sources: As Table 1.3.

minority of manual workers calling themselves working class – but not by much. Among all manual workers the number who thought of themselves as working class *and* at least sometimes noticed other people's class *and* considered it a little difficult to have cross-class friendships amounted to only 13 per cent; the number who thought of themselves as working class and regarded the fact as at least a slight disadvantage came to a mere 14 per cent. Whether these figures would have been higher in the 1950s and 1960s is impossible to say; but they do suggest that in the 1980s the Labour Party faces a working-class electorate with only a minimal sense of class interest. This is not to deny the strong, perhaps growing, *group*-consciousness and solidarity of categories of worker, as the occasional trade union militancy of the 1970s testifies (and items in the 1979 election study corroborate);[15] indeed, there lies the rub for the Labour Party. Nor is it to rule out the possibility that manual workers would develop a stronger sense of class in response to a lead from the Labour Party.

This raises the third possibility: that fewer manual workers now support Labour not because they have ceased to regard themselves as working class, but because they no longer regard the Labour Party as working class. It is often suggested that since the 1950s, for reasons to do with the embourgeoisement of Labour MPs and ministers, the dominance of the right in the Cabinet, electoral strategies to 'capture the middle ground', not to mention the hard realities of governing, the Labour Party has abandoned its class image.[16] But this assertion has always been based on mere impression, not hard evidence; what evidence exists suggests the opposite. If we consider all the dimensions to the Labour Party's electoral appeal – all the different things that electors say they like about the Labour Party – and ask to what extent references to Labour as the party of the working class have declined, the answer is: not at all. The very reverse; as Table 1.9 shows, among the electorate – and indeed manual workers and Labour identifiers – positive references to Labour as the party of 'the worker', the 'ordinary working man', the 'trade unionist', etc., were higher in 1979 than 1964. It is true that positive appraisal in these terms was made by only a minority, so that there remains an opportunity and incentive for Labour to strengthen its image in this respect; but on these data it is difficult to attribute Labour's electoral decline to the supposed shedding of its class appeal. Table 1.9 also shows that positive references to Labour as the party of 'the left', 'socialist principles', etc., have risen, although only slightly; but, as always, socialism is a conscious source of attraction to only a miniscule proportion of the electorate, and indeed to only a tiny minority of Labour supporters. It is to this aspect of Labour's electoral decline that we turn next.

Table 1.8 *Aspects of Manual Workers' Class-Consciousness, 1979*

	% of all manual workers who . . .	*% of manual workers thinking themselves 'working class' who . . .*
'Think that being working class, rather than middle class, makes life a bit/a good deal harder'	28	35
Think it makes no difference	60	55
Usually notice other people's social class	25	29
Say it is hard to have friends of another social class	8	13
Say they usually/sometimes notice other people's social class and it is hard/a little difficult to have friends of another social class	26	34

Source: 1979 British Election Study, cross-section survey.

Table 1.9 *Changes in Proportion Making Positive References to Labour Party as Party of 'Socialism' and Party 'for the Working Class', 1964–79*

	1964	*1979*	*Change, 1964–79*
% of *all* respondents referring to Labour as party of:			
socialist/left principles, ideas	4	7	+3%
working class/trade unionists	19	26	+7%
% of *manual workers* referring to Labour as party of:			
socialist/left principles, ideas	4	5	+1%
working class/trade unionists	24	32	+8%
% of *Labour identifiers* referring to Labour as party of:			
socialist/left principles, ideas	6	10	+4%
working class/trade unionists	36	49	+13%

Sources: 1964: Butler and Stokes Election survey; 1979: British Election Study cross-section survey. In both surveys the question was: 'Is there anything in particular that you *like* about the *Labour* Party? If *YES*, what is that? What else do you like about the Labour Party?'

Ideological Sources of Labour Partisanship

On the fanciful assumption that a party's supporters were overwhelmingly committed to its basic objectives, and its strategy for attaining them, we would expect their allegiance to be unimpaired by dissatisfaction with this policy, or that leader, or with a particular spell of office. Doubts and disappointments can be more easily swallowed if one believes in what the party stands for. But, as even the occasional analyst of polls and election surveys well knows, actual and potential Labour voters are indifferent and sometimes actively hostile to many aspects of Labour Party policy; and in favour, sometimes enthusiastically, of certain aspects of Conservative Party policy. And here the asymmetry mentioned earlier comes into play: among Conservative voters convergence with their own party's policy, and divergence from Labour's is far stronger.

This is vividly demonstrated by Table 1.10, which sets out the electorate's attitudes to the main proposals in the Labour and Conservative parties' 1979 election manifestos. Manual workers, Labour's natural sympathisers, were on average slightly more in favour of Conservative than Labour proposals (the same is true of young manual workers). Comparison on individual items is particularly revealing. For example, manual workers were as much in favour of cutting the *top rate* of income tax (the Conservative proposal) as of introducing a wealth tax (the Labour proposal). More sided with the House of Lords, whose powers Labour proposed to reduce, than with trade union officials, whom Labour proposed to place on company boards. There is another telling comparison. Not surprisingly, both Conservative and Labour voters were more likely to approve of their own party's proposals than of the other side's. But the pattern of approval was not balanced. Whereas the majority of Conservative voters (temporarily swelled in 1979, moreover, by many without deep Conservative commitments) explicitly opposed Labour's proposals, a substantial majority of Labour voters (reduced in 1979 to a loyal core) actually supported Conservative proposals.

This last table, however, has the drawback as well as the attraction of simplicity. It is based on dichotomous responses ('good idea/bad idea') to one-dimensional policy slogans; contains no information on electors' *perceptions* of where the parties stand (as opposed to our own assumptions); and does not measure, and so cannot compare, the relative distance between electors and the two parties. These defects are avoided in the more precise measures of the relative policy distance between each of the Labour and Conservative parties and their supporters (and non-supporters) which are provided in Figures 1.1–1.8. These consist of electoral pictures, drawn from the 1979 British Election Study, for eight 'position' issues, that is, issues on which the parties adopted distinct policies and objectives in the 1979 campaign.

Table 1.10 *Support for Various Conservative and Labour Manifesto Proposals*

	All	*Manual workers under 35*	*Manual workers*	*Con. voters*	*Lab. voters*
% saying it would be a good idea to:					
Conservative proposals					
Ban secondary picketing, that is the picketing of a company not directly involved in a strike	91	86	90	96	96
Have a free vote in the House of Commons on the death penalty	90	89	92	94	88
Sell more council houses to tenants	80	82	79	89	69
Stop social security payments to the families of strikers	60	46	56	81	38
Cut top income tax rate for people with large incomes	57	61	56	67	49
Put up VAT in order to reduce income tax	51	47	45	70	30
Average	71·5	68·5	69·7	82·8	61·7
Labour Proposals					
Take tougher stand against the Common Market's agricultural policy	94	94	94	94	94
Give government subsidies where that is necessary to protect jobs	79	84	82	66	91
Introduce a wealth tax	49	56	57	30	73
Give trade unions seats on the boards of major companies	45	49	46	33	62
Reduce the powers of the House of Lords	43	46	48	21	66
Average	62·0	65·8	65·4	48·8	78·2

Note: 'Don't knows' were excluded from the percentage base; all other respondents said 'bad idea'. The question was: 'I am going to read out some of the proposals that the different parties have put forward in this election. In each case I would like you to say whether you think the proposal is a good idea or bad idea.'
Source: Gallup survey for BBC Television. 2–3 May 1979.

The issues are:

(1) *Unemployment:* reliance on private capital *vs* government spending to create jobs.
(2) *Industrial relations:* whether or not the further regulation of trade union activities should be through changes in the law.
(3) *Wages:* incomes policy *vs* free collective bargaining.
(4) *Nationalisation:* further nationalisation *vs* denationalisation.
(5) *Social services:* more spending *vs* cutting back.
(6) *Race relations:* Stopping immigration *vs* tackling housing and unemployment in inner cities as the best way of improving relations.
(7) *Taxes:* income tax cuts *vs* maintenance of health, education and welfare services.
(8) *EEC:* whether Britain should become more or less co-operative on EEC economic policies.

These by no means exhaust the issues which had a non-trivial impact on the vote in 1979 (e.g. the list excludes such non-position issues as 'prices' and 'law and order') but it probably accounts for a large proportion of those that helped determine people's vote. On each issue respondents were asked to give their own view, and their perception of the Labour and Conservative parties' position. Each is depicted as a 7-point scale running from 1 (far right wing) to 7 (far left wing), on which is plotted (1) the position of the Labour and Conservative parties (as perceived by the electorate as a whole), (2) the position of the electorate as a whole, (3) the position of manual workers and (4) the position of committed Conservatives, uncommitted Conservatives, Liberals, uncommitted Labour supporters and committed Labour supporters.[17]

What emerges from an inspection of Figures 1.1 to 1.8 is, quite simply, that on six of the eight contentious issues of the 1979 election the Conservative Party was more representative than the Labour Party of the views of the electorate. This will not come as a surprise to seasoned survey sifters. More surprising – and disturbing for the Labour Party – is that on these same six issues the Conservatives were the closer of the two parties to the *working-class* electorate, and to the uncommitted and thus convertible Labour supporter. The two exceptions are Britain's posture in the EEC and (against expectations) the priority of tax cuts versus the maintaining of existing public services. But on unemployment policy, race relations, incomes policy, industrial relations law, social welfare benefits and nationalisation all but the committed Labour supporter (the 29 per cent of the electorate describing themselves as 'very strong' or 'fairly strong' Labour) are nearer in their views to the positions they associate with the Conservative Party than to the positions they associate with the Labour Party.

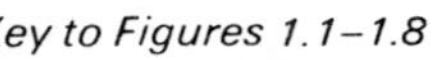
Key to Figures 1.1–1.8

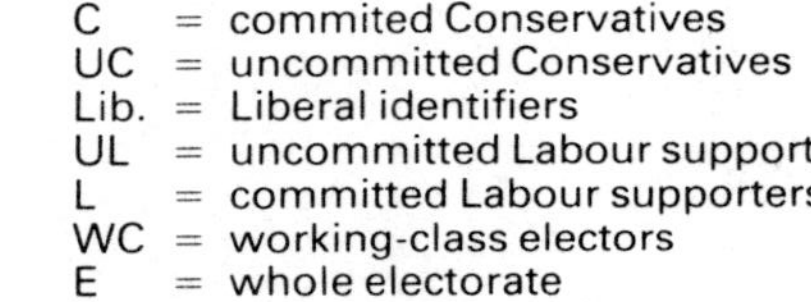
C = commited Conservatives
UC = uncommitted Conservatives
Lib. = Liberal identifiers
UL = uncommitted Labour supporters
L = committed Labour supporters
WC = working-class electors
E = whole electorate

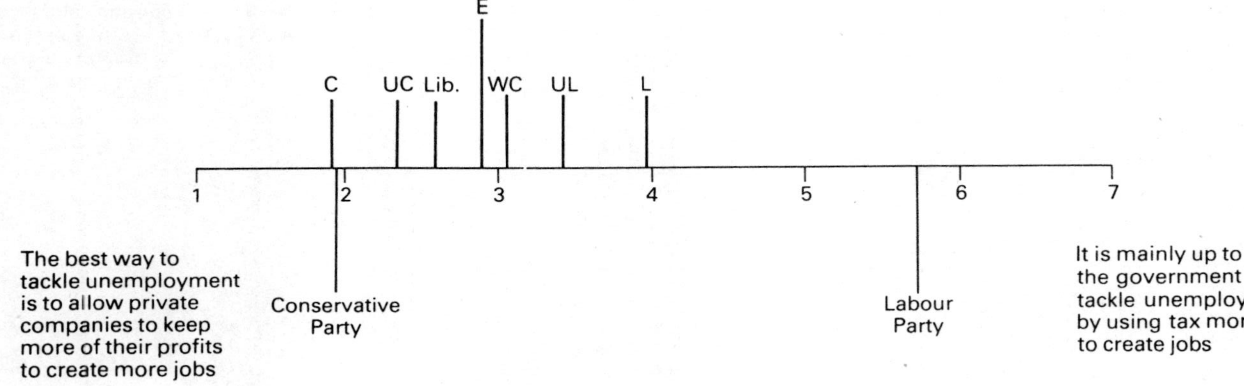
E
C
UC
Lib.
WC
UL
L
1
2
3
4
5
6
7
The best way to tackle unemployment is to allow private companies to keep more of their profits to create more jobs
Conservative Party
Labour Party
It is mainly up to the government to tackle unemployment by using tax money to create jobs

Figure 1.1

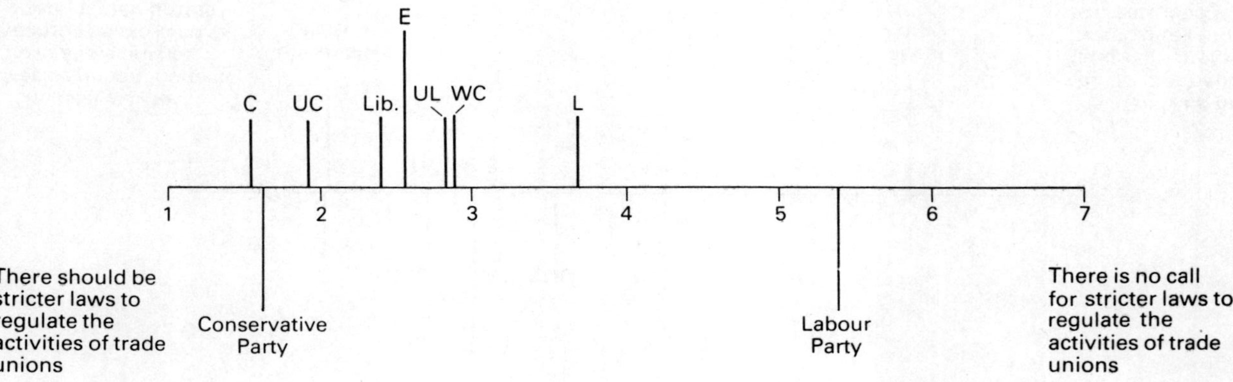
E
C
UC
Lib.
UL
WC
L
1
2
3
4
5
6
7
There should be stricter laws to regulate the activities of trade unions
Conservative Party
Labour Party
There is no call for stricter laws to regulate the activities of trade unions

Figure 1.2

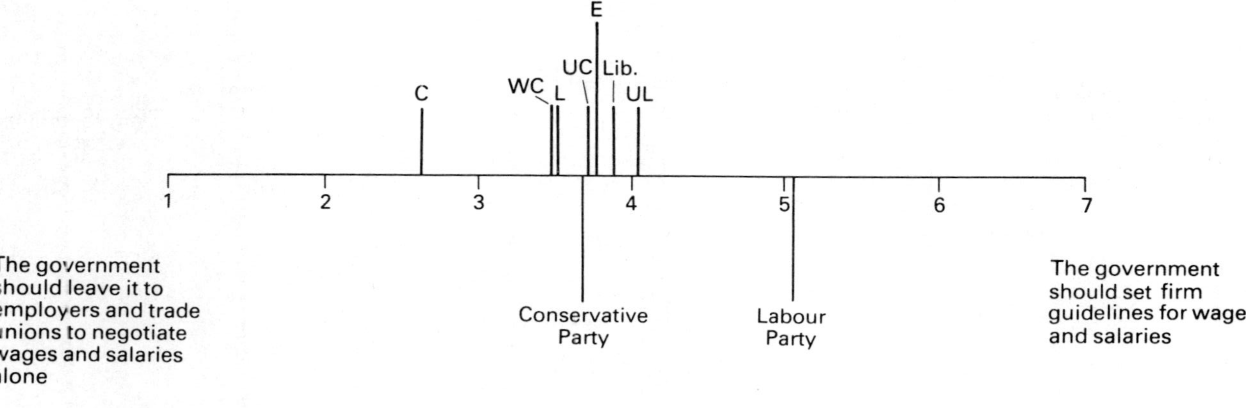
E
UC
Lib.
C
WC
L
UL
1
2
3
4
5
6
7
The government should leave it to employers and trade unions to negotiate wages and salaries alone
Conservative Party
Labour Party
The government should set firm guidelines for wages and salaries

Figure 1.3

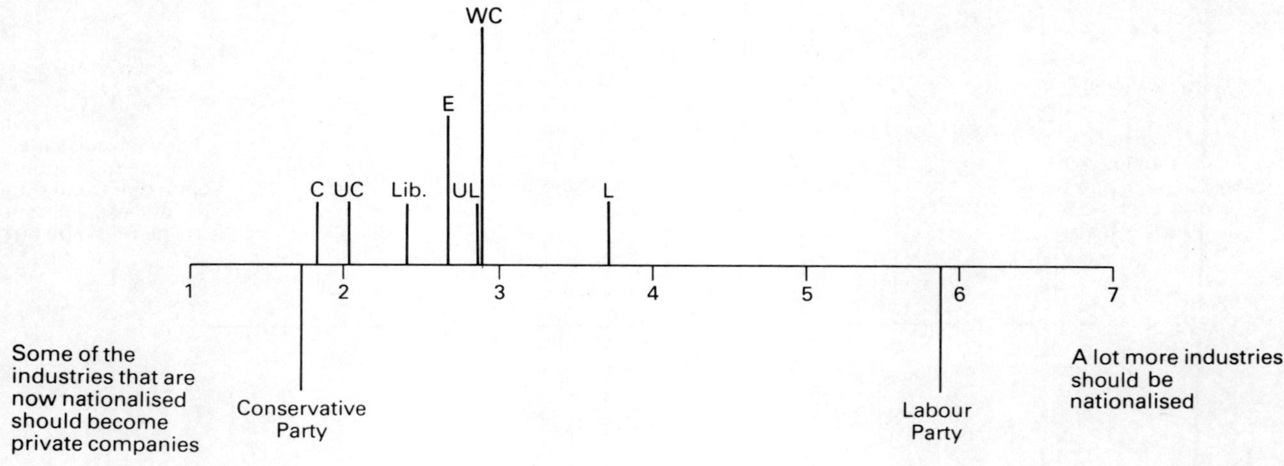
WC
E
C UC
Lib.
UL
L
1
2
3
4
5
6
7
Some of the industries that are now nationalised should become private companies
Conservative Party
Labour Party
A lot more industries should be nationalised

Figure 1.4

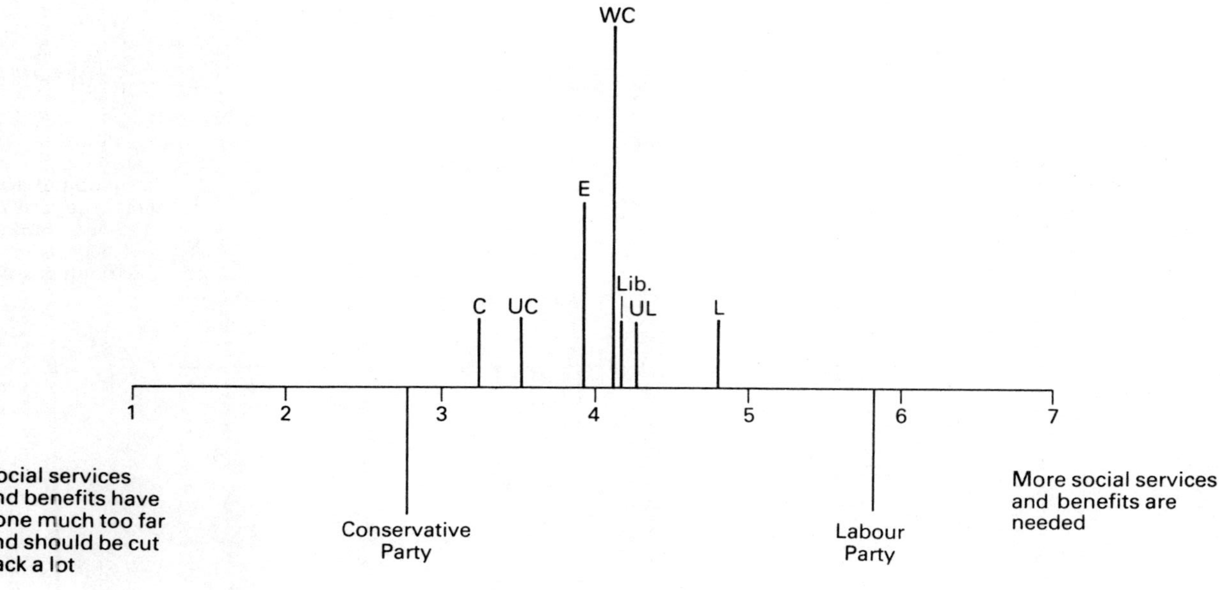
WC
E
Lib.
C
UC
UL
L
1
2
3
4
5
6
7
Social services and benefits have gone much too far and should be cut back a lot
Conservative Party
Labour Party
More social services and benefits are needed

Figure 1.5

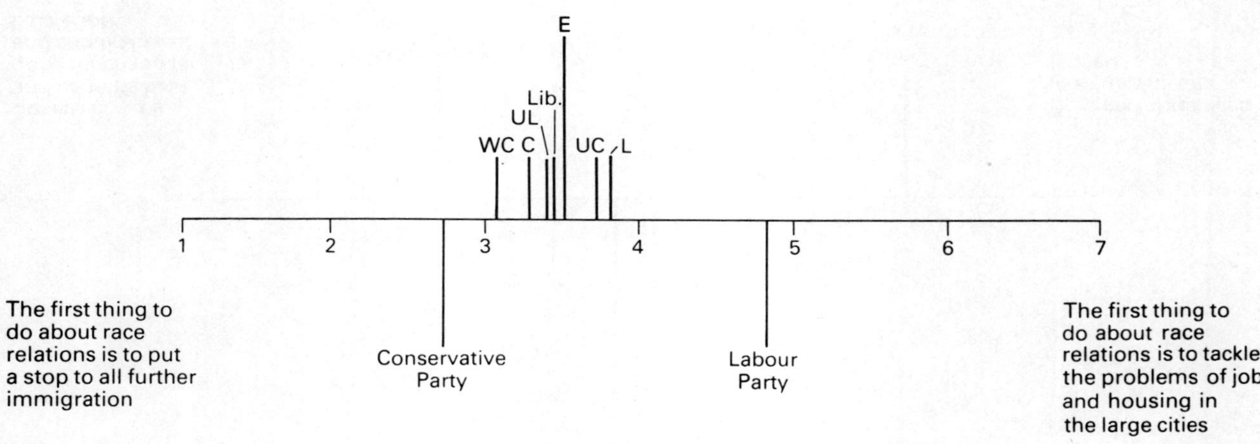
E
Lib.
UL
WC C
UC
L
1
2
3
4
5
6
7
The first thing to do about race relations is to put a stop to all further immigration
Conservative Party
Labour Party
The first thing to do about race relations is to tackle the problems of jobs and housing in the large cities

Figure 1.6

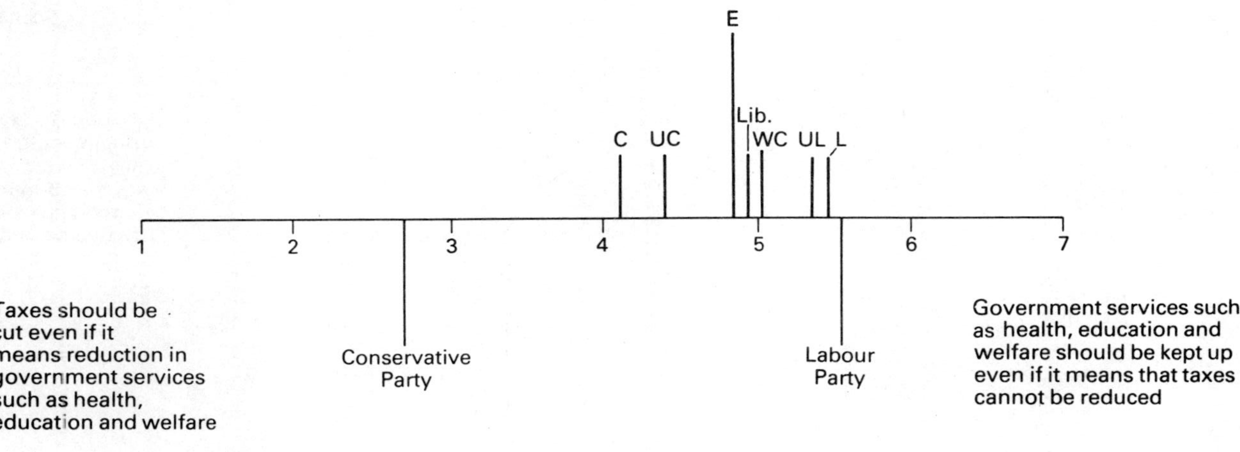
E
Lib.
C
UC
WC
UL
L
1
2
3
4
5
6
7
Taxes should be cut even if it means reduction in government services such as health, education and welfare
Conservative Party
Labour Party
Government services such as health, education and welfare should be kept up even if it means that taxes cannot be reduced

Figure 1.7

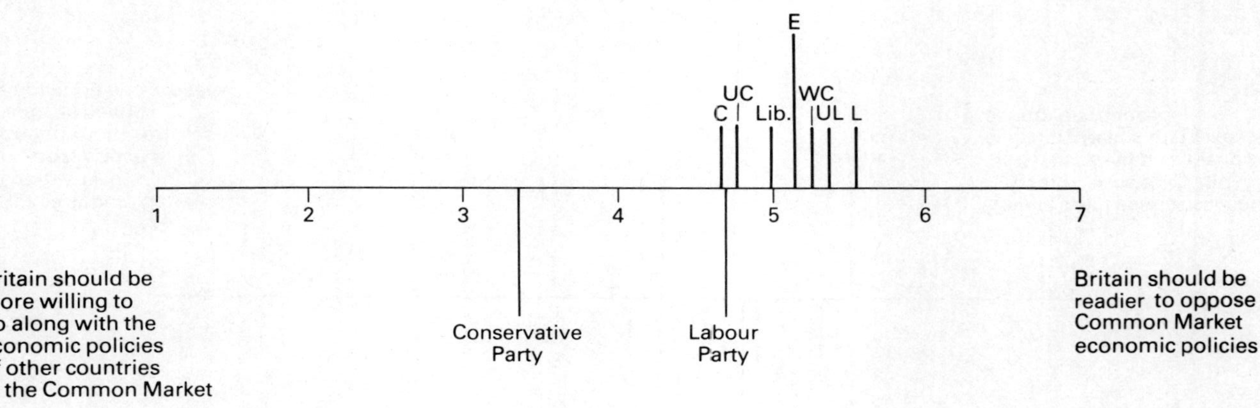
E
UC
WC
C
Lib.
UL
L
1
2
3
4
5
6
7
Britain should be more willing to go along with the economic policies of other countries in the Common Market
Conservative Party
Labour Party
Britain should be readier to oppose Common Market economic policies

Figure 1.8

The pattern of policy distances between the electorate and the two parties, both within and across issues, does not fit in with the conventional assumptions of either revisionists or fundamentalists in the Labour Party. It is not the case, *pace* the fundamentalists, that the Conservatives can only attract working-class support by crude appeals to traditional morality, xenophobia, or authoritarianism. At least in 1979 (contrary to my own earlier speculations)[18] the Conservative Party had positioned itself nearer than the Labour Party to working-class views on a series of issues relating to workers' rights and benefits. Nor is it the case, as revisionists like to believe, that Labour lost votes because the electorate occupies the ideological centre ground and the Labour Party staked out a distant position to the far left. This picture can only be drawn for nationalisation and wages policy (if incomes policy is placed on the left, free collective bargaining on the right); even so Labour was not seen as *far* to the left, only more left-of-centre. On two other issues – unemployment policy and trade union law – the electorate put the Labour Party on a limb to the right. On the EEC, if obstreperousness is 'left' and co-operativeness is 'right', the electorate positioned itself further to the left than both parties. This was the only example of an issue that might meet the fundamentalists' visions of a radical electorate awaiting a radical Labour lead; and even here a leftward shift by the Labour Party would lose rather than win votes if the electorate's views remained unchanged.

This divergence between particular policies of the Labour Party and the views of its supporters is nothing new. As much was discovered in the early 1950s.[19] For at least the last fifteen years people have voted Labour despite its policies, Conservative despite its leaders. What needs to be explored is the long-term trend in attitudes towards Labour's broader principles and basic strategies. This is attempted in Table 1.11, which reveals a quite exceptional movement of opinion. Among Labour's ranks there has been a spectacular decline in support for the collectivist trinity of public ownership, trade union power and social welfare. In 1964 a clear majority of Labour identifiers approved of further nationalisation (57 per cent) and repudiated the idea that trade unions were too powerful (59 per cent); an overwhelming majority wanted more spending on the social services (89 per cent). By 1979 support for each of these three tenets was down to barely a third; among manual workers in general, and the electorate as a whole, support was of course even lower.[20] What was already an ideological split in the 1960s had turned into an ideological chasm by 1979.

One should not make *too* much of these figures. They are based on three indicators only; the question wording is not ideal; they cover a period in which public ownership, trade union power and social welfare expenditure had all increased; and there is some contradictory evidence in the polls.[21] They encompass the broad means towards Labour's goals of equality and redistribution, rather than the goals themselves, for which there remains substantial support. For example, the 1979 British Election Study found that a clear majority of manual workers (and a comfortable majority of Labour supporters) said it was very or fairly important for the government to take steps to 'give workers more say in the running of the place where they work', 'spend more money to get rid of poverty in Britain' and 'redistribute income and wealth in favour of ordinary working people'. Equally, there remain a variety of more specific Labour proposals which undoubtedly command popular support. None the less, a commitment to an extensive and widening system of public ownership, social welfare and trade union rights is surely a defining characteristic of the Labour Party; and the trend figures in Table 1.11 undoubtedly show a dramatic drop in their electoral appeal.

Discussion and Conclusions

The distinction between psychological, social and ideological sources of Labour partisanship is an analytic one; in reality they are interconnected such that the shrivelling of one puts extra 'strain' on the others. The importance of policies and objectives in securing party loyalty has probably become more important over the last fifteen years. Until the mid-1960s class and partisan allegiance sustained Labour supporters' loyalty even when it was under strain through dissent from Labour policy. As, for various reasons, the strength of those class and psychological ties has dissolved, that electoral insulation has been less effective. Labour now enters elections with a major handicap: unlike the Conservatives, its basic, traditional principles run against the popular grain. In opposition this ideological disadvantage might be compensated for by the temporary unpopularity of a Conservative administration. But when in government the Labour Party enters the electoral arena without the protective clothing of ideological sympathy among its traditional supporters; the result is the kind of mauling it suffered in 1979.

Such conclusions, however, do not offer the Labour Party any clear guidelines for climbing out of electoral trouble. The survey data do not suggest solutions so much as underline the party's ever-present problem: the lack of appeal that socialist *policies* (although not ultimate goals), of almost any variety, hold for a large – and growing – portion of the working class. Despite the assumptions of both revolutionary Marxists and gradualist Fabians, there is no historically predestined *rendez-vous* between socialism and an industrial working class, least of all in Britain. Indeed, the *raison d'être* of the Labour Party, itself an alliance of socialists and organised labour, is to bring the two together.

Table 1.11 *Support for Further Nationalisation, and for More Spending on Social Services, and Attitudes to Trade Union Power among Labour Identifiers, 1964–79*

	1964	*1966*	*1970*	*Feb. & Oct. 1974 (average)*	*1979*	*Change, 1964–79*	
% of Labour identifiers:							
in favour of nationalising more industries[1]	57	52	39	53	32	—25	
who do not believe that trade unions have 'too much power'	59	45	40	42	36	—23	
in favour of spending more on the social services	89	66	60[2]	61[23]	n.a.	—28	(1964–Feb. 1974)
saying that 'more social services and benefits are needed'	n.a.	n.a.	n.a.	43	30	—13	(1974–9)

Notes: n.a. = not asked. Percentage bases exclude the 'don't knows'.

1 Saying that either 'a lot more' or 'a few more' industries should be nationalised.

2 Excludes the small numbers who said that only spending on pensions should be increased (coded separately in 1970 and February 1974, but not in 1964 or 1966).

3 Taken from the 1970–Feb. 1974 panel sample.

Data Sources: Butler and Stokes Election surveys for 1964, 1966 and 1970; British Election surveys for February 1974, October 1974 and 1979.

Questions: 'There has been a lot of talk recently about nationalisation, that is, the government owning and running industries like steel and electricity. Which of these statements comes closest to what you yourself feel should be done?' (A lot more should be nationalised/Only a few more industries should be nationalised/No more industries should be nationalised, but industries that are now nationalised should stay nationalised/Some of the industries that are now nationalised should be denationalised, i.e. become private companies)

'Do you think that the trade unions have too much power or not?' (Yes, too much power/No, not too much power)

'Do you feel that the government should spend more on pensions and social services, or do you feel that spending for social services should stay about as it is now?' (The government should spend more/Spending should stay as it is now)

'Now we would like to ask what you think about social services and benefits. Which of these statements do you feel comes closest to your own views?' (Social services and benefits have gone much too far and should be *cut back a lot*/Social services and benefits have gone somewhat too far and should be *cut back a bit*/Social services and benefits should *stay much as they are*/*More* social services and benefits are needed)

But the hard task of sustaining the marriage saddles the Labour Party with a chronic dilemma: whether to change the nature of its socialism or the nature of the working class. The survey evidence presented here is grist to the mills of both pragmatists and fundamentalists. To the pragmatists it demonstrates the urgency of bringing the parties' policies (again, not its ultimate goals) in line with a changing electorate; to the fundamentalists, the urgency of bringing the electorate (back) into line with the party's unchanging principles.

The fundamentalists' insistence on an unswerving adherence to traditional positions has the merit of principle and the attraction of faith. But is it practical politics? Is it realistic to assume that a sizeable proportion of the electorate can be won over to 'socialism' in the space of a few years? Fundamentalists cite four ways in which this could be done. The first is the launching of a concerted and substantial educational campaign by the Labour movement: conferences, schools, festivals, cultural activities and, most important of all, a renewed attempt to establish a popular daily socialist newspaper. Yet even if adequate resources were made available (which is unlikely) it is difficult to believe that educational programmes can touch more than a fringe of the electorate, at least in the short term. The preconditions for a successful educational campaign – willing pupils, trusted teachers and exclusive access – do not exist. The electorate is relatively uninterested in party politics, and deeply sceptical towards politicians and political propaganda. It is also subject to a predominantly anti-socialist culture, especially in the press, as fundamentalists are the first to point out. This is not to deny that electoral benefits accrue from educational campaigns; only to suggest that the return is relatively small, and long in coming.

A second means of 'mass conversion' would be the proselytising activities of local party workers. This argument envisages a two-step process by which the adoption of fundamentalist, socialist principles mobilises an enthusiastic band of party activists who, with a 'party worth working for', will in turn mobilise voters. But there is little evidence that the Labour Party is short of party workers in winnable seats, or that the number and dedication of local activists makes more than a negligible difference to the result, at least at a general election.

A third strategy for 'mass conversion' relies on the power of bold and imaginative socialist rhetoric to evoke a response from the electorate. It assumes that the public will follow the path laid down by a Labour Party leadership demonstrably committed to radical policies; and that the evidence from surveys, being no more than a distorted echo of what political leaders say, is irrelevant. The argument is often accompanied by the claim that Labour tends to win elections on radical manifestos and lose them on cautious ones.[22] The arguments rest on what might be dubbed the 'sleeping beauty' theory of British voters – the belief that within the electorate lies a long-dormant socialism awaiting the kiss of life from a bold socialist prince. This is almost certainly make-believe. If a significant portion of the electorate had been hankering after radical socialist policies some evidence would be available by now: growing public support for the leaders and policies of the left within the Labour Party, and for socialist parties outside the Labour Party. But not a hint of this is suggested by the survey evidence, or by a general election in which disillusioned one-time Labour supporters defected to the right, and the far left parties polled below the National Front and newly formed Ecology Party.[23] Even the fairy story does not say the sleeping beauty was invisible.

The fourth argument in favour of the fundamentalists' strategy, however, cannot be dismissed so easily. It rests on the assumption that Labour is bound to be swept back to power on a tide of anti-Conservative revulsion. This reasoning has some plausibility. The survey evidence does suggest that elections resemble plebiscites on the outgoing government's record rather than choices between two ideologies or sets of policies. The majority of electors judge parties in terms of their past or potential record, or the interests they represent, not their specific proposals or ideological principles; many are unaware of, or under misconceptions about, a party's policies, and among the more knowledgeable electors are many who support a party despite misgivings about particular policies. It is therefore not unrealistic (if a little unprincipled) to advocate that given the likelihood of a return to office, Labour can afford to write its manifesto with little thought for public opinion.

Yet Labour's inadequate general election 'victories' of 1964 and February 1974 reveal how risky such a strategy is. Moreover, the Conservative government may well regain some popularity by tax-cutting budgets in 1982 and 1983 (floated by the North Sea oil revenues) whilst the constituency boundary revisions and the intervention of maverick right-wing Labour candidates will together require an exceptionally large anti-Conservative swing (of at least 6 per cent, probably) to install a Labour government with an adequate majority. A more important consideration is that a failure to close the ideological gap between the Labour Party and its voters would leave a future Labour administration vulnerable, once again, to an immediate and strong backlash when the going in government got rough. To ignore the electorate's growing disaffection from Labour policies may not preclude a Labour victory at the next election, but make the re-election of the subsequent Labour government – an essential condition for radical changes to endure – very improbable.

Yet a serious examination of the survey data suggests that the pragmatists' strategy of bringing Labour Party policy more into line with public opinion, or, more specifically, working-class opinion (the difference is rarely substantial), is not as simple or practical as it might seem. The difficulties lie not only in the conservative fundamentalism of sections of the Labour Party, or in the inconsistencies and profligacies of a 'public opinion' that, unlike governments or even oppositions, is not responsible for making policies and meeting their consequences. The nub of the problem lies in the sheer gulf that separates the policies and principles *of all wings* of the Labour Party from what the public say it wants.

The magnitude of the difficulty is revealed by Table 1.12, which provides a summary guide to public opinion in 1979 on a wide range of issues. The table is based on virtually all the 'issue' questions asked in both the 1979 British Election Study and the BBC/Gallup election-day survey. The thirty-seven issues are categorised in two ways: first, according to whether they are ones on which the Labour Party takes a firm and united stand (top half of table) or an ambivalent and divided stand (bottom half); and secondly, according to whether they are ones on which the public largely takes a 'left-wing' position (left-hand side of table), or is fairly evenly divided (middle of table), or largely takes a 'right-wing' position (right-hand side of table).[24]

The table reconfirms that there are many more issues on which the substantial majority of the electorate opposes than supports the Labour Party (compare the top right with the top left box). These issues are not confined, moreover, to such familiar populist-authoritarian measures as restoring the death penalty or increasing defence spending; most are 'bread and butter' matters of social and economic policy. Nor are they issues on which the Labour Party is seriously divided between right and left or on which the right is ambivalent. A glance at the table shows that a purely pragmatist strategy would be no more congenial to social democrats than to socialists. It is true that bringing party policy into line with public opinion would oblige the left to abandon some of its major principles (defence cuts, further public ownership, an extension of trade union rights); but it would oblige the right to shed as many of its own (libertarianism, concerted action on behalf of racial minorities, internationalism, foreign aid, constructive membership of the EEC, foreign aid, incomes policies).

For both the social democratic and socialist wings of the Labour Party Table 1.12 contains an even more disturbing feature. Many of the issues on which the electorate – indeed the working-class electorate – were ambivalent or outright hostile towards Labour policies in 1979 were ones on which the party was not only united, but clear as to where working-class interests lay. For example, the party is largely opposed to the Conservatives' policy of encouraging local authorities to sell council houses to tenants; but 85 per cent of the electorate and 86 per cent of the working-class electorate were in favour. The whole of the Labour Party wants to complete its programme of replacing grammar schools by com-

Table 1.12 *Public Opinion and the Position of the Labour Party on Thirty-Seven Issues, May 1979*

	Public opinion united and pro-Labour	*Public opinion divided*	*Public opinion united and pro-Conservative*
Labour Party united and firm	More money should be put in the NHS (93%) More money should be spent to get rid of poverty in Britain (91%) ˣIn favour of government subsidies where necessary to protect jobs (79%) *Agrees that government services such as health, education and welfare should be kept up even if it means that taxes cannot be reduced (71%) Income and wealth should be redistributed in favour of ordinary working people (67%) Workers should be given more say in the running of the place where they work (65%) Coloured immigrants should *not* be sent back to their own country (63%)	Attempts to ensure equality have *not* gone too far (56%) Recent attempts to ensure equality for coloured people have *not* gone too far (51%) ˣAgainst putting up VAT in order to reduce income tax (49%) ˣIn favour of introducing a wealth tax (49%) ˣIn favour of reducing the power of the House of Lords (43%) In favour of giving more aid to poorer countries in Africa and Asia (43%) ˣIn favour of cutting top income tax rate for people with large incomes (43%) In favour of increasing state control of land for building (42%) *The first thing to do about race relations is to tackle the problems of jobs and housing in the large cities (41%)	Stiffer sentences should be given to people who break the law (97%) The right to show nudity and sex in films and magazines has gone too far (94%) ˣIn favour of banning secondary picketing (91%) Council house tenants should be given the right to buy their houses (85%) *There should be stricter laws to regulate the activities of trade unions (80%) Feel that the change towards modern methods in teaching children at school has gone too far (79%) Feel that the welfare benefits available have gone too far (75%) The death penalty should be brought back (75%) *The best way to tackle unemployment is to allow private companies to keep more of their profits to create more jobs (74%)

	Public opinion united and pro-Labour	*Public opinion divided*	*Public opinion united and pro-Conservative*
			*Social services and benefits should be cut back (71%) Not in favour of establishing comprehensive schools in place of grammar schools throughout the country (61%) ˣIn favour of stopping social security payments to the families of strikers (60%)
Labour Party divided, ambivalent, or uncommitted	More efforts should be made to protect the countryside and our finest buildings (97%) *Britain should be readier to oppose Common Market economic policies (75%)	British troops should be immediately withdrawn from Northern Ireland (54%) *The government should leave it to employers and trade unions to negotiage wages and salaries alone (57%) ˣIn favour of giving trade unions seats on the boards of major companies (45%)	Tougher measures should be taken to prevent communist influence in Britain (85%) *Not in favour of the nationalisation of more industries (83%) Feel that the availability of abortion on the NHS has gone too far (79%) There should be further expansion of the nuclear power industry (61%)

Note: All the issue statements have been drawn from the 1979 British Election Study cross-section sample and from the BBC/Gallup election day survey. Where there was adaptation of questions, the BES survey was used. Respondents answering 'Don't know' or a neutral, intermediate category have been excluded from the percentage base; all other responses were dichotomised. The figure in parentheses after each statement is the proportion opting for that 'side' of the issue. Statements marked with an asterisk (*) are those for which the 'opposite' statement consists of a *different* policy, not the negation of the statement. The wording of these 'opposite' statements can be found in Figures 1.1 to 1.8.

Issue statements marked with an 'ˣ' have been taken from the BBC/Gallup survey.

prehensives; but only 39 per cent of the electorate (and 48 per cent of the working-class electorate) share the same enthusiasm. Right and left within the party take it as axiomatic that the regeneration of the economy and creation of jobs will depend on state rather than private investment; but only 26 per cent of the electorate (and 29 per cent of the working-class electorate) agree. The party is united in its opposition – whether out of scepticism or on principle – to the use of the law to regulate trade union activities; yet 80 per cent of the electorate (and 75 per cent of the working-class electorate) are in favour. Within the party there is no dissent about the need to extend and improve social services; but 71 per cent of the electorate (and 67 per cent of the working-class electorate) wanted to see the social services cut back (at least in 1979). All these issues are ones on which the Labour Party is united and committed, and on which it sees a self-evident coincidence of socialist principles and working-class interests; yet in 1979 all were ones on which a decisive majority of the working class embraced a Conservative position.

No doubt the size of this gap between the electorate and the Labour Party was temporarily inflated by the political circumstances of 1979 and will narrow under a Conservative government; but the gap will not disappear. The Labour Party must face the fact that the divorce between Labour principles and working-class opinion results partly from changes of working-class *interests* over the last twenty years. Even if Abrams's assumptions about continuing economic growth were over-optimistic, some aspects of working-class life have sufficiently altered (usually for the better) to create new interests that are not obviously served by the Labour Party's traditional faith in the steady growth of public expenditure, welfare benefits, trade union power and public ownership. The rapid growth of house-ownership among manual workers (40 per cent were outright owners or mortgagees by 1977)[25] has created aspirations among those still renting their houses, for whom cheap mortgages and the opportunity to purchase one's council house are important policy considerations. As the income tax net has spread more widely, so an increasing proportion of manual workers are attracted to tax-cutting policies, at the expense of those welfare benefits which do not serve their direct interests (e.g. unemployment benefits in the case of those with secure jobs in expanding industries; family allowances in the case of those without dependants)[26] The capacity of strong unions in expanding sectors of the economy to secure wage rises that match price inflation makes free collective bargaining in the interest of some workers; progressive, flat-rate incomes policies the interest of others. There is no simple division within the working class, but rather a fragmentation of interests, between skilled and unskilled, high wage and low wage, expanding and contracting industries, private and public sector, and strong and weak unions: divisions that partly overlap and that tend to be reinforced by differences of race and sex.

Conflicts of interest within the working class have always existed; differences between skilled and unskilled, 'respectable' and 'rough', and Protestant and Catholic were recurring themes of Labour Party politics in the north and Scotland earlier this century. But today's divisions may be more entrenched and less reconcilable not least because of the trade union and pressure group militancy that is frequently encouraged by most sections of the Labour Party. It is therefore especially difficult for the party to construct a package of *policies* with broad electoral appeal, because so many of the policies favoured by the party promote some working-class interests at the expense of others. Are there, then, any over-arching principles on which an electoral strategy might be based? One possibility for the party is to concentrate on its ultimate goals and fundamental values, especially economic and political equality. As Table 1.12 shows (see top left box), proposals for the redistribution of wealth and power, for the elimination of poverty and for adequately financed public services continue to evoke a favourable response from the bulk of the electorate. Another option for the Labour Party is to persuade the electorate that it has the edge over the Conservatives on such 'performance' issues as inflation, unemployment, industrial relations and economic growth – that it is better at managing and governing. Skilful economic management and sound administration in the service of socialist ends is neither an original nor a glamorous appeal; but it is perhaps the only one that can simultaneously unite the party and convince the electorate.

Notes: Chapter 1

1 Mark Abrams, Richard Rose and Rita Hinden, *Must Labour Lose?* (Harmondsworth: Penguin, 1960). Mark Abrams was a survey researcher and subsequently the Labour Party's pollster; Richard Rose was a political scientist and co-author of the 'Nuffield' election study of 1959; and Rita Hinden was founder and secretary of the Fabian Colonial Bureau, and editor of *Socialist Commentary*.

2 See David Lockwood, Frank Bechhofer and Jennifer Platt, *The Affluent Worker, Vol 1I: Political Attitudes and Behaviour* (Cambridge: Cambridge University Press, 1969). While they showed that affluent workers did not necessarily come to vote Conservative, they also showed that they could not be *relied* upon to be unswervingly Labour voters either. Their argument that working-class political attitudes were increasingly 'instrumental' rather than 'solidaristic' is not inconsistent with the heavy swing to the Conservatives among working-class voters in 1979.

3 See BBC TV's Gallup survey on 2–3 May 1979; Market and Opinion Research International, *British Public Opinion: General Election 1979* (Final Report) (London: MORI, 1979),pp.6–7; and the 1979 British Election Study at the University of Essex which will be reported in a planned book by Bo Särlvik, David Robertson and myself. This chapter will draw mainly on the BES survey.

4 See Ivor Crewe, 'Why the Conservatives won', in Howard Penniman (ed.), *Britain at the Polls* (Washington, DC: American Enterprise Institute for Public Policy Research, 1981), and mimeo., based on the BBC Gallup survey.

5 David Butler and Donald Stokes, *Political Change in Britain*, 2nd ed (London: Macmillan, 1975), pp. 247–75.

6 See Ivor Crewe, Bo Särlvik and James Alt, 'Partisan de-alignment in Britain, 1964–74', *British Journal of Political Science*, vol. 7 (1977), pp. 129–90, esp. 148–61.

7 Moreover, these three countries are subject to deep divisions other than those of class (urban/rural, linguistic, religious) which cannot be cited in explanation in the case of Britain. These international comparisons are based on Thomas T. Mackie and Richard Rose, *The International Almanac of Electoral History* (London: Macmillan, 1974) and the updates published annually in the September issue of the *European Journal of Political Research*.

8 See 'The district elections: why there's no euphoria on either side', *The Times*, 6 May 1980, table 11.

9 In 1979 50 per cent of Conservative identifiers were 'very strongly' against the Labour Party; 42 per cent of Labour identifiers 'very strongly' against the Conservative Party. In October 1974 the proportions were 55 and 49 per cent (BES 1979 and October 1974 surveys).

10 See James Alt, *The Politics of Economic Decline* (London: Macmillan, 1978), ch 6 and 7, and 'The dynamics of partisanship in Britain', mimeo., May 1980.

11 Crewe *et al.*, 'Partisan de-alignment in Britain', pp. 142–8.

12 Respondents answering 'none' or 'don't know' to the first question are asked 'Do you generally think of yourself as a little closer to one of the parties than the others?' and if they mention a party in reply are counted as 'not very strong' identifiers.

13 The one exception I have so far found is that the rate of partisan weakening has been faster among Labour trade unionists than Labour non-trade unionists (0·40 as opposed to 0·22). A possible reason, as yet untested, is that Labour trade unionists in 1979 included more non-manual workers than in 1964; non-manual Labour identifiers tend to be slightly less strongly partisan than their manual counterparts.

14 This finding is reinforced by the results of two Gallup surveys on 'life satisfaction', conducted in February 1973 and January 1976. The two surveys found that the majority of the working class – usually a substantial one – were satisfied with five 'life domains' out of nine, including leisure, work, housing, their standard of living and their children's education. Moreover, working-class levels of satisfaction were only fractionally lower (by 4 percentage points) than middle-class levels. The downturn in the economy and exceptional price inflation between 1973 and 1976 appeared to have little impact on 'life satisfaction'; indeed, working-class levels rose marginally, while middle-class levels marginally declined. For further details see Richard Rose, *Politics in England*, 3rd ed (London: Faber, 1980), pp. 343–4.

15 For example, trade union members were asked whether 'your own trade union at the place where you work is too ready to take industrial action or not'. The answers were: far/a little too ready, 16 per cent; about right, 52 per cent; not quite/nearly ready enough, 28 per cent.

16 The decline of manual workers' class-consciousness, and the fading of Labour's image as a party for the working class might also reflect some of the achievements of Labour governments. The Labour Party's educational policies – and successes – are a notable case in point. One of the main justifications for the replacement of secondary modern and grammar schools by non-selective comprehensive schools – a process that was near to completion by the late 1970s – was that it would break down the social and cultural barriers of class. The expansion of higher education, especially polytechnics, has been supported by the Labour Party on similar grounds.

17 It is important to appreciate some of the limits to this method of analysis. For one thing, it is difficult to apply to those issues (sometimes described as 'valence' as opposed to 'position' issues) on which the electorate shares a near-identical goal and disagrees only on the relative ability of the parties to achieve it, e.g. a reduction in the

rate of inflation or crime. On these issues one can only discover which party is preferred by electors. For another, not all 'position' issues are unidimensional: although the issue of nationalisation can be represented by a line running from 'nationalise the lot' to 'denationalise the lot', there would be no obviously correct location for the voter who believed in nationalising some industries and denationalising others. Thirdly, the 'position' on the line for any group of electors is only the average of a scatter of positions of the individuals composing the group; and the degree of scatter itself varies across issues and between groups. Fourthly, the position attributed to the two parties is based on the perceptions of the electorate as a whole, not on those of a particular subgroup. However, perceptions of the two parties' positions do not vary sufficiently to affect the conclusions drawn in the text. These and other technical points are discussed in more detail in Ivor Crewe and Bo Särlvik, 'Popular attitudes and the Conservative Party', in Zig Layton-Henry (ed.), *Conservative Party Politics* (London: Macmillan, 1979).

18 See Crewe and Särlvik, 'Popular attitudes and the Conservative Party'.

19 See, for example, R. S. Milne and H. C. McKenzie, *Marginal Seat 1955* (London: Hansard Society, 1958) pp. 117–21.

20 More detailed analysis of trends in subgroups shows that the sharpest declines occurred among the post-1950 cohort of working-class identifiers; the most gentle among the post-1950 cohort of middle-class identifiers.

21 For example, the Gallup polls report that the proportion (of the general public) who say that the government is spending too little on the health service has increased from 30 per cent in 1960 to 66 per cent in 1979; on education from 34 to 52 per cent. On the other hand, the proportion agreeing that 'generally speaking, and thinking of Britain as a whole, trade unions are a good thing' has gradually fallen from 69 per cent in 1952 to say 58 per cent in 1979.

22 The historical evidence offers scant support for this claim. Labour's most radical manifesto since the war was that of 1959 when it promised to nationalise 500 leading private companies; the election resulted in a Conservative majority of 100. One of Labour's blandest manifestos was that of 1966 ('Time for Decision'); the election resulted in a Labour majority of 96. To cite the radicalism of the 1945 manifesto, as proponents of this claim usually do, is to ignore the crucial fact that Labour's leadership had been in a coalition government for the previous five years. Even if a positive correlation between the Labour vote and the radicalism of its manifesto could be established, this would prove little unless it could also be shown that both were not the result of a third, decisive, factor – whether or not Labour was in office.

23 The far left parties did spectacularly badly. The thirty-eight communist candidates, all standing in overwhelmingly working-class constituencies, averaged 0·9 per cent of the constituency vote. The Ecology Party obtained 1·1 per cent; the National Front beat the Communist candidate in ten of the twelve seats in which they competed against each other. The Workers' Revolutionary Party did worse still, always coming bottom of the poll (except where an independent stood).

24 This table can only be treated as a broad, summary guide, and is open to objections on details. The labelling of issues as ones on which the Labour Party is united and firm or divided and ambivalent is my own. The definition of a 'divided public opinion' as that which splits within the range 40–60 per cent is inevitably arbitrary. And the dichotomising of responses to all the questions, whatever their original answer format, is a crude form of standardisation.

Readers should note that a similar table constructed for the working-class electorate only would look very similar. The mean difference between the opinion of all electors and working-class electors was only 4 percentage points. The only issues on which the gap was substantially greater were: the reduction of the powers of the House of Lords (manual workers were 11 per cent more in favour); increased state control of land for building (10 per cent more in favour); establishing comprehensive schools in place of grammar schools (9 per cent more in favour); redistributing income and wealth in favour of ordinary working people (9 per cent more in favour); introducing a wealth tax (8 per cent more in favour).

25 Calculated from Office of Population Censuses and Surveys, *General Household Survey 1977* (London: HMSO, 1979), p .29, table 3.15.

26 For an impressionistic but persuasive argument along these lines, see David Donnison, 'New times, new politics', *New Society,* 2 October 1980, p. 25.

2 Changing Styles of Labour Leadership

PHILIP WILLIAMS

I

Every leader of a major British party must try to reconcile several objectives: to unite his followers, persuade the electorate and eventually govern the country. Sometimes these aims converge. Harmonious parties are the likeliest to win elections or govern well. Electoral victory helps to unite party members, and the prospect of it holds a party or a government together. When an administration is successful, floating voters pay as little heed to the opposition parties as its own supporters do to the rebels in its ranks. Yet the three aims may also point in different directions. The uncommitted, who decide elections, may be put off by the cherished plans of the party zealots or seduced by imprudent promises which become a handicap in government. Concessions to the zealots may be essential for uniting the party, but can frighten the voters or prove unworkable or damaging in practice. A recognition of realities and a choice of priorities are required to govern successfully, but are often likely to offend either the activists or the electorate.

No politician reaches the front rank without showing some capacity in all three tasks. But each displays a different combination of skills and a different range of priorities. Party leaders have sometimes been classified into three types: the Dreamer who inspires and alarms; the Fixer who is admired but not trusted; and the Regular who generates public confidence but not excitement – pejoratively, the Wild Man, the Con Man and the Plodder; sympathetically, the Pathfinder, the Problem-Solver and the Stabiliser. (Gladstone, Lloyd George and Baldwin come to mind, though individuals often combine the characteristics of different types, or display them at different times, so that pure specimens are rare). When a leader departs, owing to unpopularity or simply to age, the country or the party will often prefer a successor of another type, who may well choose deliberately to capitalise on the contrast.[1]

British parties tend to give their confidence much more frequently to the third type than to the first two, except in crises – and even these have been resolved within the normal rules of the political system, which are hardly ever suspended in time of peace. That is perhaps not surprising, for the Stabilisers are always sound party men; and in normal conditions strong parties, and a prolonged parliamentary apprenticeship for their prospective leaders, have usually screened out those aspirants whose dynamism, flamboyance, or waywardness has earned suspicion rather than admiration from their colleagues. The Pathfinder, feeling a duty to lead in a particular direction, will have his own vision and destination in mind, and they may not appeal to all his followers; the more cautious ones may be put off by the very enthusiasm and passion he can sometimes excite. In the Conservative Party until recently the leader 'emerged' after private consultations which put a heavy premium on acceptability to the main factions and chieftains – so that although authority, once attained, commanded deferential loyalty as long as it was exercised successfully, it was usually conferred only on candidates who were thought unlikely to provoke division. For quite different reasons, turbulent and potentially divisive characters were regarded with equal suspicion in the Labour Party – with its extra-parliamentary origins, and the emphasis upon solidarity and collective decisions which it derives from its trade union base. Reconcilers rather than mobilisers – or Stabilisers rather than Pathfinders – therefore enjoy an advantage among the relatively few selectors in both parties, which is only accentuated by the context in which the selectors operate. Both parties must appeal to an electorate which is rarely passionate about politics, normally prefers comfortable moderation to disquieting trenchancy, and thus values at most times exactly the unspectacular qualities in which the Stabilisers excel.

Somewhat similar considerations limit the appeal of the Problem-Solving types, whose special talent is to produce novel answers to the intractable problems of the moment, and whose drawback lies precisely in the absence of that long-term consistency of purpose which marks the Pathfinder. Their very assets of ingenuity and unpredictability can easily become liabilities among prospective colleagues for whom that kind of leadership would make it hard to calculate their course in their own interest or the party's; while in the ordinary voter, wishing only to keep the ship of state 'steady as she goes', the same qualities tend to evoke deep suspicion. Consequently few Problem-Solvers attain leadership, and while those few may enjoy reputations that glitter for a time, they are liable in the long run to suffer complete eclipse.

Party leaders do not operate in a vacuum, but interact with a specific following in a specific context. Within any political system dominated by two big parties, each must be a heterogeneous coalition including sections to which, in some conditions, a rival leader can successfully appeal. These conditions depend on circumstances and on the traditions of the party. Thus the Conservative Party began as an adjunct to its parliamentary leaders, and has attached great virtue to loyalty – unlike right-wing parties in France or Germany or the United States. (It has been particularly wary of Pathfinders, which may partly explain why both observers and participants find the current British scene somewhat abnormal.)

II

'Only after the Labour Party has obtained a clear majority, when it has shown whether and to what extent it can accomplish its aims, will it be possible to say what it is . . . only after it has survived the inevitable disappointments, when the messianic hopes nourished even by its doughtiest champions, are broken, and the myth lies shattered, will the stuff of which it is made be known. Only then will it become clear what the Labour Party stands for.'[2] So wrote Egon Wertheimer in the most perceptive study of the Labour Party, published just before MacDonald's second government.

The Labour Party is subject to centripetal and centrifugal forces both of which are different from those which act upon the Conservatives, and its essential character differs too. A party seeking changes in society is vulnerable to internal quarrels about the pace and direction of the march, while one aiming at preventing or containing change finds it easier to hold together, except in times when there is as good a case for concession as for diehard resistance. Both for these general reasons and because of their respective histories, most Conservatives have usually and consciously given a higher priority to retaining power than to preserving the purity of their principles, whereas in the Labour Party – which for half its life to date was a body of propagandists remote from real power – the opposite priority has appealed more widely and prevailed more frequently. The difference has not disappeared in the second half of Labour's existence. For previously the different perspectives of the power-seekers (whether pure pragmatists or practical reformers) and of the utopian purists had been easily glossed over. Measures welcomed by the latter as first steps towards the new Jerusalem could be presented by the former to a sceptical electorate as reforms necessary in their own right. When Labour seemed far from power, and the immediate grievances of its natural supporters were acute, its pragmatic leaders could avert trouble in the ranks by stirring rhetoric about a far future, knowing that their visionary dreams would not fall to be implemented in their political lifetimes and would therefore never return as nightmares to haunt them on the eve of poll. But the unity so achieved rested on fragile foundations, as Wertheimer foresaw.

Sixteen years passed before his condition was fulfilled. But after 1951, when the early programmes had been enacted and the early grievances remedied, different wings of the party began trying to bring rhetoric and reality into harmony. Some sought to scale down the rhetoric to match only those proposals which did or might enjoy popular support; others, to scale up the proposals to match the sweeping promises of the rhetoric; others still to shelve the effort to harmonise as far too dangerous, preferring a comfortable accord on an ambiguous objective to which everyone could attach his own meaning, to the risk of disruption entailed by any attempt to achieve intellectual clarity. Contrary to legend, the three tendencies did not really divide leaders from the 'rank and file', but could each be found, in different proportions at different times, at all levels in the party.

Arguments over power and principles by no means constituted the only difference between Conservatives and Labour. The former were a governing-class party seeking to build support in the country for the men who wielded power; the latter, a party of provincials and outsiders, built from the ground up, in opposition to the governing class, and instinctively allergic to deference, social or political. Its origin and base were in the organised working class, and to Labour people it is a point of both duty and pride that the party speaks for the workers, so that when a leader can plausibly claim to articulate their authentic voice, that voice carries a powerful resonance – from which some surprising figures have drawn political profit. (Labour has always attracted sympathisers of bourgeois origin. As Wertheimer put it in 1929: 'In contrast to their Continental colleagues, the British workers . . . make use of men born with an understanding of tradition and a ruthless will to power [rather] than limit their choice to men of their own class.'[3] This has been just as true – or even truer – of the radical left as of the orthodox right, and the 'prolier than thou' note is regularly sounded by trumpeters of rather dubious working-class credentials.)

There is also a distinctive Labour attitude to leadership itself. To some extent this is the outcome of the long years out of office, which – as with rank-and-file American Republicans ever since the New Deal – have secreted a marked opposition mentality. But that is not the only reason, as the impact of James Ramsay MacDonald showed in one generation, and that of Harold Wilson in another. It was not always so. MacDonald, though he inspired little confidence in many of his colleagues, attracted more public adulation from his followers than any successor. Moreover, shortly before the trauma of 1931 Wertheimer observed – and he was not referring to MacDonald alone – that whereas in Germany the socialist leader 'goes his way unloved . . . [and] half anonymous in the party ghetto', in Britain on the other hand 'the cult of the individual leader knows no limits ... Instead of loyalty to that almost metaphysical concept – the movement – we often find in England a personal loyalty to the individual leader.'[4] Two years later the three best-known figures in the party defected, leaving a permanent scar on its collective psyche. Sometimes a newcomer may enjoy a brief honeymoon, but normally, ever since 1931, the actions of Labour leaders are scrutinised with suspicion, while insurgent prophets of the ancient verities are heard with respect or even credulity.

History has also endowed the party with a federal structure, which has two crucial features. First, the main trade unions are much the largest component of the party. They founded it, they finance it and they control its formal decision-making machinery. Yet in their own decisions, political alignments take a poor second place to the needs of the union in the industrial and organisational spheres. Secondly, the federal constitution affords rival leaders a political base and an alternative career ladder outside the parliamentary party. Among the Conservatives, the road to power *for* the party at Westminster is the only road to power *within* the party; the careers of Lord Randolph Churchill in the last century and Enoch Powell in this one point that moral.

Labour's situation is quite different. For prospective party leaders, National Executive membership provides a position of influence and prominence which Wilson and Callaghan enjoyed for many years, to the great advantage of their standing within the party, which Foot also had for a shorter period, but which Gaitskell acquired late and Healey held only briefly. More important still, its constituency section has since 1937 elected its own members independently of the unions, and has afforded successive spokesmen of the parliamentary minority – Cripps, Bevan, Foot when he chose, and Benn – the official platform which they were denied at Westminster. Since 1952, indeed, that section has been a stonghold of the left, giving its representatives like Crossman, Barbara Castle, Mikardo, or Heffer high visibility with the party membership.

A Labour leader therefore has two specific problems, besides those familiar to his opposite numbers in other parties. In the first place, his dealings with the big trade unions are not confined to the economic policies of his actual or prospective administration; he needs also to cultivate their support in any current argument, even purely political, which arouses serious controversy within the Labour ranks. Secondly, the extremist critics with whom any party leader must reckon are, in his case, often championed by influential rival politicians, seeking party power by a different route. The leader's own assets vary with his followers' expectations of power. He is strong when seen as a potential premier on the verge of victory, stronger still when it has just been won; weak as a newcomer to the leadership of the opposition, or in office when defeat looms; very vulnerable when an election has just been lost. His influence also depends on his expected tenure. A goose who may lay golden eggs is a more attractive bird than a lame duck.

From 1935 to 1980 there were eight Conservative leaders, six German chancellors, and eight American presidents; but the Labour leadership was held by only four men. The incumbent may find himself suspected and harassed but, unlike his Conservative opposite number, he has little reason to fear ejection from his position or any serious threat to it. The Conservatives, for whom 'fitness to govern' is a value and personal leadership a presumed electoral asset, give their leaders more freedom to act during a more precarious tenure; Labour, seeking to base its appeal on its policies, believes much less in the potential influence of individual leadership and therefore attaches less importance to the leader's personality. (Besides, the party and unions, while ungenerous about the conditions of work of the movement's own employees in all ranks, do recognise their claim to enjoy job security like everyone else.) In consequence, the post has usually been vacated suddenly – by MacDonald's switch, Gaitskell's death and Wilson's resignation; so that only Attlee and Callaghan have stayed on as prospective premiers until it was clear that a successor must soon be chosen.

III

Clement Attlee was a classic Stabiliser, and survived for twenty years. Yet he was at first a stop-gap, chosen when the unions, deeply suspicious of politicians since the defections of MacDonald and Mosley, were forcefully reasserting their power. It was their spokesman Ernest Bevin who had toppled Lansbury, the previous parliamentary leader, and who was to buttress Attlee against his rivals – Morrison in 1945, Cripps in 1947. The left was also suspect to them for toying with separatist or breakaway movements – the ILP, the Socialist League, the United and Popular Fronts; Cripps was expelled in 1939, returning in 1945 as a moderate man of government. But in 1937 the unions made one concession – autonomy for the constituency parties in National Executive elections – which, fifteen years later, was to give the left its first foothold within the machine.

Before the war Attlee was a self-effacing leader; the main policy change – over British rearmament – was taken against his wishes. He became an efficient and decisive minister in the wartime coalition, and a strong Prime Minister both in external affairs – India, defence and foreign policy – and in choosing and sometimes dismissing ministers. He looked for men of substance rather than factional spokesmen, but promoted the principal left-winger, Aneurin Bevan (who duly adjusted his conduct in office). Attlee was aloof and taciturn, with few friends and no group of personal followers. In Cabinet or NEC he doodled through discussions, giving no lead but summing up at the end when the weight of opinion had become clear. He held the balance judiciously between ambitious and mutually mistrustful colleagues, and his government's policies satisfied most Labour supporters. When it ended, his own position was unchallenged. But its heavy dependence on Cripps and Bevin became evident after both men fell ill and died.

The Korean War, the impending election and the rivalries within the Cabinet had revived old tensions between the different wings of the party. Attlee, persisting in his old habit of hoarding his personal prestige, repeatedly allowed wounds to fester and become inflamed. Stronger action earlier could have averted the resignation of Bevan (together with Harold Wilson) in April 1951, which gave the left-wing critics a powerful leader for whom they were a useful lever to overturn the existing hierarchy. In 1952 the Bevanites won six of the seven constituency seats on the NEC, which have been held by the left ever since. Two years later they nearly defeated the leadership over German rearmament, winning over the majority of the constituency parties though not of the unions (a split verdict which, contrary to legend, happened very rarely).[5] In 1955, after a year in which Bevan abandoned his previous restraint and directly challenged both the union and party leaderships, he was narrowly saved by Attlee at the last minute from a rash attempt to expel him from the party; and Attlee thus acquired undeserved credit for averting a crisis which would never have arisen but for his own reluctance to clarify his intentions in good time.

Attlee stayed on after turning 70 largely in order to damage the chances of his deputy, Herbert Morrison, with whom both he and the union leaders had for years been at odds. As Morrison's skills diminished with age and Bevan's aggressions grew with disappointment, support grew for the youngest contender, Hugh Gaitskell. Bevan had antagonised too many people, and Morrison's inevitably brief tenure could bring only a short lull in the succession struggle. Gaitskell, who was gradually shedding his previous combative image, came to seem both the most acceptable to the electorate and the likeliest to unite the party and so to defer the next leadership contest, it was supposed, for twenty years. At the end of 1955 he was elected in a three-cornered contest, winning about 60 per cent of the votes cast.

Gaitskell was a Pathfinder, a rarity among British party leaders.[6] He wanted Labour to abandon its ingrained opposition-mindedness, and took more personal initiative than his predecessor or successor in pointing his followers in the right direction. But he did so at first by cajolery not confrontation, and it was only after the 1959 election, when his leadership was directly challenged, that he was driven into an open conflict with many of his followers which revealed his fighting qualities to the nation.

He had first entered the House of Commons only ten years before becoming leader, the shortest apprenticeship this century and less than half the average length. Like those who have undergone a normal period of socialisation, however, he too began by seeking to show himself acceptable to all within the party, and spent his first three years in living down his past reputation as a hatchet-man of the right. He succeeded in reconciling first Bevan's ablest allies, Harold Wilson and Richard Crossman, and then Bevan himself. Up to the 1959 election, the left was quiescent and there was little opposition on either domestic or foreign policy – apart from a last-minute challenge over unilateral nuclear disarmament from Frank Cousins, the new general secretary of the Transport Workers (Bevin's old union and the largest of them all). Gaitskell was a sharp contrast to Attlee – both far more gregarious and far more willing to give a strong and early lead. When the second habit brought him under furious attack and he fell back on the few friends he could trust, he acquired a much-exaggerated reputation for cliquishness.

Though not at first blamed for the 1959 election defeat, he provoked a storm by an ill-prepared and maladroit attempt to dilute the party's vague commitment to sweeping future nationalisation: not an assault on a disputed policy but an affront to a symbol and a myth. It played into the hands of his left-wing critics, for it shook the confidence of the unions on whom he had hitherto relied – although at that time few of them sought any actual nationalisation at all. When the Campaign for Nuclear Disarmament aroused a big movement of (largely non-political) opinion in the country, Gaitskell's critics took it up and defeated the leadership – narrowly, but for the first time ever on a major issue – at the 1960 party conference in Scarborough. Doubts about Gaitskell's ability to reunite the party were so widespread that neither the NEC nor party headquarters gave him reliable support. But the Labour MPs reacted differently, and when Wilson stood against Gaitskell claiming that he could reconcile the factions, he lost by over two to one. Then the next conference overwhelmingly repudiated unilateralism, and in 1962 Gaitskell conciliated his less intransigent opponents by his vehement opposition to the terms proposed for entering the Common Market. But his leadership cannot well be compared with that of his peers, since they are naturally judged by their performance as prime ministers rather than in the preparatory roles of opposition spokesmen and election campaigners. Alone among those who have led a major party for long in this century, Gaitskell never reached Downing Street, dying suddenly in January 1963.

Harold Wilson was elected to succeed him, on the second ballot. Most trade union MPs favoured George Brown, whose impulsive personality inspired little confidence elsewhere; and the Shadow Cabinet – but few others – preferred James Callaghan. Wilson, the ablest parliamentarian of the three, was supported by the left wing with whom he had intermittently associated but never really agreed: an appropriate ambiguous start for the first Fixer – or Problem-Solver – in the regular line of Labour leaders.[7] His tenure saw two long-term changes, in the character of the

Labour left and in the conduct of the major unions; and two cycles in the party's fortunes, twice from opposition to precarious office and then, once only, to a secure position in government. These similar processes occurred in very different moods and contexts.

In the optimistic 1960s it was hoped that Labour could transform itself simultaneously into a party of government and a party of modernisation, achieving prosperity through technological progress without radical decisions or divisive conflicts. Wilson enjoyed many advantages: the leader's authority restored, the principal left-wingers co-opted, his own governmental experience and tactical skills recognised as indispensable – so that even a single-figure parliamentary majority became a personal asset. But the frenzied early activity, and the subsequent endless administrative tinkering and ministerial reshuffling, concealed a deep conservatism, buttressed by optimism, about the major problems of the country's future. The parity of the pound was to be defended without the cost being examined, a presence East of Suez maintained without the requisite military resources being supplied. Similar inveterate optimism prevailed over Vietnam, where Britain sought to remain detached from the war while still exercising influence in Washington, and over Rhodesia, where sanctions were supposed to overcome resistance in weeks rather than months. Concentration on balancing factions in ministerial appointments kept the party together – but produced a Cabinet of able but quarrelsome seniors, and others who apparently qualified for high office mainly by personal allegiance, or benefited from the Prime Minister's reluctance to remove anyone. He trusted his own entourage, who enjoyed little confidence elsewhere. But he regarded his leading colleagues with ill-disguised suspicion and preferred to deal with them individually, or in committees which he could manipulate, rather than in the Cabinet itself.

There was therefore little team spirit to help keep the government together when the optimism, which had persisted until the 1966 election victory, suddenly and rapidly faded. At home, the deflationary measures of July 1966 destroyed the early expansionist hopes – without averting the devaluation which the Prime Minister had refused even to contemplate until it became inevitable. Punctilious fulfilment of manifesto commitments to legislate did not prevent the disillusionment of Labour supporters when social services suffered and unemployment rose. Abroad, Britain's enforced retreat led both to a withdrawal East of Suez and to an application to enter the Common Market – on which Wilson's consummate tactical skill achieved near-unanimity in the government. On the left, the unilateralist politicians of 1960 served without visible discomfort in an administration which kept and built Polaris submarines; only Cousins, never at home in the House of Commons, resigned in 1966 to lead his union's opposition to the incomes policy which he had half-openly resisted in office. (Cousins was replaced as Minister of

Technology by Anthony Wedgwood Benn – as he then was – who promptly set about cultivating his early image as a technocrat with all the assiduity he later displayed in his new incarnation as a champion of popular participation.) On the right wing, several resignations expressed unhappiness at some domestic policies, or frustration at the style in which the government was managed: bad blood at the top is usually far more evident in Labour than in Conservative Cabinets, but this time No. 10 was in the thick of it. On the whole, however, the backbenchers remained faithful, and the Prime Minister was even able occasionally to mobilise them against his own colleagues.

Collective responsibility, frayed at the end of the Conservative government, was fast eroded in this one by leaks (usually from highly placed cisterns) and semi-public quarrels. Efforts to modernise in industry were hampered by the reluctance of the unions, which might have yielded in an expansionist climate but was reinforced by economic stagnation. Whether party victory or successful government was the criterion, the results were dismal. By 1968 local and by-elections showed an unprecedented record of disaster. Party conferences defeated the leadership twelve times – on one major issue, incomes policy, by five to one; these votes were ignored, storing up resentment against their leaders among those who stayed in the party. (Officially, individual menbership rose by a third under Attlee's government, but fell by a sixth under Wilson's, declining every year; by less artificial and more realistic estimates, the fall was much greater.)[8] The forced devaluation at the end of 1967 drove James Callaghan from the Treasury, and badly damaged the prestige and influence of the Prime Minister who had sacrificed so much to avoid it. In 1968–9 the government lost its major items of legislation. House of Lords reform was successfully filibustered because it would have increased the Prime Minister's patronage; and a Trade Union Bill, to which he fully committed his personal authority, failed when the strenuous TUC objections found growing support among politicians. By this time Wilson, who had always openly advocated reconciling the irreconcilable, and seeking to conceal disunity behind ambiguous phrases, was himself in sharp confrontation with the unions on whom the party had always depended so heavily – and found most of his own political colleagues defecting to the other side. James Callaghan began the revolt when, openly defying Cabinet solidarity, he voted against the penal clauses in the Labour Party NEC, but could not be dismissed because too many MPs and ministers shared his view.

The long-delayed economic upturn came too late and seemed too precarious to save Wilson's government at the general election in June 1970. In opposition, Wilson kept a very low profile and followed a line of no resistance. The old Bevanite left, which he had so successfully neutralised, was giving way to a new left wing, much more working class in composition. Its position within the party was much stronger. The two largest unions (Transport Workers and Engineers) and the fastest-growing ones (in the public sector) had left-wing leaders; widespread disillusionment had eroded confidence in the whole front bench; and a growing hostility to the Common Market, which Edward Heath's government was determined to join, threatened the positions of Labour's right wing who mainly favoured entry. Though he had himself sought to go in, Wilson judged it imprudent to resist the trend; some who tried to do so, including the deputy leader Roy Jenkins, resigned from the Shadow Cabinet. By 1972 the left was in control of the party machine. It repealed the old rules which kept people with communist or Trotskyist associations outside the party, and ceased to protect MPs whose local parties fell under extreme left control. It was not long before they were to choose an avowed Trotskyist as Labour's official youth organiser, and to brush aside the national agent's formal warning against planned Trotskyist infiltration in the constituencies.

In 1974 the electorate repudiated Heath over the miners' strike, and Wilson was returned to another precarious period of office, without a parliamentary majority. The mood was quite unlike that of ten years earlier. The two major parties now commanded only 60 per cent of the electorate between them, 7 per cent fewer than in 1964 (and 20 per cent fewer than in 1951). Labour regained office with less hopeful followers and less self-confident leaders, and though a second election after eight months gave it a tiny majority for a short time, its survival depended on the divisions among its various opponents.

Wilson's style of government was also very different and more collegial. With many experienced colleagues, the Prime Minister was far less obtrusive, and personal relations were not nearly so strained. The most divisive issue, the Common Market, was evaded in 1975 by a referendum and a formal suspension of Cabinet responsibility (unprecedented except in the 1931 coalition government). The hitherto intransigent left was conciliated by the inclusion of its leader, Michael Foot, whose 'social contract' with the trade unions did nothing to check the inflationary pressure which reached a peak in 1975. Soon the government had to retreat, with deflation and a loan from the International Monetary Fund in the following year, and a formal pact with the Liberals in 1977. But by then it was no longer led by Harold Wilson, who had suddenly retired in March 1976.

On the third ballot Callaghan was elected against Foot, who became his deputy leader without opposition. It was a symbolic alliance of two men from the old parliamentary right and left wings, now both conspicuous conciliators, each outpolling rivals like Jenkins and Benn who, within the opposing tendencies, seemed to stand for clarity and confrontation. Foot was to prove an invaluable guardian of the new leader's left flank, as Bevan had for Gaitskell, and to undertake many functions of liaison within the party. Henderson had performed similar services for MacDonald, Morrison for Attlee, and Callaghan himself in Wilson's previous government; while Gaitskell after Bevan's death in 1960, and Wilson through reluctance to recognise an heir-apparent in 1964–70, had suffered by the absence of such a figure,

Callaghan was a Stabiliser, miscast by the press as another Harold Wilson and all the more determined to behave differently. He entered the Labour movement through birth rather than conversion – the only leader ever to have served as a trade union official, and the only one of the last four not to have attended a university. He had been on the Parliamentary Committee for twenty-four years, a long apprenticeship during which he had always stayed close to the centre of gravity of Labour opinion and to the party and union machines. He had served thirty-two years in Parliament, the longest of any non-Conservative party leader this century. In office, he had done his share of fixing in the past, but he had also shown, notably over Northern Ireland in 1969, an ability to elicit general public confidence which his predecessor enjoyed for barely three of his twelve years at the helm.

As Prime Minister he, like Wilson, balanced carefully between the factions. But he was more respectful of the Cabinet's collegiate traditions, less devious with and suspicious of his colleagues, less obsessed with short-term crisis management and more interested in larger and longer-term issues, and more concerned with getting his own way than with protecting his own position. Michael Foot's new role left a vacuum on the left, filled by Tony Benn as the new champion of a younger generation hoping to reshape the party in opposition in the next decade. Carefully avoiding either offering his resignation or openly courting dismissal, Benn tested the outer limits of tolerance in detaching himself from his colleagues; prime ministers might feel strong enough to shift him to a lesser office as Wilson had done, but not to remove him altogether from the government.

Callaghan presided over three years in which the inflation rate fell back to single figures, thanks largely to Jack Jones, Cousins's left-wing successor as leader of the Transport Workers. By sponsoring a voluntary wage limit on union claims, the TUC gave the mass of workers a welcome opportunity to escape from the inflationary spiral. But in deciding not to go to the country in October 1978, Callaghan was gambling heavily on the policy's lasting appeal, while after Jones retired there was no trade union leader of sufficient stature to take his place. The government had committed itself to devolution in Scotland and Wales, which helped to keep it in office but was unpopular among many English backbenchers. They filibustered a Bill covering both countries, and then frustrated a separate measure for Scotland, while the corresponding

Welsh Bill failed in a referendum. Nearly all the smaller parties then joined to defeat the government (by a single vote) on a motion of no confidence. The electorate, which had blamed the previous government for mishandling industrial relations five years earlier, now penalised Labour for the unpopular strikes of the preceding winter. A 5 per cent swing (a postwar record) carried the Conservatives back to power.

Wertheimer's prediction, that the character of the Labour Party could be judged only after it had held full responsibility, has now been tested three times. Under Attlee in 1945–51, the first majority Labour government alienated much of the middle-class support it initially enjoyed, but fully satisfied its working-class followers, as the collapse of its communist and independent left critics proved. Those activists within the party who were unhappy over some aspects, particularly of foreign and defence policy, therefore found little sympathy among the mass of Labour voters. Under Wilson and Callaghan the outcome was different. Both sought, as Gaitskell had done by different means, to turn Labour into a party which saw government, rather than opposition, as its natural role. Both, taking power in difficult economic and social circumstances, disappointed their followers – not so much by neglect of the manifesto commitments to which politicians attach such disproportionate importance, but by failures in economic management. Judged on performance, not promise, they failed to satisfy either their electoral followers, who voted Tory or stayed at home, or the activist party members who turned sharply to the left. Within the Labour Party, Attlee and his principal colleagues had been vigorously criticised but also vigorously defended after 1951; their influence and standing were diminished but not destroyed. When the two later Labour prime ministers left office in 1970 and in 1979, the collapse of their authority was far more dramatic and complete.

In 1979, back in opposition with a leader whose tenure could not continue for many more years, Labour's succession crisis – only the second in its history – became entangled with the old conflict over the type of party it wished to be. While Mrs Thatcher's government proclaimed with relish its intention to dismantle the 'Attlee consensus', Labour mounted no effective protest. Instead, the NEC revived all the issues which in former years had most bitterly divided the party – Common Market membership, unilateralism, sweeping nationalisation (in some cases now proposed without compensation) and even the House of Lords. But mainly it concentrated on reshaping the party's structure. As its activist members became fewer and fewer, and less and less typical of Labour voters, it pressed more earnestly in the name of democracy its claims to expand its authority over the party's elected representatives. Benn now led the NEC in open, repeated and humiliating challenges to the parliamentary leadership. The main changes proposed were designed to maximise the opportunities for ousting Labour MPs who offended their local activists, to remove the choice of leader from the parliamentary party, to weaken a Labour prime minister's power by eliminating his right to choose or place his colleagues, and to deny them collectively any formal say in the terms of the election manifesto which they were supposed to implement in office. Callaghan and Foot tried to foil this assault by delay and compromise, hoping that the major unions – exasperated at financing a declining party preoccupied with endless internal wrangling – would come to their rescue at the 1980 conference. To many on the right wing of the party, their strategy offered a hope of escape from the pressure of the unpopular left only by accepting and making even more visible the dominance of the equally unpopular trade union leaders: an unlikely way to revive Labour's electoral fortunes.

IV

During the last half-century, social changes have made it harder for a party leader to achieve any of his aims, and far harder to pursue them all successfully. The electorate has become much more volatile and suspicious. Politicians have grown more recalcitrant as parties have become more fragmented, factions more entrenched, individuals more independent; in the House of Commons a loyal and disciplined generation of backbenchers – Tory knights of the shire and Labour trade union officials – has been supplanted by a younger breed of advertising and public relations men, journalists and lecturers. Meanwhile, as interest groups have grown assertive, social deference has vanished and political legitimacy has been challenged; so that government by consent has grown increasingly difficult.

In the past, the party in office always found it necessary at times to pursue policies which its active supporters did not expect or welcome. At home, when the political climate changed before 1951, a weak Labour government began dismantling controls, as before 1964 a Conservative one reverted to planning, and as Labour curbed public expenditure and began monetary restraint before 1979. Abroad, great changes in the country's course have often commanded general assent thanks to sponsorship by the leaders of the very party which might otherwise have protested most; adherence to NATO in the 1940s, decolonisation in the 1950s (or, across the Atlantic, Richard Nixon's recognition of China). But the zealots on both sides – perhaps because of underlying resentment at the national decline – are far less tolerant and more rebellious than they once were; such surprises are therefore more likely to be seen as betrayals, and to afford another opportunity for challenging the judgement or authority of the leader.

All these changes affect leaders in either major party, but the two special problems on the Labour side have also grown harder to handle. That of the status of the unions, though in principle posed ever since the party became a serious claimant to power, has in practice been deferred for two generations by a confident, skilful and moderate union leadership. Today those men lack true successors, and the problem seems more intractable than ever before.

In countries like the United States or Germany or Holland, where the unions are powerful allies of a big political party, the problems arising from that relationship resemble those between any party and a friendly pressure group with a mass membership. The British situation is different. The unions are integrated into the structure of the party and, as organisations, their procedures and decisions may determine its policy on major political questions. As a result, before each conference the chiefs of the opposition or even of the government must persuade or conciliate the unions' principal spokesmen, who as individuals may cohabit with the elected politicians in positions of leadership, and collectively as a General Council will deal with Cabinets and Shadow Cabinets on almost equal terms. The difficulties arising from that relationship, which are of many kinds, are of a different order of magnitude from those elsewhere. Thus in 1931 a Labour Cabinet was split and a Labour Prime Minister expelled when the General Council condemned his financial policy. In 1969 another Cabinet retreated, abandoning the industrial relations legislation to which the TUC objected and shattering the prestige of the Prime Minister who had committed himself to it. In 1979 a third Cabinet was rejected by the electorate which, resentful at the industrial activities of some unions, exacted the price from the political party associated with them and the Prime Minister who, more than any predecessor, had built his career on union goodwill.

These conflicts did not follow the old ideological fault-lines. In 1931 Labour's right as well as its left opposed the policies of its former leaders. In 1969 the objectionable legislation was resented by the 'right-wing' trade unionists in the Cabinet, and promoted by Barbara Castle, a 'left-wing' minister who justly claimed to be acting in the tradition of Aneurin Bevan. That lifelong bugbear and scourge of the union leaders had always fiercely resisted their efforts either to support the policies of a parliamentary leadership to which he did not belong, or to impose their own upon one to which he did. In 1979 the strikers' unpopularity damaged the electoral prospects, not just of one wing or the other, but of the whole party.

The character of the conflicts differed too. In 1931 the General Council saw themselves as protecting working-class standards and the Labour ministers who wished to cut unemployment benefits as betraying the common cause. In 1960, in opposition, union votes were mobilised to impose a defence policy on the political leaders who would have to take the responsibility for recommending or implementing it. In 1969 the TUC as an organised interest in effect demanded a veto on changes in the legal terms on which that interest could operate. In 1979, specific actions by a handful of unions provoked a reaction from the voters.

Yet the underlying problem was the same. To outsiders the unions appeared as a powerful sectional interest enjoying great privileges – whether they were objected to as an obstacle to economic modernisation, or as a body with pretensions to share in policy-making in fields where they should not interfere, or as an industrial force capable of causing frequent inconvenience and an occasional lapse into local anarchy. But from inside the party the perspective was different. As its active membership became increasingly middle class, as it parliamentary spokesmen became more absorbed into the procedures of Westminster, as it grew less certain of its ideological destination, the union link appeared even to many non-unionists as the last guarantee that Labour would still represent the interests of the workers and the poor, and the last bulwark preventing a collapse into a band of professional politicians seeking only re-election and career advancement. The Labour Party has always worshipped solidarity and loyalty to collective decisions – a loyalty given to it because of the working-class identity of which the trade union link was the visible symbol. Thus for emotional reasons, quite as much as for the more familiar financial ones, the Labour Party could hardly live without the unions – yet it was becoming harder and harder for a Labour leader to convince the country (or himself) that it could live with them.

In any case, he could never neglect the unions because of their numbers, their resources, their social weight, and the growing salience of the problems which concern them most deeply: incomes policies and industrial relations. His relations with them are therefore probably the more difficult of his two special difficulties. Yet the other, that of his relationship with the zealots, has also become harder to manage since they ceased to believe that leaders and members all share the same distant aims. That change – the collapse of the old faith in an ambiguous 'socialism' which had different meanings for different speakers and audiences – has come about not just through disagreement about the location of the objective or the cost of the journey, but also through open distrust of the credentials of the guide.

The acceptance of personal leadership, which Wertheimer regarded as extraordinary in 1929, suffered a grievous blow two years later. As he foresaw, there was a testing time after Labour's first successful majority government, which made untenable in the long run the party's comfortable ambiguity about its nature and purpose which had been masked for so many years. After Gaitskell's premature effort in 1959 to settle the ambiguity by open debate in opposition, Wilson sought to solve the problem by stealth – hoping that performance in government would reveal the party's true character to the voters, while rhetoric about principles would divert the attention of the zealots. But by alienating all sections alike, his administration left the doubts unsettled and bequeathed to his successor an almost impossible task.

Disillusionment spread still further after another spell of government in adverse conditions. Old conflicts revived and new ones developed, in which policies and symbols, the identity of the next leader and the distribution of power within the party were all at stake – and all were fought out against a new background of mistrust and recrimination between the parliamentary leaders and their most single-minded and articulate followers, in a party which now, for the first time in its history, recognised no enemies and excluded no recruits among the revolutionary left. The disputes, moreover, were conducted in a glare of publicity which impeded any concession or compromise, since every blow to the prestige of any participant was underlined and magnified. The old arguments were therefore harder than ever to settle, and new ones always likely to arise. For the new propensity of the zealots to rebel in turn affects the parliamentarians, since any ground for resentment against the existing leader can so readily be exploited by a rival searching for a resonant theme.

Of course, party revolts are nothing new, and often they follow familiar patterns. Their leaders may be upstarts early in their careers, like Cripps in the 1930s or Crossman ten years later; or, as in the 1950s, middle-rankers like Bevan whose further advance seems blocked, or disgruntled ex-ministers without hope of office like Shinwell or even Morrison; or occasionally prominent figures who seem indifferent to it, as Foot did for many years. Their appeal to the average MP varies with their personality and the circumstances, and according to stages in the electoral cycle: with only one exception (1955), every lost election since the war has seen the Labour Party lurch to the left, though so far the approach of the next election has always pulled it back again. When the situation of an individual politician changes, his attitudes may change too: so Callaghan as Prime Minister rebuked Benn for flouting collective Cabinet responsibility by showing on the National Executive the same open dissent from government policy that Callaghan had himself shown under Wilson a few years earlier. (That too fitted a pattern of relations between prime ministers and their awkward colleagues. For Benn protested that ministers could not be bound over future party policies as distinct from present government ones, just as Joseph Chamberlain had done when he defied Gladstone in the early 1880s – and as Gladstone himself had, when he offended Palmerston twenty years earlier.)[9]

Today's challengers rightly rebuke the media for attributing these clashes merely to personal ambition: for whether or not that is present, their challenge finds an echo only if it articulates feelings and demands more widely shared. Yet while repudiating that explanation of their own conduct, they invoke it to explain that of the many others who have left the Labour Party altogether. Between the wars, many politicians had been recruited to Labour from other parties, usually the Liberals; in the twenty years after the last war, those few minor figures who changed allegiance might either join it or desert it; but in the last fifteen years the defections from Labour have been numerous, and have reached to the most senior levels. Including ten ex-ministers, two of them former deputy leaders of the party, this massive drain on the right is unprecedented in a potential governing party since the Liberals began to break up almost a century ago. No more than the newly intransigent and far-reaching character of the revolts on the left can it simply be explained away by reference to character defects of the politicians concerned. Both developments, indeed, are symptoms of the same malaise: the growing doubt whether the old 'broad church' Labour Party can or should survive much longer. Callaghan's successor will have to display exceptionally strong and skilful leadership to dispel that doubt and maintain the coalition as a viable political force.

V

Since this chapter was written, that successor has been elected. In exercising – no doubt for the last time – their newly challenged prerogative, Labour MPs made a revealing choice. In recent years the country has become harder to govern, and the Labour coalition harder to keep together. The parliamentary party, in preferring Michael Foot to Denis Healey, by 139 to 129 on the second ballot, indicated that in the eyes of MPs it was already the latter objective that took priority. But the new leader, like his predecessor, will be judged on his ability to press forward simultaneously towards those three familiar, distinct and perhaps conflicting aims: unity, victory and successful government.

Notes: Chapter 2

1 The classification is, of course, impressionistic, imprecise and highly personal. I would regard as Stabilisers: Campbell-Bannerman, Asquith, Bonar Law, Baldwin, Chamberlain, Attlee, Eden (*before* his premiership), Home, Callaghan. As Problem-Solvers: Balfour, Lloyd George, Macmillan, Wilson. As Pathfinders: MacDonald (before 1931), Churchill (at least 1940–45), Eden (as PM), Heath, Thatcher. Among those who never were PM, perhaps Foot (as leader) may fit the first category, Butler the second, Gaitskell the third.

2 E. Wertheimer, *Portrait of the Labour Party* (London: Putnam, 1929), p.xvi.

3 ibid., p.145.
4 ibid., pp. 168–9.
5 M. Harrison, *Trade Unions and the Labour Party since 1945* (London: Allen & Unwin, 1960), ch. V, especially pp. 138–40.
6 P. M. Williams, *Hugh Gaitskell* (London: Cape, 1979), ch. 12 on his election to the leadership, chs. 14–i and 27–ii on his leadership style.
7 Arthur Henderson, leader for a few weeks after MacDonald defected, might also qualify.
8 For instance, P. Seyd and L. Minkin in *New Society*, 20 September 1979, pp.613–16.
9 Gladstone and Chamberlain exchanged many letters on the subject between 1883 and 1885, some of them quoted in Joseph Chamberlain, *A Political Memoir 1880–1892*, ed. C. H. D. Howard (London: Batchworth Press, 1953) pp. 88–97, 111–19; and in J. L. Garvin, *Life of Joseph Chamberlain* (London: Macmillan, 1932), vol, II, pp. 558–9. J. Morley, *Life of Gladstone* (London: Lloyd, 1908 edn), vol. I, pp. 571, 581, quotes Palmerston's similar complaints against Gladstone in 1864–5; and see also vol. II, pp. 264–5) Gladstone's letter to Granville about one of the incidents with Chamberlain.

3 The Labour Left in Parliament: Maintenance, Erosion and Renewal

HUGH BERRINGTON

Introduction

The constitutional controversies within the Labour Party during the last decade have focused on the powers and membership of the Parliamentary Labour Party. It is here, in the PLP, that the left is weakest. The left, therefore, and especially the left outside Parliament, has emphasised the need for changes to decrease the powers of the PLP, and to strengthen the dependence of MPs on their constituency parties.

However, there is nothing immutable about the present ideological balance of the parliamentary party. The strength of the left has fluctuated in the past, but in the last fifteen years or so it has grown quite steadily. The aim of this chapter is to look at the ways in which the size of the left has either increased or diminished as a result of various changes which have occurred both within and outside the House. How far have deaths, retirements, the influx of new MPs after an election victory and the defeat of old members in an election setback affected the strength of left and right within the PLP? What changes of ideological affiliation occur among the continuing members of the House?

First, however, we must ask whether it is possible to speak of a left or right ideology within the PLP? Secondly, what were the effects of various kinds of change in the composition of the party? To what extent were the influxes of new MPs, brought into the House by the pro-Labour swings of 1964, 1966 and 1974, more left-wing than existing members? Did the defeats of 1970 and 1979 strengthen the right? Has there been a long-term shift to the left within the PLP as a result of the normal process of deaths and retirements? And are there any regional differences in the ideological preferences of new recruits to the PLP? Questions of this sort focus on changes, short term and long term, in the membership of the PLP. Such alterations, however, may be retarded or accelerated by changes in the ideological allegiance of continuously serving members. It may be that the mere fact of experience in the House dampens the socialist zeal of the left-wing MP. Perhaps, despite changes in composition, the whole party is moving to the right because of the mellowing effects of parliamentary or governmental experience.

Indeed, fears that service in the House of Commons may seduce members from their socialist commitment presumably underlie the call for mandatory reselection. As will be seen, the available data do not permit any emphatic judgement on the effects of parliamentary service *per se*, but they make it possible to assess the effects of governmental experience. Moreover, it may be possible to identify particular categories of members whose socialist commitment is more likely than that of others to wane.

Briefly, it does seem likely that the new intakes of Labour's good years – 1964, 1966 and 1974 – contained a disproportionate number of left-wingers; however, the defeats of 1970 and 1979 did not reduce the left's representation as sharply as the victories had increased it, because of a long-term tendency when older, right-wing stalwarts retired or died for them to be replaced by young left-wing enthusiasts. The left clearly does better when the party as a whole does well; but even in defeat the left seems to succeed in inching forward towards a majority of the PLP. The flow of the tide carries the left forward, but the ebb takes the left back only a little way.

Left and Right: a Bogus Dichotomy?

The words left and right are a convenient short-hand term for describing the ideological make-up of the PLP. Butler and Stokes have shown how few ordinary voters think in terms of left and right and how even fewer of those who do, give them the meaning attributed to them by political activists or sophisticated political commentators.[1] But though such terms may be misleading when applied to the mass electorate, or even to the Parliamentary Conservative Party, they remain indispensable for any discussion of the cleavage within the Labour Party. Whatever the words may lack in accuracy, they gain in usefulness.

Left and right are a summary way of describing the attitude of an individual to a range of apparently separate issues. Belief in unilateral nuclear disarmament does not logically entail any belief in far-reaching measures of public ownership, or a high and increasing level of public expenditure. Almost certainly, however, most of those Labour MPs who favour a large extension of public ownership are also committed to unilateral renunciation of nuclear weapons, while most supporters of the mixed economy oppose unilateral, and favour multilateral, nuclear disarmament. The belief systems of Labour MPs, in short, are likely to be characterised by a high degree of 'constraint'.[2] A 'left' position on an issue tends to be accompanied by a 'left' position on other questions. Traditionally, some opinions tend to go hand in hand. It is this characteristic which gives left and right within the party their basic cohesion and continuity. Although particular issues may change in importance, and new ones, such as nuclear weapons, may appear, it is possible today, as in the 1930s to distinguish a left and a right within the party.

Such a division is not inconsistent with considerable fluidity on issues that do not fall easily into a left/right pattern. Thus, on German rearmament, in 1954, the Bevanites were able to recruit allies from the centre and right who found the deliberate rearming of the West Germans hard to accept, and in an even more pronounced way the left was able to win substantial support from the centre and right on the issue of the Common Market. There are questions, too, such as devolution which tend to cut across the party's ideological boundaries and in leadership elections it is clear that some MPs are swayed by non-ideological matters.

These qualifications, however, do not detract from the importance of the left/right division. There are many issues which do not fall easily within its scope and numerous competing and cross-cutting loyalties, but it remains the single most important continuing source of cleavage within the PLP.

Changes in the relative strength of these groups have not been easy to assess, partly because the criteria for assigning members to them tend to be subjective. In 1962 Leon Epstein, on the basis of a floor revolt, expressed the cautious view that the evidence indicated

> that a modestly higher percentage of new MPs than of old MPs rebelled in December 1960. The last finding suggests the interesting likelihood that new Labour MPs subsequently chosen in a general election would more frequently be rebels than the new MPs chosen in 1952–60. But nothing in this study indicates that the number of new rebels would be so great as itself to be the cause of a drastic shift in the PLP's balance of power between left and right.[3]

The general verdict of politicians and political commentators is that the left is stronger today, within the PLP, than it has ever been. The decisive votes which elected Mr Foot as leader of the PLP may have come from men of the centre and right, anxious to avoid a confrontation with the party outside Parliament, or from those expressing their liking for Mr Foot as a man – but such votes would have been of no account if the strength of the left had not grown markedly during the last twenty years.

Sources

The sources for the information in this chapter consist of a data-set of Early Day Motions for the period 1959–76, and of constituency and biographic data on MPs. A number of divisions have also been added to the data-set. The very high inter-correlations between sessions, reported on p. 73, demonstrate the reliability of this source, for determining the ideological position of Labour MPs, and the correlation between the EDM scores, and behaviour in floor revolts, confirms the validity of the measures used. Unfortunately, although data right up until the end of the 1975–6 session are now available in machine readable form, the sheer bulk of the material has delayed its exploitation and only seven sessions have so far been analysed in any detail – the sessions of 1960–1, 1961–2 and 1962–3 during the Macmillan parliament, the sessions of 1967–8, 1968–9 and 1969–70 in the 1966 parliament and the session of 1972–3 in the Heath parliament. In order therefore to examine changes which have taken place since 1973 it has been necessary to take as a measure, membership of the Tribune Group.

Methodology

Details of the methods used are given in the appendix, and only an outline will be provided here. The EDM signatures were subjected to factor analysis and for six of the seven sessions a factor emerged as the main factor (VF1) which seemed from its content to approximate to the traditional left–right scale.[4] For 1972–3 the second factor (VF2) seemed similar in nature to the first factor in earlier years. Factors generally correlated well with one another within each parliament indicating that the scales measure highly consistent phenomena.

Table 3.1 shows the inter-correlation of VF1 for the sessions in the 1960s. It can be seen that the correlations are generally high.[5] Thus VF1 for 1960–1 correlates at 0·80 with that for 1961–2 and the correlation between 1961–2 and 1962–3 is marginally higher. In the 1966 parliament the inter-correlations are almost as impressive.

Measures of Ideological Location

A member's location in the left–right scale in different sessions is given by his factor scores. For the 1959 parliament, factor scores for the 1961–2 session were used. For the 1966 parliament scores relate not to a single session but to a composite analysis of the three sessions 1967–8, 1968–9, 1969–70, giving us a measure called VF1 1967–8–9. This factor correlates well with those of the three individual sessions (at 0·85 with VF1 for 1967–8, at 0·61 with 1968–9 and 0·78 with 1969–70).

Table 3.1 *Inter-correlation of Factor Scores (VF1) (within parliaments)*

	1959 parliament	
	1961–2	1962–3
1960–1	0·80	0·69
1961–2	—	0·81
	1966 parliament	
	1968–9	1969–70
1967–8	0·75	0·85
1968–9	—	0·73

Table 3.2 *EDM Factor Scores and Tribune Declaration*

Ideological position	*Signatory of Declaration*	*Non-signatory*	*Total*
(1)	—	55	55
(2)	1	55	56
(3)	16	40	56
(4)	43	12	55
Total	60	162	222

Factor scores derived from EDMs have been correlated with behaviour in left-wing floor revolts. The correlation between VF1 for 1961–2 and participation in four floor revolts on defence issues between 1960 and 1963, is 0·75. Similarly five significant floor revolts under the Wilson government of 1966–70 were identified. VF1 for 1967–8–9 correlates with these floor revolts at 0·71.[6]

Finally, we can relate these factor scores to signature of the Tribune Declaration in July 1967. The Declaration was a manifesto, published by *Tribune* on the first anniversary of the deflationary measures introduced by the Wilson government in 1966. The Declaration, which called for a radical socialist solution to the economic crisis was signed by sixty-nine Labour MPs (and one peer). Table 3.2 shows the distribution of factor scores among the signatories. Most of the most left-wing quartile signed the Declaration; so did a significant minority of the 'centre-left' group, but only one of the centre-right and none of the most right-wing quartile.

Stability of Ideological Affiliation

The left/right cleavage is noteworthy for its persistence, from session to session, and from parliament to parliament. Members to the left of their colleagues in one session tended to occupy the same position in later sessions. Butler and Stokes[8] have shown the very high level of instability of response by ordinary voters to policy questions. The EDM data, on the contrary, show a remarkable degree of stability, as already indicated by the high inter-correlations between different sessions in the same parliament. These inter-correlations demonstrate the continuity, over the short term, of the ideological boundaries within the parliamentary party. If the boundaries were less rigid, if adhesion to the different factional groups were less clear-cut, if ideological affiliation were more volatile from session to session, then presumably the party's internal conflicts would be less embittered, and more susceptible to negotiation. The fact that the correlations are so strong indicates that short-term change is unlikely. Table 3.3 shows that the inter-correlations *across* parliaments remain high.

Table 3.3 *Inter-correlation of Factor Scores (across parliaments)*

	1961–2	1972–3
1961–2	—	0·54
1967–8–9	0·77	0·62

Note: This table shows the correlation of factor scores, in the specific sessions, of MPs who were backbenchers in each of the two sessions to which the correlation coefficient relates.

The relatively small element who remained continuously on the backbenches between 1961 and the last three sessions of the 1966 parliament retained their order of 'leftness' in a remarkable way. The correlation between 1961 and 1967–8–9 is if anything somewhat higher than that between the individual sessions of the 1966 parliament. This figure in itself shows the persistence of ideological allegiance from one parliament to another. It may well be, of course, that the party as a whole shifted, either to the left or to the right, in an absolute sense during this time. Such a change is something that EDM data cannot measure though, impressionistically, it might well seem that the backbench party did move to the left in this way. However, what is important here is the extent to which the *relative* positions of members changed between the two periods. They changed very little.

Table 3.4 shows the persistence of ideological orientations of Labour MPs in a different way. Members who served continuously on the backbenches from 1961–2 to the election of 1970 have been divided into quartiles, the first being the most right wing and the fourth the most left wing. More than half the members fell into exactly the same quartile in the late 1960s as they had in 1961–2 and most of the others were found in adjacent quartiles.

Table 3.4 *Factor Scores 1961–2 and 1967–8–9*

		VF1 1961–2				
		1	*2*	*3*	*4*	*N*
	(1)	11	6	4	1	22
VF1	(2)	7	12	2	1	22
1967–8–9	(3)	3	2	13	4	22
	(4)	1	2	3	14	20
	N	22	22	22	20	86

Note: The table shows the number of MPs in each quartile for both periods. Thus, two MPs who were in the second quartile of VF1 for 1961–2 were in the fourth quartile of VF1 for 1967–9.

The period from 1967–8–9 to 1972–3 seems to show a rather higher degree of erosion though the correlation is still high. Over the full eleven-year period between 1961–2 and 1972–3 the correlation diminished, however, to 0·54. There are, then, signs among the continuing members of some blurring of the earlier cleavage lines within the parliamentary party over this period. The general picture, however, remains one of the persistence of the ideological boundaries over this decade – even though, as will be seen, the salience of particular issues changed markedly.

Apparent Change in the Character of VF1

Factor analysis yields objective scales in that the factors which emerge depend on the statistical relationship between different items – the items in this study being signatures to backbench motions.

High scores for VF1 have been taken as an index of left-wing attitudes. The scope of left EDMs naturally changes as the Labour Party changes its role from opposition to government. The change in the character of VF1 for Labour between the early and the late 1960s is vividly exemplified by comparison between the sessions selected for special study – 1961–2 and 1967–70. In 1961–2 eight EDMs had loadings on VF1 of 0·50 or more; all but one of these fell unambiguously into the peace/defence category. Five were concerned with nuclear weapons, and two with British policy towards South-East Asia. Even the one exception had a defence connotation, despite its being essentially concerned with civil liberties.

VF1 in the 1967–8 session seems to cover a much more diverse array. Of twenty-one EDMs with loadings of 0·50 or higher, twelve were of a defence and foreign policy kind but none of them referred to the issue of nuclear weapons. Among them South-East Asia again contributed two, but four were on Rhodesia and South Africa and three on Greece. What is most striking, however, was the increased number of domestic economic motions. Two criticised the Governor of the Bank of England, one opposed the Labour government's income policy, while two more attacked cuts in social welfare expenditure, and two were critical of private industry.

What is 'left' in the Labour Party depends as much on the situation as on the nature of the demand. Had the Labour Party been in opposition, the leadership would almost certainly have censured the incomes policy, the cuts in social welfare and the views expressed by the Governor of the Bank. On defence and foreign policy the party leadership either in or out of office remained faithful to the Western alliance; but on economic and social questions it freely criticised Conservative governments for decisions not unlike those it made itself when it had the responsibility of ruling. So the agenda of the left is extended whenever a Labour government is in office, to embrace social welfare and economic policy.

In fact, the measure used in this paper, VF1 for 1967–8–9, is dominated by EDMs concerned with foreign affairs. Of the sixty-six motions selected, twenty-two had loadings of 0·50 or above. Fifteen of these dealt with foreign issues – mostly with the Third World. Only three clearly belonged to the realm of domestic economic and social policy. Only two of them, however, emphasised defence questions in contrast to the overwhelming importance of nuclear weapons in 1961–2.[9]

Ideological Constraint

It has already been shown that, whereas opinions on issues among the mass electorate in Britain are extremely volatile, and change markedly within two or three years (or perhaps even more rapidly) the locations of Labour MPs, relative to one another, along the left–right scale are highly stable. Another and related contrast between the opinions of the mass public and Labour MPs lies in the extent to which attitudes form a recognisably consistent pattern.

Among the mass electorate, even after excluding respondents whose opinions change from interview to interview, there is little tendency for left-wing opinions on, say, nuclear weapons to go hand in hand with left-wing views on nationalisation.[10] The belief systems of members of the mass public are characterised by little or no constraint.[11] Attitudes tend to cut across one another. Electors react to each separate issue, without reference to their opinions on other issues. Their responses are not informed by any general philosophy. It would not be easy to predict the views on capital punishment of a particular citizen by knowing his views on trade union reform. The highly involved, however, typically show much higher levels of constraint. The correlations in Tables 3.1 and 3.3 illustrate not only the stability of the ideological affiliations of Labour MPs, but also the heavily ideological character of Labour MPs' thinking. Despite the apparent change in the content of VF1 over the two periods, the backbenchers kept roughly the same location on the factor in 1967–70 as they had occupied in 1961–2. It is possible to know, with considerable accuracy, what a Labour MP thinks of social expenditure cuts made by a Labour government, from his attitude to nuclear weapons several years earlier. Hostility to the use of nuclear arms, indifference or opposition to the NATO alliance, go hand in hand with resentment at government cuts in public expenditure, and at government attempts to impose an incomes policy even when a Labour administration.

Changes In Ideological Composition

Changes in the ideological balance within a parliamentary party can occur for a number of reasons. First of all, some members of Parliament may freely change their minds. An MP might move from left to right within the parliamentary party. Changes of this kind might occur either as part of the general experience of ageing – it is sometimes suggested, notwithstanding the examples of Gladstone, Campbell-Bannerman and Tony Benn, that men tend to move towards the right as they grow older. Some changes may reflect the socialising influence of the House of Commons as an institution, and some may occur because of experience acquired, or appetite whetted, as a minister. After a year or two in office an ardent crusader may come to believe that proposals which seemed simple and beneficial, seen from the back benches, are in fact full of complication and hazard. Sometimes movement may occur because of pressures from constituency parties or, alternatively, because of pressure from parliamentary leaders, or because of the member's ambition to become a minister or to benefit from some other act of patronage.

Other shifts in opinion can arise from changes in the membership of the parliamentary party. Its membership will alter when members are defeated, or when new members are elected at by-elections, or at a general election at which there has been a favourable swing. Deaths and retirements too can help to change the ideological balance. Such changes focus attention upon the mechanism and process of selection. The apparent increase in the strength of the left within the PLP during the last fifteen to twenty years raises the question whether there has not been some kind of systematic tendency for constituency parties to select more left-wing members than hitherto.

Such analysis depends, however, on assessing the ideological affiliation of those MPs who die or retire during, or at the end of, a parliament, of those who are defeated, and of the newcomers who have won seats from other parties or replaced those who have died or retired from the House.

Turnover of Membership

It is often forgotten how large the turnover of membership of the House of Commons is. Among backbenchers, turnover is particularly high. Thus there were 207 Labour members continuously on the backbenches in the period from November 1960 to October 1963. Of these 207 only 86 were still backbenchers for the whole of the period November 1967 to June 1970. Clearly, a considerable number had been appointed to government office, so a more realistic test would be to take the change in the composition of the whole of the PLP between 1961 and 1972. Although there were 255 in the PLP in November 1961 and 289 in 1972, only 100 members were there at both times. This large turnover in a relatively short period gives some indication of the scope for quite rapid change in the ideological balance of the parliamentary party.

Changes In Membership, 1961–7

The changes in the physical composition of the party were substantial between 1961–2 and 1967. Altogether forty-two Labour MPs retired from the House at the general elections of 1964 and 1966 and by-elections were precipitated by a further thirty-one retirements or deaths between November 1961 and November 1967.[12] There was also a large influx of new members, some of them occupying the seats of those who had retired or died, and others who had won their seats from the Conservatives or indeed the Liberals. Table 3.5 shows the ideological orientation of the Labour backbenchers who died or retired during this period. For this purpose the party has again been divided into four quartiles: the first quartile can loosely be called the right, the second the centre-right, the third the centre-left and the fourth the left (see Table 3.5).

Backbenchers who died or retired were drawn very evenly from the four groups. However, more than half of the replacements who were backbenchers from 1967 to 1970 were in the late 1960s in the more 'leftward' half of the backbench party (excluding those for whom we have no information about their ideological leanings). It is worth, however, looking a little more closely at the pattern of replacements. It is notable that when leftish members retired or died they were often replaced by middle-of-the-roaders or right-wingers. Thus, for instance, the four North

Table 3.5 *Ideological Orientations of Labour MPs: Leavers and Replacements, 1963–7*

Leavers in 1960–1–2 data-set (*Ideological position, 1961*)		*Replacements for leavers in 1960–1–2 data-set* (*Ideological position, 1976–8–9*)		*Replacements for leavers not in 1960–1–2 data-set* (*Ideological position, 1967–8–9*)
(1)	14*	(1)	—	
		(2)	—	
		(3)	4	
		(4)	1	
		No info.	8	4
(2)	16	(1)	—	
		(2)	5	
		(3)	4	
		(4)	4	
		No info.	3	2
(3)	16†	(1)	3	
		(2)	4	
		(3)	1	
		(4)	3	
		No info.	3	1
(4)	12	(1)	—	
		(2)	2	
		(3)	4	
		(4)	4	
		No info.	2	2
Total	58		55	9

* One member was defeated by a Conservative in 1964 who held the seat in 1966.
† Successors of two members were defeated at by-elections.
Note: As explained in the text, MPs have been divided into quartiles according to the VF1 scores in 1971 and 1967–8–9. The table shows the distribution of 'leavers' according to their 1961 location on VF1 and the distribution of their replacements on the VF1 scale for 1967 8 9. The first quartile is the most right-wing position, the fourth the most left-wing. No information means that the replacement was excluded from the 1967–8–9 data-set, usually because he or she held government office.

Staffordshire members died or retired between 1964 and 1968. Three (Stephen Swingler, Ellis Smith and Harriet Slater), and arguably the fourth, Barnett Stross, were of the left, but by 1969 all four seats had been filled by men of the centre and right (John Golding, Jack Ashley, John Forrester and Bob Cant).

It does not look, summarising the evidence so far, as though there was any *systematic* tendency in the early and mid-1960s for left-wing candidates to be chosen in safe Labour seats.

If the right appears to have lost ground because of deaths and retirements it was not necessarily because the left held onto its own and encroached on the territory of the moderates. The pattern was much more fluid, suggesting that at this time it was untypical for a constituency party which had been represented by a member from left or right to go on to choose a successor from the same wing of the party.

Table 3.6 *Ideological Orientation of Other New MPs, 1961–7*

Ideological position	*Won seats from other parties*
(1)	8
(2)	21
(3)	18
(4)	29
Total	76

Note: This table spans the years 1961–7, whereas Table 3.5 covers a shorter period, 1963–7. The reason for this difference in treatment is that a member who left the House or died between November 1961 and October 1963 is not included in the 1960–1–2 data-set.

Table 3.7 *Summary of Changes in Composition of PLP 1963–7*

Ideological position	*Leavers*	*Replacements*	*Winners*	*Gain* (+) *or Loss* (–)
(1)	14	7	8	+1
(2)	16	13	21	+18
(3)	16	14	18	+16
(4)	12	14	29	+31
No info.	9	16	—	+7
Total	67	64	76	+73

Detailed examination of high scorers in 1961 who left the House, or died, between 1963 and 1967 shows that nine of their replacements leant to the right and only twelve belonged to the left half of the 1967–70 backbench party. However, the replacements for the right-wingers included a substantial number of leftish recruits. More important, as Table 3.6 shows, were the widespread gains made by Labour in 1964 and 1966 (plus gains in by-elections between 1961 and 1963). Table 3.7 consolidates the information shown in Tables 3.5 and 3.6. These tables show a distinct leftward shift, with what might be called the normal process of moving slightly to the left as a result of deaths and retirements being perceptibly speeded up by the election of a considerable number of new Labour MPs in 1964 and 1966.

Changes in membership, 1967–72

Even in a period of electoral setback, changes in the composition of the party continued. Between November 1967 and November 1972 the PLP lost seventy-six MPs as a result of retirements, deaths, peerages, and so on, and a further sixty-two as a result of defeat in the general election of 1970.

Table 3.8 *Ideological Orientations of Labour MPs: Leavers and Replacements, 1967–72*

	Leavers ideological position, 1967–8–9		*Replacements ideological position, 1972–3*
(1)	17	(1)	3
		(2)	3
		(3)	8
		(4)	3
(2)	12	(1)	3
		(2)	—
		(3)	7
		(4)	2
(3)	5	(1)	3
		(2)	—
		(3)	—
		(4)	2
(4)	4	(1)	2
		(2)	—
		(3)	2
		(4)	—
No info.	26	(1)	4
		(2)	3
		(3)	7
		(4)	12

The implications of this change for the ideological composition of the party can be seen from Tables 3.8, 3.9 and 3.10. (Because of the rounding of factor scores for 1972–3 problems have arisen about a number of members on the borderlines between two quartile positions. Where this problem has occurred, the allocation of members to a particular quartile has been determined by chance. It is most unlikely that this defect in the data affects the nature of the findings.)

Table 3.9 *Ideological Orientations of Defeated MPs, 1970*

Ideological position 1967–8–9	
(1)	6
(2)	8
(3)	10
(4)	20
No info.	18

Table 3.10 *Summary of Changes In Composition of PLP, 1967–72*

Ideological position	*Leavers*	*Replacements*	*Losers*	*Gain* (+) *or Loss* (–)
(1)	17	15	6	–8
(2)	12	6	8	–14
(3)	5	24	10	+9
(4)	4	19	20	–5
No info.	38	—	18	–56
Total	76	64	62	–74

Note: This table shows the distribution of MPs who retired or died or were defeated, according to their ideological location, in 1967–8–9, and that of the replacements of the leavers, according to their location in 1972–3.

The right lost because the leavers were concentrated among its members in a disproportionate way, the left because so many of the recruits of 1964 and 1966 were defeated in 1970. The large number of retiring MPs about whom we have no information for the years 1967–70 (that is, those holding government office) makes it difficult to assess the effect on the ideological balance of the party. The likelihood, however, is that the ex-ministers who left the House were recruited heavily from the right – an expectation confirmed by examination of their scores in 1961. It seems, despite its losses at the hands of the Conservatives, that the left was relatively stronger in the new parliament than in the old.

1974 and 1979

As indicated earlier, the EDM data for 1974–6 have not yet been analysed. Membership of the Tribune Group, however, affords a useful surrogate measure.

Not all members of the Tribune Group are committed left-wingers. Some may join for cosmetic purposes, to safeguard themselves in their dealings with their local parties. There are indeed likely to be some MPs outside the group who are to the left of some of those who belong. It is hard to see any systematic error being caused by our using Tribune Group membership as a measure of 'leftness'. The probability is strong that a Tribune Group member who replaces a retiring Labour MP who did not belong to the group will be to the left of the retiring member.[13]

To what extent were the left, as defined in this way, strengthened or weakened by deaths and retirements and the opportunities they presented, and by the ebb and flow of electoral opinion? Between November 1972 and October 1974 forty-one MPs retired from Parliament, died, or left the party. Ten were defeated (excluding those who regained their seats between March and October 1974). Forty-eight new MPs gained seats from the Conservatives, or won constituencies newly created by boundary revisions. The ideological distribution in 1972–3 of the outgoing members was as shown in Table 3.11. Of their replacements twelve were members of the Tribune Group and a further twenty-three of the forty-eight successful Labour candidates who had won their seats in either February or October 1974 joined the Tribune Group (see Table 3.12).

We can bring the examination of these changes up to date by looking at the situation after the election of May 1979. Many left-wing Labour MPs sat for marginal seats which had been gained from the

Table 3.11 *Ideological Orientations of Labour MPs Leaving Parliament, November 1972 to October 1974*

Ideological positions	*Leavers*	*Defeated*	*Replacements Tribune Group members*	*non-members*	*Seats lost through redistribution*
(1)	12	3	2	5	5
(2)	12	4	5	7	—
(3)	9	1	3	2	4
(4)	3	1	1	2	—
No info.	3	1	1	2	—
Total	39	10	12	18	9

Source: Membership of Tribune Group calculated from lists in *Political Companion*, Spring 1975.

Table 3.12 *Labour MPs Gaining Seats in 1974 Elections from Conservatives (or through redistribution)*

Tribune members	non-Tribune members
23	25

Source: As Table 3.11.

Table 3.13 *Labour MPs by Tribune Group Membership, October 1974 to May 1979*

	Member	*non-Member*
Retired or died	7	49
Defeated	17	28
Total leaving House	24	77
Elected Oct. 1974–May 1979	19	37

Sources: I am grateful to Patrick Seyd for information about new MPs. Data for retiring and defeated MPs, etc., from *Political Companion*, Winter 1978.

Conservatives either in 1966 or at one of the two elections of 1974. It might have been expected, therefore, that members of the Tribune Group would suffer disproportionately from Mrs Thatcher's sweeping victory in 1979. That does not seem to have happened, however. In early 1975 the Tribune Group boasted seventy-nine members and in late 1978, just before the election, seventy-one members. In 1980 the membership stood at seventy.[14] What has happened is that the heavy losses within the Tribune Group caused by the marked swing to the Conservatives have been largely offset by further left-wing advance into the safe and comfortable seats held by people who retired or died.

Table 3.13 shows a further strengthening of the Tribune Group in the five years which followed the general election of October 1974. Because of losses in Labour marginals the group lost twenty-four MPs during this period – about a quarter of all Labour MPs who left the House, either by defeat, retirement, or death. But a third of the newcomers joined the Tribune Group, almost making up, in an absolute sense, for the members who had died or been defeated and testifying to the increasing penetration of safe and comfortable seats by the left. In contrast, seventy-seven MPs outside the group died or left the House and only thirty-seven came in.

Ideological Balance and Constituency Geography

Let us, however, explore the general question of the change in composition caused by replacements and by Labour election victories more closely. It has been shown that in the earlier period there was little sign of a systematic tendency for left-wing members who died or retired to be replaced by other left-wingers. This suggests that up to the mid-1960s at least, constituency parties had been swayed by personal or sectional considerations rather than by the ideological orientation of candidates (or alternatively that factional control of parties changed markedly over, say, fifteen years). A change can be detected from 1974 as the left penetrated the comfortable and safe seats, with the death or retirement of right-wing members. The question arises as to why this should have occurred. If there were systematic forces at work from, say, the early 1970s, were these the result of conscious decisions to ensure the selection of left-wing candidates or were they the by-product of other forces?

One possible explanation for the increase in the number of left-wing members replacing right-wingers who died or retired would be a change in the pool of candidates. If the pool of candidates as a whole shifts to the left this is likely to be reflected, other things being equal, in the kind of people who are selected to replace retiring MPs. The possibility remains that there were conscious attempts to place left-wing candidates in the safer seats. In the past decade there have been a number of celebrated controversies between sitting MPs and their general management committees about the MPs' ideological moderation. It has been suggested, for example, that in areas undergoing rapid change the continuity of the constituency parties would have been disturbed and it would be very easy, with marked population changes, for newcomers to seize control of what had become a largely moribund party. Some limited evidence in support of this can be found from our data. The correlation between VF1 scores for 1967–8–9 and the percentage who moved into or out of the constituency in the five years before 1966 was a positive one of 0·15. We find a similar correlation of 0·13 for 1972–3. However, in a regression analysis the independent contribution made by this variable was vestigial.

Marginality of Constituencies

Downsian theories of party competition would predict that the marginal seats would have been represented by the most moderate MPs on each side.[15] At first sight, therefore, it seems strange that the most extreme members should have been elected for the least safe seats. The link between attitudes and constituency marginality can, however, be explained by the marked change in the character of candidates who had been selected after 1959 and the heavy Labour advances of 1964 and 1966. What is decisive here is not marginality but intake. Members newly elected in 1964 and 1966 tended to have marginal seats. Members newly elected in 1964 and 1966 were relatively left-wing.

What is interesting, however, is that this propensity to choose left-wing candidates seems to have been most marked in particular regions of the country – broadly those regions where Labour did not have much traditional strength: the South-East, South-West England, East Anglia, the East and West Midlands and North-West England. Table 14 shows the regional distribution of MPs according to their ideological orientation. At first sight it might seem that this relationship was also spurious but in fact, within the marginal seats, and also among members elected for the first time in 1964 and 1966, the relationship appears very strong.

Thus, if we compare north Britain and Wales with southern and central England we find a striking difference in the attitudes of MPs who were first elected in 1964 or 1966. Similarly, if we detach North-West England, as not being one of Labour's bedrock areas and add it to the south and midlands, the contrast becomes even more pronounced.

Table 3.14 *Ideological Orientation of Labour MPs First Elected 1964–66*

(a)

Ideological position	*North Britain (and Wales)*	*Southern England*
(1)	5	9
(2)	25	5
(3)	17	14
(4)	11	27
Total	58	55

(b)

Ideological position	*Traditional Labour regions*	*New Labour regions*
(1)	4	10
(2)	17	13
(3)	11	20
(4)	2	36
Total	34	79

Notes: Traditional Labour regions are defined as Scotland, Wales, Northern England, Yorkshire and Humberside. New Labour regions embrace all other regions in Great Britain. North Britain consists of the traditional Labour regions and the North-West; Southern England of the South-East, South-West, East Anglia and West and East Midlands. Regions used are the official standard regions.

Why was it that in the 1960s (though not later) left-wing candidates had a much bigger appeal to constituency parties in southern England than in northern England and Wales? It has been suggested that the difference can be accounted for by Labour's greater local government strength in the north and Wales than in the south. Continuing power at the local level, the hypothesis runs, brings with it a breed of activist whose chief satisfaction is derived from the opportunities and psychological perquisites of council work. These, it is argued, are likely to lose interest in party work if deprived of these satisfactions, so leaving constituency Labour parties open to domination by left-wing ideologues. Between 1959 and 1961, when Labour was unpopular, the party lost many of the local government gains it had made in earlier years. Perhaps, as a result, control of constituency parties passed to new activists, more interested in the application of socialist principles to national and international problems than in the mundane issues of local services.

Any test of such a hypothesis is bound to be crude, partly because constituencies often embrace several boroughs or districts, partly because in the bigger towns a borough contains several constituencies, and partly because of the difficulty, with available information, of reducing the notion to a form that is both precise and meaningful.

Comparison of the ideological location of new members, who came from constituencies where Labour remained strong in local government in the bad years of 1959–61, with that of MPs who represented seats where Labour had not survived so well at local level, gives no support to this hypothesis. Members from English constituencies which contained, or formed part of, local government areas where Labour was in control even before the recovery of 1962 were as likely to be left-wing as those in areas where Labour had lost local power before 1962, or had never enjoyed it. For every Gordon Bagier or Bernard Conlan, representing areas in Labour's local government heartland, the left could put forward an Albert Booth or a Stan Orme.

Whatever the cause of this regional difference, the consequence is that the ideological composition of the PLP depends to some extent on the regional distribution of swing. So in 1979 the left may have suffered relatively more as a result of the heavy pro-Conservative swing in southern England, and the right may have benefited from the relatively low swings in northern England and Scotland.

Political Experience and Change in Ideological Location

Examination of retirements and deaths, and their replacements, and of the ideological complexion of new members and those who are defeated, can throw some light on the apparent change in the ideological balance of the PLP. It must be emphasised that the scores do not measure the degree of 'leftness' in any absolute sense; the data simply show the order of leftness in any one session. We must beware, therefore, before we assume that a member who occupies a markedly left position in one session is necessarily more left-wing than someone occupying a right position in another session. Strictly speaking, the scores are not comparable from session to session.

How far does this difficulty undermine the problem of determining whether the new entrants of the 1960s and 1970s were, say, to the left of those who retired or died? The limitations of ordinal data are not denied but it would seem odd, for instance, to argue that the low scorers of 1959 who left the House between 1963 and 1967 would have been to the left of the new members who came in in 1964 and 1966. Such an argument would seem all the more perverse given the tendency for the colleagues of the low scorers who had left the House to keep their position relative to their more left-wing fellows of 1961–2, a position clearly much more right-wing than that of most of the new intakes.

Even while the process of replacement and election victories are strengthening the left, the rump of the party could be moving to the right simply because membership of the House, or greater understanding of the apparent difficulties in achieving socialist goals, might have a general dampening effect. Again, ordinal data are silent here. It is possible, however, that individual members could move to the right relative to others, so creating a more fluid factional pattern. Perhaps particular experiences influence such movement.

To what extent does membership of the House or the holding of government office influence a person's ideological outlook? Is there a tendency, as is sometimes affirmed, for the House to exercise a taming or conservatising influence upon its members? Does appointment to government office, with all the immediate practical problems which this brings, or do the psychological and material advantages of office, have a similar effect? 'If we're honest,' wrote Barbara Castle after attending a Downing Street dinner held in President Nixon's honour, 'it is moments like this, when one is in the inner circle and conscious of not being awed by it, that are the consolation for all the work and strain.'[16]

It is not easy to trace with ordinal data the effects on members' ideology, of service in the House. It is, of course, possible to estimate the extent to which *particular* members move from left to right along the scale. But since the data are ordinal their moving rightwards must in the very nature of things be compensated for by others moving leftwards. Two members may both, in one session, rank high on the left–right scale; ten years later one may have moved towards the right, while another remains on the left. As both have served for the same additional period of time, it is hard to attribute the rightward movement of one to the effects of membership in the House.

On the other hand, it is possible to distinguish between members who move sharply along the ideological continuum from those who simply make relatively small adjustments. While we cannot attribute any movement to a further length of time in the House, since this would have affected all MPs equally, we can pose the question whether there is perhaps some critical point in the career of a left-wing Labour MP at which he is likely to move sharply to the right. Is there a tendency, for instance, for the socialist enthusiasm of the newcomer to wane markedly, after a given number of years in the Commons? Alternatively, is there a critical point when an older MP or a long-serving member is likely to change his views?

An attempt was made to test for such influences by looking at the members of the backbench party in 1960–1–2 who survived and remained on the backbenches until 1972–3, and also at those backbenchers who served in 1967–8–9 and were still backbenchers in 1972–3.

The party in each period was divided into three groups. (Because of problems in the data for 1972–3 the groups for that year are not equal in size).[17] It seemed unwise to attribute much significance to a movement from the leftmost group to the intermediate group and the comparisons therefore were restricted to those members who moved from top (i.e. the most left) position in the earlier period to the least left group in the later period.

Difficulties were compounded by the very small number of MPs who did move across the spectrum in a dramatic way – eight between 1961 and 1972, and seven in the period from 1967–8–9 to 1972–3. These small numbers reflect partly the limited character of the changes in ideological allegiance which took place, partly the high turnover of members.

Age, Membership of the House and Changes in Ideology

It must be emphasised that it is hard to draw firm conclusions on such tiny numbers. Age, as such, does not seem to have been linked to ideological change. There are more grounds for identifying length of service in the House; only two of the twenty-two of the most recently elected changed between 1967–8–9 and 1972–3. Those who did change were likely to be the longer-serving MPs. It may be that after a long period as a committed left-winger the socialist zeal of a member may decline.

Experience of Government Office

There can be few parliamentarians who have shared Tony Benn's experience, and moved to the left after working as a minister. 'It would be more usual', wrote Mr Benn, 'for a radical MP to be converted to respectability the moment that he receives his Seals of Office.'[18] Nothing, it is often averred, tames a rebel so much as executive responsibility. However, though we can point to individual MPs such as, say, Bert Oram, who after a spell in government return to the backbenches and seem much less militant than they were before they went into office, the very sparse evidence at our disposal does not support this interpretation.

MPs who returned to the backbenches after holding ministerial office did not change significantly, relative to other Labour MPs; that is to say, there was no sign of any distinctive behaviour by ex-ministers. It must be stressed that the data deal only with backbenchers; members who were elected to the Shadow Cabinet after serving in government would be excluded from the figures. Perhaps members who moved to the right after holding office tended, to a disproportionate degree, to win places on the opposition front bench.

Adverse Electoral Swings

An attempt was made to assess whether members were likely to change their location because of an abnormally high electoral swing against them in the election of 1970. Once again analysis is hampered by small numbers. For what it is worth, there was some tendency for those members who had experienced below-average swings against them to be confirmed in their leftness whilst the handful of members who moved across the scale tended to have suffered higher adverse swings. (There was, incidentally, a low negative correlation between 1972/3 factor scores and the 1970 swing, i.e. the left-wing members fared better at the polls.)

Conclusion

Attempts to reduce the status of the PLP have been a crucial part of the left/right struggle, even if members of the Tribune Group have sometimes reacted to proposals for constitutional change more as members of Parliament and less as the vanguard of the left. Three main constitutional changes have been put forward: mandatory re-selection of MPs, the selection of the leader by either Annual Conference or an electoral college, and the location of authority for the contents of the election manifesto with the National Executive Committee, instead of responsibility being shared between the Parliamentary Labour Party (the Cabinet when Labour is in office) and the NEC. The reason why some elements of the left have put so much emphasis on these changes, which must weaken the authority and role of Labour MPs, has been because it is within the PLP that the left has been weakest. The left has enjoyed significant, if not always consistent, victories at Annual Conference; it broadly controls the National Executive Committee. But the PLP retains a right-wing or at any rate a non-left majority, and the power of the left within the PLP depends largely on the extent to which members of the right and centre can be detached on specific issues from their normal allegiance. This occurred, for instance, over British entry into the Common Market, and over the election of Mr Foot as leader of the parliamentary party.

This chapter has attempted to look at some elements, external to the House, which appear to have pulled the Parliamentary Labour Party to the left in recent years. It has also sought to examine the influence of government office, service in the House and electoral swing, on ideological orientations.

The most clear-cut findings concern the extent to which right-wing MPs have been replaced, either directly or indirectly, by left-wing members. In the earlier period, left-wing progress occurred mainly because of the pro-Labour swings of 1964 and 1966. The candidates who captured the crucial marginals in those two elections were drawn heavily from the left. In the 1970s, as well, constituency parties became increasingly likely to choose left-wing candidates to replace outgoing Labour MPs. Even when Labour suffers electoral defeat, the left is able to consolidate its power; when Labour wins, the left is likely to advance rapidly. Constituency redistribution and mandatory re-selection are likely to accelerate what has hitherto been a gradual, if cumulatively considerable, movement to the left.

Substantial change of ideological position by individual members relative to others seems surprisingly rare – at least among backbenchers. In the next few years, as the left extends its grasp on the leadership of the party, factors which may have favoured the right in the past are likely to work on the left's behalf. Distaste for intra-party controversy and a desire to please the leadership are likely to solidify the left-wing orientations of individual backbenchers. It looks as though only a propensity, as yet unmeasured, for the parliamentary party as a whole to move, over the years, to the right, or a spectacular change in the character of constituency parties, can sustain the right's present precarious majority.[19]

Methodological Appendix

Signatures to politically significant EDMs were recorded as were, for the earlier sessions, votes in a number of selected divisions. EDMs with fewer than ten signatures from a party, those which dealt with regional and local issues, or the claims of particular interest groups, party squibs and motions of a congratulatory or highly specific and technical nature were excluded (except for one session, that of 1969–70.) The decision whether to record an EDM was made after discussion between two of the researchers. (One hundred and fifty EDMs were recorded for Labour for 1960–3 and 319 for 1967–70.)

The data were subjected first to cluster analysis and then to factor analysis (varimax rotation). Three main factors were extracted for each session (and in addition a group of sessions) and an attempt was made to determine the character of each factor and see how well it correlated with factors in other sessions. For six of the seven sessions a factor emerged as the main factor (VF1) which seemed to approximate to the traditional left–right scale. In 1972–3 a similar factor was generated as the second factor. Factors generally correlated well with one another within each parliament.

It might be argued that these high correlations have perhaps been magnified by a number of MPs who signed very few or no EDMs in any session. A member who consistently signs only a handful of EDMs is likely to achieve a low factor score. However, exclusion of MPs who consistently signed few EDMs does little to diminish the strength of the correlations.

Ordinal Data

The factor scores for members have, of course, no absolute significance as an indicator of 'leftness'. The data employed for most of this study are ordinal in character. We can say with considerable confidence that some MPs are more left than others but what we cannot say is that any member has achieved a particular absolute threshold of leftness, nor indeed, strictly speaking, can we be sure that an MP who scores highly in one session is farther left than one who scores low in another session. Absolute measures which might be supplied by, say, interview responses at two or more periods are not available. In the last resort we cannot therefore claim on the basis of such data that the PLP as a whole was more left in, say, 1969 than it had been in 1961. Nevertheless, ordinal measures, despite their limitations, can help to throw light on some of the changes which have taken place. Whether or not it is right to interpret the departure of low-scoring MPs at the end of one parliament and the arrival of high-scoring MPs at the beginning of another as a sign of a leftward shift must depend on how plausible it seems compared with other interpretations, and on information or impressions from other sources.

Notes: Chapter 3

The basic analysis of the EDM data reported in this chapter was undertaken by Norman Squirrell and the late John Leece. Collection and analysis of these data was undertaken by the author, Mr Squirrell and Dr Leece, and financed by a grant from the Social Science Research Council, whose help is gratefully acknowledged.

1 D. Butler and D. Stokes *Political Change in Britain*, 2nd edn (London: Macmillan, 1974), pp. 323 ff.

2 P. Converse, 'The nature of the belief systems of mass publics', in D. Apter (ed.), *Ideology and Discontent* (Glencoe, I11.: The Free Press, 1964).

3 L. Epstein, 'New MPs and the politics of the PLP', *Political Studies*, June 1962.

4 As commonly used, the left–right scale in Britain refers, *inter alia*, to the ownership of the means of production and the question of government control of the economy, as well as to questions of defence and foreign policy. Questions of ownership and control play a relatively minor part in the scales used here, and Third World issues a heavy part. It would never be possible to achieve agreement on the composition of an ideal 'left–right' scale and therefore there will always be some uncertainty about the claims of any scale purporting to measure left–right attitudes and about the location of particular members. Thus in most sessions it is possible to point to a handful of MPs who appear to be somewhat farther left, and one or two considerably farther left, than a more impressionistic approach would place them. Such cases are at worst rare and are most prominent, though still uncommon, in 1972–3.

5 The correlations after consistent low signers had been excluded were 0·75 for 1967–8 and 1968–9, 0·73 for 1968–9 and 1969–70 and 0·83 for 1967–8 and 1969–70.

6 The divisions taken for the 1959 parliament were Div. 86, 1960–1 (Air Estimates); Div. 29, 1960–1 (Polaris submarine base); Div. 192, 1961–2 (Thailand and Laos); Div. 17, 1962–3 (Polaris submarine base). The divisions for the 1966 parliament were Div. 207, 1967–8 (National Health Service Charges); Div. 241, 1967–8 (Prices and Incomes Bill, Clause 1); Div. 7, 1967–8 (IMF – letter of intent); Div. 28, 1969–70 (Vietnam); Div. 117, 1969–70 (Cambodia).

7 *Tribune*, 21 July 1967.

8 Butler and Stokes, op. cit. pp. 277–84.

9 This change in content of the general left–right factor as the party moves into opposition is confirmed by the experience of 1972–3. Once again, Labour was in opposition; it is noteworthy that of the eight EDMs with loadings of 0·50 or above on VF722, seven have a foreign policy (including Third World) or defence character.

10 Butler and Stokes, op. cit., pp. 319–21.

11 Converse, op. cit.

12 Details of retirements, etc., taken from various issues of *The Times Guide to the House of Commons*, and of by-elections from the Nuffield General Election Studies. Readers are advised that apparent discrepancies between figures cited in the text and in the tables can occur because, while retirements, deaths, gains and losses, etc., relate to the full party, only members who were continuous backbenchers for the period in question would be included in the relevant data-set.

13 The conclusion, based on membership of the Tribune Group, that the left was strengthened by the election of May 1979, is supported by analysis of lists of signatories to resolutions or letters following the vote on the selection of the leader at the 1980 annual conference. Fifty-six Labour MPs called on the PLP to suspend standing orders so as to allow Michael Foot to take over as leader. Twenty-one belonged to the intake of May 1979, constituting 38 per cent of the signatories. New entrants, however, accounted for only 18 per cent of the full backbench party.

Only four MPs of the 1979 intake signed a letter from sixty-two MPs to the Shadow Cabinet urging that election of a new leader should go ahead before the special conference called to draw up a new method of choosing the leader. The figures of signatories rise to twenty-two and eight respectively if members elected at by-elections between October 1974 and May 1979 are included. On either definition new MPs were heavily over-represented among the signatories of the first letter, and under-represented among the signatories of the second.

14 Information from Patrick Seyd. The figure of seventy includes Mr Litherland, elected

at a by-election later in 1979. The figures of membership just before the general election of 1979 are derived from the *Political Companion*, Winter 1978.

15 Anthony Downs, *An Economic Theory of Democracy* (New York: Harper, 1957), and David Robertson, *A Theory of Party Competition* (London: Wiley, 1976).

16 Diaries (entry for 25 February 1969), *Sunday Times* 20 January 1980.

17 The factor scores for 1972–3 were only available in rounded form and not in the original. It was therefore not possible to choose the cutting points in such a way as to divide the party into three equal groups. By making the rightmost group larger, rather than smaller, than one-third, the potential size of the number of ideological changers was increased.

18 Tony Benn, *Arguments for Socialism* (Harmondsworth: Penguin, 1980), p.16.

19 This chapter was written before the formation of the SDP. This development has further weakened the right, though the growth of the 'soft-left' will have strengthened the right in terms of style or spirit, if not in policy preferences. The NEC, too, is now split, almost evenly between left (including 'soft left') and right.

4 Still the Workers' Party? Changing Social Trends in Elite Recruitment and Electoral Support

DENNIS KAVANAGH

> A political labor movement without deserters from the bourgeoisie is historically as inconceivable as would be such a movement without a class-conscious proletariat.
> (Robert Michels, *Political Parties* (New York: The Free Press, 1962), p. 304)

This chapter looks at the changing social composition of Labour elites and the Labour electorate. The embourgeoisement of the former, in Parliament and the NEC, has continued for many years. However, the loss of working-class support in the electorate and the steady growth of a middle-class electoral following is a recent development. In view of the decline of the working-class base of the party both in the House of Commons and in the country, two questions are posed: in what sense is Labour still the workers' party, and is the decline connected with an erosion of the party's commitment to socialism?

I: Labour and Social Class

The British Labour Party has always had an ambiguous attitude to social class. On the one hand there is the familiar rhetoric about the need to defend 'our people', 'the working class', 'working people and their families'. This rhetoric is a staple of Conference, parliamentary and election speakers. It represents an awareness of a shared identity, a common political purpose and a defined constituency. It is joined to a frequently stated belief that people from a working-class background are best able to represent this interest. On the other hand, the party leaders, particularly in government, have invariably wanted to show that Labour rules in a national, not a class or sectional, interest, and that it is not beholden to the trade unions. In electoral terms social class has been a source of strength as well as a limitation, providing a guaranteed floor of support, and at the same time cutting the party off from other sections. Since its formation in 1900 the Labour Party has been *a* party of the working class but rarely *the* party of the working class. Indeed it was not until 1945 that it gained more than half of the working-class vote.

In 1900, at the founding conference of the party, the attempt by the Social Democratic Federation to commit the party to socialism and 'a recognition of the class war' was decisively defeated.[1] Instead the new party more modestly sought 'a better representation of the interests of labour in the House of Commons'. There were many reasons for the formation of the new party. One factor was a demand for social representation of the working class and trade unions; this was fuelled by the refusal of constituency Liberal parties to choose working men as Liberal candidates. Yet the demand did not entail that representation of the working class would only be by working-class MPs. In 1918 the party constitution stated that its aim was to promote the interests of 'workers by hand and by brain'. Of the authors of the constitution, Henderson was always concerned to add a leavening of middle-class intellectuals to the party's trade union base, and Sidney Webb, as a Fabian, was a firm believer in meritocracy. The Fabians assumed that the commitment to socialism would appeal to the middle class. As McKibbin notes, Clause 4 was adopted in part as 'a sop to the professional bourgeoisie'.[2]

II: Labour Elites

The novel feature about the twenty-nine Labour members of Parliament returned in 1906 was that they so clearly came from working-class backgrounds. Historically, membership of the House of Commons had been confined to men of high birth and breeding and, even today, men of upper-class background retain a large presence in Parliament. The intrusion of Labour on to the political stage in the early decades of the twentieth century introduced men whose social backgrounds and political socialisation were very different from those of the conventional politician. Eighty years later it is still the case that penetration of the political elite by members of the working class (either in terms of parental background or the individual's occupation) is almost entirely a consequence of the rise of the Labour Party, even though the party's role in providing such an avenue has declined over the years.

Before the war there were stark differences in the social backgrounds of Conservative and Labour MPs. Conservative MPs were drawn largely from the upper-middle and middle classes and they had usually been educated at a public school, followed by attendance at Oxbridge. Most Labour MPs, by contrast, came from the ranks of manual workers or trade union officials and, before 1922, few had attended a university. The party amply fulfilled its early goal of increasing representation of the working class in the House of Commons. Between 1906 and 1918, 89 per cent of Labour MPs came from working-class occupations, and even between 1922 and 1935 the figure was still 71 per cent. The great majority of Labour MPs were sponsored by trade unions in solidly working-class constituencies. After the war the party managed to attract middle-class and well-educated recruits, usually refugees from the ranks of the Liberals. In 1918 Labour became a national party, open to members of any social class, and gradually embraced candidates outside the ranks of the working class and trade union officials. But even in 1935 only 11 per cent of Labour MPs had been to a university, compared with 69 per cent on the Conservative side. In terms of parliamentary representation we may talk of the party system at that time as institutionalising class difference.

Since 1922, and particularly since 1945, however, an embourgeoisement on the Labour side has produced a remarkable narrowing of this social 'gap'. The term 'bourgeois' is used here to refer to middle-class employment, or professional, managerial and clerical work.[3] Both parties now draw their MPs mainly from the ranks of the professions and the graduate middle class, though Labour still has a (shrinking) minority from the working-class (skilled, semi-skilled and unskilled manual work). Since 1945 an average of 34 per cent have been former workers. The total of 'workers' among Labour MPs is exaggerated, if we include the large number of ex-trade union officials (twenty-seven in 1980) in the total. Even trade union sponsorship, originally a device for recruiting workers to Parliament, is increasingly being offered to university graduates and people with little experience of industry. The unions are now more concerned to sponsor specialised representatives who may not necessarily be members of the union.[4]

The main 'switchboard' for entry to politics now is attendance at a university, usually by way of public school and then Oxbridge for a Conservative MP, or by grammar school and then non-Oxbridge for a Labour MP (though Oxbridge for Labour ministers). Emphasis on academic achievement for political recruitment and promotion has particularly affected the type of Labour MP. In 1945, 43 per cent of Labour MPs had only an elementary education, the minimum provided by the state. Since then that proportion has steadily declined to only 15 per cent in 1979. The 1944 Education Act enabled more children from the working and lower-middle classes to enter grammar schools and universities and thereby achieve social mobility. That generation has come into its own, as ability for local selection committees increasingly appears to be reflected in the possession of a university degree and professional qualifications.

The shift to recruitment by educational merit is shown in Table 4.1, which presents figures on the educational backgrounds of MPs after the general elections of 1945, 1959 and 1979. This shows the proportion of MPs whose education has been purely prestigious (attendance at public school only), purely meritocratic (attendance at non-public school and university), prestigious and meritocratic (attendance at both public school and university) and lacking both prestige and merit. The most striking change has occurred on the Labour side, with the median MP changing from one whose education lacks both merit and prestige in 1945 and 1959 to one who now has merit, that is, a university degree. Between 1945 and 1979 the proportion of graduates grew on the Conservative side from 59 to 69 per cent, while on the Labour side it grew from 33 to 57 per cent.

Table 4.1 *Prestige and Merit in the Education of Politicians*

	1945	*1959*	*1979*
Conservatives			
Pure prestige	29%	24%	20%
Pure merit	3%	12%	16%
Prestige and merit	56%	48%	52%
Neither	12%	16%	12%
Numbers	213	365	339
Labour			
Pure prestige	4%	2%	1%
Pure merit	18%	23%	37%
Prestige and merit	15%	15%	17%
Neither	61%	58%	45%
Numbers	400	258	269

Note: See text for details.

Sources: Data for 1945 extracted from Colin Mellors, *The British MP* (Farnborough: Saxon House, 1978). For subsequent elections they are drawn from Nuffield election studies.

There are, however, two distinct types of middle-class members on the Labour and Conservative benches. First, although we lack authoritative data, many Labour MPs appear to be middle-class *arrivistes*. They are first-generation middle class – having come from working or lower-middle class homes, making their way via grammar schools and university into the professions, and thereby acquiring skills useful for politics. Another contrast is that middle-class Labour MPs are usually employed in the non-commercial parts of the public sector, often in the service sphere, as teachers, lecturers, political organisers, welfare and social workers. Conservative middle-class MPs, on the other hand, usually come from comfortable upper-middle-class families, have been to the most prestigious and expensive public schools and are drawn from the commercial and private sector, being lawyers, accountants and business executives.[5]

Table 4.2 *Number of 'Talking' Professions in Labour Party*

	1951	*Oct. 1974*	*1979*
Lecturers (consultants and scientific researchers)	24	55	28
Teachers	18	38	36
Journalists, publishers	33	22	13
Politicians, organisers	6	8	13
Total of Labour MPs	81	123	90
Percentage of Labour MPs	26	38	30
Total of Labour candidates	163	267	267
Percentage of Labour candidates	27	43	43

Source: Derived from successive Nuffield election studies.

The important change in occupational background is shown in Table 4.2. A crucial distinction is between 'established' professions (such as law, medicine, accountancy) and what Finer calls the 'talking' professions (such as lecturing, teaching, journalism and political and group organisers).[6] The proportion of Labour MPs from the former groups has remained steady at between a fifth and a sixth in postwar parliaments. But the 'talkers' rose from a quarter in 1951 to two-fifths in 1974 and then fell back to 30 per cent in 1979. The fall is not surprising because most safe Labour seats are held by union-sponsored MPs, who are more often manual workers than 'talkers'; consequently the loss of seats at an election normally entails a fall in the proportion of middle-class Labour MPs. But if we look at the bottom line of Table 4.2, which shows the occupational backgrounds of Labour candidates, as opposed to MPs, the change is more startling; the proportion of 'talkers' rose from 27 per cent in 1951 to 43 per cent in 1979. The rise in the number of teachers and lecturers among Labour MPs in postwar Parliaments almost exactly matches the decline in the number of workers. Indeed, the growth of the middle class among Labour MPs is almost solely a function of the growth of the teachers. The party is now a more heterogeneous coalition of workers, 'new' professionals and 'old' professionals.[7] And it is easy to understand why the *arrivistes* should be so concentrated in the teaching profession. Kelsall's study of university graduates[8] shows that the well-educated children from working-class and lower-middle-class families were more likely to aspire to becoming teachers rather than members of more prestigious and exclusive professions. Graduates from established middle-class families were more likely to go into these professions. The change in the occupational structure in the last two decades, particularly the growth in the education and related sector, has provided the opportunity for upward social mobility and a 'take-off' into a political career.

These two trends – to a graduate body of Labour MPs and to one that is more middle class – parallel changes in British society in these directions. But the scale and rate of the change is far more dramatic than that for society. The consequences of this change for the character of the party in Parliament are discussed below (pp. 105–6).

If we turn to Cabinet appointments, the more interesting change is again on the Labour side. A feature of political recruitment in Britain, as in other societies, is that the higher one ascends the political hierarchy, the more socially and educationally exclusive it becomes. Cabinet ministers are usually of higher social and educational status than ministers outside the Cabinet, who, in turn, usually stand above backbenchers.

In terms of social background, most Labour ministers have fallen into one of three broad groups.[9] The party has always found a place for the *patricians* (MPs who come from established upper-middle-class professional families, attended the public schools and Oxbridge, and entered one of the professions). Attlee, Dalton, Cripps and Gaitskell represented this genre and, more recently, Crossman, Gordon-Walker, Jay, Benn and Owen. In the interwar years the party's willingness to find a place for men and women of high social standing, who often had previously been associated with other political parties, contrasted sharply with the practice of socialist parties on the Continent.[10]

This group supplemented the *proletarians* (MPs from working-class families, who left school at an early age and then became manual workers, trade union organisers, or lowly clerical workers). Many of the prewar leaders came from this second background. Aneurin Bevan, who contested the 1955 leadership election with Hugh Gaitskell, and George Brown, who was runner-up to Wilson in 1963, were in this group. Table 4.3 shows that the Labour Cabinets of MacDonald, Attlee and Wilson in 1964 drew about half of their members from such people. During Mr Wilson's leadership, however, there was a steady exodus of proletarians from the Cabinet and they were replaced by the graduate middle-class ministers; by 1970 only three Cabinet ministers were of working-class background. Although Mr Callaghan restored the social balance somewhat (the Labour Cabinet in 1979 contained Eric Varley and Roy Mason, both former miners, Stan Orme, an ex-engineer and Albert

Table 4.3 *Social and Educational Composition of Labour Cabinets, 1924–76*

Date	*Size*	*Aristocrat*	*Middle class*	*Working class*	*University*	
					All	*Oxbridge*
1924	19	3	5	11	6	6
1929	20	2	4	12	6	3
1945	20	—	8	12	10	5
1964	23	1	14	8	13	11
1974 (March)	21	1	16	4	16	11
1976 (March)	22	1	13	7	15	10
Average	20	$1\frac{1}{2}$	10	$8\frac{1}{2}$	$11\frac{1}{2}$	$7\frac{1}{2}$

Notes: Aristocrats are those who had among their grandparents a holder of a hereditary title. *Working class* includes those whose fathers appear to have had a manual occupation when they were growing up.

Source: D. E. Butler and Anne Sloman, *British Political Facts,* 5th edn (London: Macmillan, 1979), p. 79.

Booth, an ex-draughtsman), the gradual erosion of ministers with a working-class background over time is clear.

The third group, now numerically and politically the most significant, is the *meritocrats*. These come from working- or lower-middle-class backgrounds, attend state schools (usually winning scholarships to grammar schools) and go on to university. In recent Labour Cabinets the group has been represented by such people as Wilson, Healey, Mrs Castle, Dell, Hattersley, Shore, Rodgers, Rees and Jenkins. These are scholarship boys and girls whose parents are from the working class, or the lower ranks of the professions, or white-collar occupations (teaching, the civil service, clerical posts and trade union organisers). After university they usually enter the professions themselves often becoming academics, journalists, consultants. In contrast to the proletarians their social mobility has been achieved prior to a political career, by dint of going to university. These are the 'new' types of men and women who, scarcely represented among Conservative MPs, have identified their career advancement with the Labour Party.

Some of the changes in the background of three generations of Labour Cabinet ministers are shown in Table 4.4. The changes in pre-political occupations and educational backgrounds are not marked for the first two periods. But the rise in ministers from the professions, who have received a selective secondary and university education, increases dramatically from 1964. Of the fifty-eight Labour Cabinet ministers who held office between 1964 and 1979, exactly half (twenty-nine) appear to be *meritocrats*, a quarter *proletarians* and a fifth *patricians*.

Table 4.4 *Labour Cabinet Ministers Contrasted*

	Period in Office		
	1916–35	*1935–55*	*1964–79*
(a) Occupation			
Landowning	2	—	—
Rentier	2	1	—
Professional	10	15	35
Commerce, industry	2	2	4
Trade union officials	14	15	12
Others	4	1	7
(b) Education: School			
Elementary, Sec. Mod.	17	18	15
Grammar	8	5	25
Public	6	11	18
Other	3	—	—
(c) Education: University			
None	20	17	21
Oxbridge	7	11	25
Other university	7	6	12
All Labour Cabinet ministers	34	34	58

Sources: Figures for first two columns are from W. L. Guttsman, *The British Political Elite* (London: MacGibbon & Kee, 1964), p. 244; final column compiled from Butler and Sloman, op. cit., and A. Roth, *The MPs' Chart* (London: Parliamentary Profiles, 1971).

There is evidence of a similar embourgeoisement in other tiers of the party. Studies of local parties indicate that the middle class is heavily over-represented and that workers are under-represented among local activists and management committees.[11] On the National Executive Committee, twenty-seven of whose twenty-nine members are now elected by the annual party conference, the shift has been in the same direction. Before 1918 its membership was uniformly working class. Since then, there has been a middle-class takeover – again, largely *arriviste* – of the non-trade union sections. According to Hanby, about a third of the new incumbents of the NEC over the past forty years had already moved upwards socially, that is, they were in middle-class occupations and their fathers were working class.[12] In one sense, of course, the middle-class takeover of the NEC is an extension of the same trend in the PLP; this is because more than half the members of the NEC since 1945 have been MPs and they have dominated elections to the non-trade union sections.

The main source of PLP members from the working class remains the trade unions, and these usually provide former officials, who have deskbound jobs. It is now extremely difficult for a working-class activist, a self-starter like MacDonald, Snowden, or Morrison, to enter politics unless it is through a trade union. In terms of such background factors as social class and education, 'the political class' is now probably more homogeneous than at any time since 1922, when a substantial number of Labour MPs were first returned. This is not to deny the differences in types and quality of education, exact location in the middle class, length of family's membership of that class and differences in political socialisation. Yet the broad similarity between the two main parties is clear.

W. L. Guttsman has described how the middle-class intellectual wing of the Labour Party formed its own 'Left-Wing Society' in the interwar years. Members met at Fabian summer schools, central London flats and weekend cottages in the home counties, and were attached to such figures as the Webbs, Dalton and the Coles. Dalton at the LSE and Cole at Oxford were extremely influential in assisting the careers of would-be Labour politicians.

> The men and women who belonged to [this group] were writers and journalists, lawyers, university teachers, and artists, left-wing professional politicians and younger administrators . . . The trade union leaders of the middle ranks, energetic and able local councillors of working-class origin, are unlikely to find their way into it.[13]

It is already possible to discern the emergence of a Labour 'establishment', based on dynastic and kinship ties. The 1974 parliament included such offspring of former Labour MPs as Jenkins, Marquand, Moyle, Benn, Janner, the Silkins, Mrs Summerskill and Mrs Dunwoody. They followed in the steps of Noel-Baker, Greenwood, Henderson, Cripps and others. If we also took account of MPs who were the sons and daughters of trade union officials, of Labour councillors, or nephews and nieces of Labour politicians, then membership of a 'political family' would emerge as an important factor cutting across social class.[14]

III: Reasons and Results of Change

Two interesting questions are raised by the social transformation of the Labour elite. The first is, why has it occurred? The second is, what is its significance? On the first it is clear that we are talking of a general phenomenon, affecting socialist parties in most industrial societies. The professional, university-educated people, usually first-generation middle class, dominate the parliamentary ranks of other West European socialist parties, and the Australian Labour Party.[15] Teachers and civil servants were always prominent in the French Socialist Party, but now manual workers have been virtually eliminated from that party's MPs. If anything, comparative perspective indicates that working-class representation in Parliament is still higher in Britain than in most other West European countries. Yet the general trend, a decline of working-class representation across countries, is clear enough. The factor common to these industrialised societies is a change in the composition of the workforce, the shift to service or white-collar employment at the expense of the manufacturing and manual workforce. The growth of this 'service' class is common to late industrial societies. The recently published Nuffield social mobility study[16] shows that in the past fifty years the proportion of adults employed in skilled and unskilled manual work fell slightly (45·7 to 43·6 per cent), the intermediate or routine non-manual also declined (from 32 to 26·8 per cent), and the service class grew (from 22·2 to 29·6 per cent). The main growth has been in the professions, senior management and employment in the public sector, covering services and state corporations. The workforce in this sector has grown from 24 per cent of the total in 1960 to a third in 1976. Employment in the local authority sector grew by 69·7 per cent between 1961 and 1975, mainly in health and social services, education and administration, and by 26·5 per cent in central government.[17]

The expansion of the education system has 'creamed off' a larger number of able working-class boys and girls. Only 1 per cent of children of skilled and semi-skilled working-class homes born before 1910 received a grammar school type of education. For those born between 1933 and 1942 it grew to 20·2 per cent and just over 5 per cent of this generation went on to university.[18] And the proportion of children from working-class homes going on to university has hardly altered over fifty years. These figures show that there were, and are still, great inequalities of educational opportunity between children of different social class backgrounds. But they also show that a larger number (if not a greater proportion) of working-class boys were able to compete for elite positions. People from working-class backgrounds could enter the professions but usually only if they had left the working class. By going to university and entering occupations with politics-related skills (like law, journalism and education), they became 'available' for a political career. Of course, other factors such as an interest in politics, activity in organisations, possession of political skills and ambition determine whether such people will try to enter politics. Here is where such factors as membership of the 'political family' and early socialisation, mentioned on p. 103, are important. The key point is that political recruitment is a selective process; the possession of high social status combined with interest and ambition are resources possessed by only a small minority. Hence the disproportionate recruitment from these ranks.

In dealing with the second problem, about significance, one has to tread cautiously in linking changes in the social composition of an elite to changes in its political style or changes in policy outcomes. There are several steps in establishing such relationships and they have to be demonstrated and not, as is often the case, taken for granted.

A familiar argument that different social backgrounds produce different policy outcomes proceeds along one of the following lines. The first is that elites from a particular class background will produce policies which favour members of their own social class. It is difficult to know how to go about testing this particular proposition.[19] The history of the Labour Party, after all, is as littered with examples of middle-class MPs who are socialist and egalitarian as it is of working-class MPs who are very conservative. Three recent left-wing contenders for the political leadership (Benn, Foot and Silkin) are the upper-middle-class sons of upper-middle-class parents. They are also sons of prominent radical politicians, an interesting example of political dynasties! The second line is that differences in social background create different predispositions and different policy preferences. On this point we do have some relevant evidence. One study has found that occupational class relates to ideology for candidates but not MPs.[20] The same survey found that among local councillors middle-class members were more radical in political outlook than working-class members, but the differences were not systematic.[21] Berrington and Guttsman found that Labour MPs from the newer professions were more likely to be rebellious on Third World and humanitarian issues than were members from the older professions and the working class.[22] Traditionally, the educated middle-class professionals have contributed an important *expressive* strand to the Labour style of politics. Study of membership of the CND twenty years ago has demonstrated that the goals of pacificism, humanitarianism and equality were disproportionately supported by teachers and welfare workers. They were the *middle-class radicals in British politics*.[23] It so happens that this social component is now the largest in the Labour Party in Parliament. In the United States, also, a similarly well-educated middle-class intelligentsia, or group of 'symbol specialists' (teachers, lawyers and journalists), has come to the fore in the Democratic Party in the 1970s. Their interests in politics have been less oriented to bread-and-butter issues and gaining office than to more abstract questions of ideology, social justice and 'quality of life'. Compared with the traditional politicians, the new elite, the 'talkers', placed 'more emphasis on the symbolic aspects of politics and less on the output of goods and services'.[24] Recent reforms and trends in both the British Labour and American Democratic parties have made the organisations more open to influence by the activists. In both cases because many of the issue concerns of the new activists are unrepresentative of the concerns of their parties' electoral followings, particularly in the working class, the party finds it more difficult to represent the views of voters.

These varied findings only suggest the possibility of there being significant differences in outlook between MPs of different occupational backgrounds. One may concede, for example, that the middle-class members are more likely to see politics in ideological terms and neglect bread-and-butter concerns of working people. What is not clear, however, is how significant or consistent such differences are, or how they compare with differences which correlate with other factors such as political ambition, political socialisation, or political careers. But the social transformation of Labour MPs may still be important for those who believe that a 'social gap' between leaders and followers is undesirable in itself, or that MPs of a working-class background are more truly 'representative' of their class and more likely to share the same values and emotions. This has been an important strand in Labour thinking. According to one MP:

> for many years to come there will be millions of people doing mundane jobs in factories, mines and desks . . . it is my contention that true political representatives of these people can only come from their own ranks.[25]

Ivor Crewe's survey evidence, reported in Chapter 1, suggests that the change has not yet affected the popular class images voters have of the two main parties. Yet a reading of the diaries of recent Labour ministers, with their revelations of the life-styles of the authors and their Labour colleagues, both in and out of ministerial office, shows that there is nothing very 'proletarian' about the Labour Party in Parliament today.

However, it is difficult to sustain the argument that the social transformation has produced a change in political ideology, that the embourgeoisement of the leadership has resulted in the party being deflected from a militant radical socialist outlook which it possessed when it was largely working class. Such an argument is frequently advanced, in both academic and more political circles.[26] It is suggested that embourgeoisement leads to a de-radicalisation of the party, and this in turn enhances its appeal to the ranks of the moderate middle class. Embourgeoisement for Michels refers both to a growth in middle-class members and to manual workers becoming middle class. Unfortunately, he also uses the term to cover the adoption of 'moderate' or 'compromising' values and political tactics as well as social composition. The process of becoming bourgeois, for Michels, links social change among the leaders with the party becoming oligarchical and anti-revolutionary, and propounding goals which are inimical to the interests of the masses. Social class is treated almost as a surrogate for political outlook. But the idea that the Labour party originally possessed such a radical, socialist outlook, in its working-class days, is a 'myth of the golden age'. From the outset the Labour Party accepted parliamentary methods, interpreted equality along meritocratic lines and disavowed the class war in its policies. Moreover, it has been the middle-class intellectuals, (Michels's 'deserters from the bourgeoisie'), from Trevelyan and Cripps to Benn, who have usually been more disposed to socialist policies.

IV: Electoral Support

Labour's loss of electoral support in the working class has been documented elsewhere in this volume. In the last four general elections, 1970–9, the party has averaged about half the working-class vote. The recent trends are a continuation of the weakening of the class basis of the party system, observable in the 1960s. In 1979 the Conservatives gained 28 per cent of the working-class vote, and Labour 45 per cent, according to a MORI poll. The Conservatives gained 59 per cent of the middle-class vote, Labour 24 per cent. Compared with 1974 (October), Labour's lead over the Conservatives in the working class fell from 24 to 7 per cent, and the Conservative lead in the middle class fell from 37 to 35 per cent. Between 1964 and 1979, as Crewe points out, there has been a swing of 5 per cent from Labour to Conservative in the working class, but a swing of 10 per cent to Labour in the middle class. The same trend is noticeable if we turn to party identification. Since 1964 the proportion of Conservative to Labour identifiers in the middle class has fallen from three to one to two to one, while party identifiers in the working class have favoured Labour by two to one. Both parties have been making their electoral gains among their 'deviant' classes.[27]

The growth of the Labour middle class may be connected to three more general social trends which affect the fragmentation of the middle class itself. The first factor, the change in the class structure and the decline of the manual working-class occupation, has already been mentioned. A separate factor is upward social mobility itself, as a person changes class in his lifetime, or his social class differs from that of his father. The Nuffield social mobility study showed that there has been a net increase in upward social mobility of some 7 per cent, simply because of the expansion of the service sector. Yet the actual proportion of boys from working-class backgrounds moving into the middle class – about one in five – has grown only slowly. Boys from service backgrounds still have four times as great a chance of following their parents into the service class as a working-class boy does of entering that class. But far from being 'closed' and self-recruiting, the middle class contains many *arrivistes*. Some two-thirds of middle-class men were born into another class. We have already noted how the top and middle echelons of leadership in the Labour Party come from these ranks and how important education has been for their rise in station. Other research indicates that some three-quarters of middle-class Labour voters had moved upwards socially compared to their fathers.[28]

Might it be that it is a particular stratum of the middle class that is more likely than another to support Labour? The Census distinguishes within the middle class A (higher managerial or professional), B (lower managerial or professional) and C_1 (skilled or supervisory non-manual and lower non-manual). Rallings found that in 1970 it was the C_1 groups who were the more likely to vote Labour. In terms of life-style (trade union membership, council house tenancy) and subjective class assessment, these routine non-manuals had more in common with the working than the middle class. They were marginal to the dominant social and political norms of their objective social class. In subsequent elections, however, Crewe has shown that Labour has made inroads and the Conservatives suffered losses across the middle class as a whole.[29]

In seeking an explanation for this change, it is interesting to note the qualitative change in social class B, the lower managerial, administrative and professional groups. Between 1964 and 1974 it became more of an employee and managerial class; the proportion of self-employed fell from 27 to 11 per cent. It also became more unionised, up from 18 to 43 per cent, and concentrated in the growing white-collar unions like NALGO, NUPE, the NUT and ASTMS. Crewe points out that many have become middle class largely through higher education, not through the possession of capital and contacts. They are found predominantly in the expanding 'new' professions of administration, teaching and 'caring', rather than commerce or the traditional ones of law and medicine, and in the public rather than the private sector.

Reference to the public/private sector divide draws attention to an emerging cleavage which cuts across the manual versus middle class division. Public sector employees depend for their livelihood on public expenditure and the 'social wage'; they have an economic interest (apart from any presumed ideological sympathies) for the growth of these state services. There has been a decline in support for many Labour principles across Labour voters since 1964. But the decline was less marked among the middle-class Labour voters; they were more likely to favour the expansion of public ownership and state expenditure on welfare services between 1964 and 1974. Similarly, 'collective modes of consumption' or life-styles (e.g. reliance on council housing and public transport), and private styles of consumption (home ownership and access to a motor car), correlate with contrasting patterns of political behaviour. Regardless of social class, dependence on collective modes of consumption aligns the voter to the political left while involvement in individualised forms aligns voters to the right.[30]

V: Conclusion

The above analysis shows the complexity of social class and the ambiguous relations between class and party. If British politics was purely about social class, then Labour MPs would be largely working class in background and Conservative MPs middle class. Alternatively, if the occupations of the two parties' MPs mirrored their electoral support then most Labour MPs and half of the Conservatives would be working class. In fact, the MPs of both parties are largely middle class, though there are still differences between them. Historically, the Conservatives have been a middle- and upper-middle-class parliamentary party, drawing voters from across the social spectrum. Historically, Labour has been based on a largely working-class vote and drawn its MPs from different social strata. It is now a largely middle-class party in Parliament drawing on a diminishing body of working-class support in the country. What remains is the rhetoric of equality, redistribution and class, while the social bases of such a style are being eroded. The change may or may not advance the cause of socialism in the Labour Party. Historically, however, the advance or retreat of that all-encompassing, but rarely defined, term has had little to do with the strength of the working-class base.

Notes: Chapter 4

1 H. Pelling, *The Origins of the Labour Party* (London: Macmillan, 1965), pp. 204, 209.
2 R. McKibbin, *The Evolution of the Labour Party 1910–1924* (London: Oxford University Press, 1974), p. 97.
3 For a sociologist's discussion of the different meanings of the term embourgeoisement, see J. H. Goldthorpe, D. Lockwood, F. Bechhofer and J. Platt, *The Affluent Worker in the Class Structure* (Cambridge: Cambridge University Press, 1968), ch. 1.
4 See W. D. Muller, *The Kept Men* (Hassocks: Harvester, 1977).
5 In 1974 39 per cent of Labour MPs had been employed in the state sector before entering Parliament. For Conservative MPs the figure was 8 per cent. Extracted from Colin Mellors, *The British MP* (Farnborough: Saxon House, 1978), p. 66.
6 S. E. Finer, *The Changing British Party System 1945–1979* (Washington, DC: American Enterprise Institute, 1980).
7 Muller, op. cit., p. 76.
8 R. K. Kelsall, *Graduates: The Sociology of an Elite* (London: Methuen, 1972).
9 This point is discussed in D. Kavanagh, 'From gentlemen to players: Changes in political leadership', in W. Gwynn and R. Rose (eds), *Britain: Progress and Decline* (London: Macmillan, 1980). See also T. May, 'A government of meritocrats', *New Society*, 12 May 1977.
10 E. Wertheimer, *Portrait of the Labour Party* (London: Putnam, 1929).
11 See the evidence in B. Hindess, *The Decline of Working Class Politics* (London: McGibbon & Kee, 1971); E. Janosik, *Constituency Labour Parties in Britain* (New York: Praeger, 1968); I. Gordon and P. Whiteley, 'Social class and political attitudes: the case of Labour committees', *Political Studies*, vol. XXVII no. 1 (January 1979).

12 V. Hanby, 'A changing Labour elite', in Ivor Crewe (ed.), *British Political Sociology Yearbook,* Vol. 1 (London: Croom Helm, 1974), p. 142.
13 W. L. Guttsman, *The British Political Elite* (London: MacGibbon & Kee, 1964), pp. 252–3.
14 R. Johnson, 'The British political elite, 1955–1972', *Archives europeénes de sociologie,* vol. 14 (1973).
15 W. Patterson and A. Thomas, *Social Democratic Parties in Western Europe* (London: Croom Helm, 1975), and M. Grattan 'The Australian Labour Party', in H. Mayer and H. Wilson (eds), *Australian Politics: A Third Reader* (Melbourne: Cheshire, 1975).
16 J. Goldthorpe, *Social Mobility and Class Structure* (Oxford: Clarendon Press, 1980).
17 R. Bacon and W. Eltis, *Britain's Economic Problems* (London: Macmillan, 1976).
18 A. Halsey, A. F. Heath and J. M. Ridge, *Origins and Destinations* (Oxford: Clarendon Press, 1980).
19 Hindess suggests that the middle-class 'takeover' has resulted in the squeezing out of working-class issues. It is not obvious, however, that many issues may be characterised in such terms.
20 P. Whiteley, 'The structure of democratic socialist ideology in Britain', *Political Studies*, vol. XXVI, no. 2 (June 1978).
21 Gordon and Whiteley, op. cit.
22 Guttsman, op. cit., and H. Berrington, *Backbench Opinion in the House of Commons 1945–55* (Oxford: Pergamon, 1973).
23 F. Parkin, *Middle-Class Radicals* (Manchester: Manchester University Press, 1968).
24 J. Kirkpatrick with W. E. Miller, E. Douvain, W. Crotty, T. Levitin and M. Fiedler, *The New Presidential Elite: Men and Women in National Politics* (New York: Russell Sage and Twentieth Century Fund, 1976).
25 Cited in Muller, op. cit., p. 70.
26 As in Hindess, op. cit., and F. Parkin, *Class Inequality and Political Order* (London: MacGibbon & Kee, 1971), pp. 132 ff.
27 See Crewe, this volume and sources cited therein.
28 See P. Abramson, 'Intergenerational social mobility and political choice', *American Political Science Review*, vol. LXVI (1972).
29 C. Rallings, 'Two types of middle-class Labour voter?', *British Journal of Political Science*, vol. 5 (January 1975).
30 P. Dunleavy, 'The political implications of sectoral changes and the growth of state employment', pts 1 and 2, *Political Studies*, vol. XXVII, nos 3 and 4 (September and December 1980).

5 The Decline of Labour's Local Party Membership and Electoral Base, 1945–79

PAUL WHITELEY

The Labour Party is in serious trouble. The current faction fighting over the issue of Conference democracy is only a visible indicator of the problems which go deep and have been with the party for many years. The most fundamental and deep rooted of these problems is the erosion of Labour's electoral base, and this has been accompanied by an equally strong decline in individual membership of the party. The electoral decline is particularly disturbing; the Labour and Conservative shares of the popular vote in general elections are graphed against the number of years since 1944 in Figure 5.1. The correlation between Labour's vote share of years was –0·85, and the equivalent correlation for the Conservatives was –0·37. Thus the decline in the Labour vote is much more rapid and more predictable than that of the Conservatives.

An equal though less conspicuous decline has taken place in the individual membership of the party, the component of total membership not tied to trade union affiliations. This can be seen in the published figures for individual membership which, as is well known, exaggerate the true levels. If we graph the relationship between the affiliated individual membership and the number of years since 1949 we observe the near-perfect linear relationship of Figure 5.2, which gives a correlation of –0·91. On the published figures the party has on average been losing more than 11,000 members per year, and the true loss of membership may well be higher than this.

The purpose of this chapter is to attempt to explain why this decline in membership and electoral support has happened. These two trends, in membership and in the vote, are considered together since it will be argued that similar factors account for both phenomena. But before discussion of trends in the membership figures it will be useful to try and estimate more accurate figures of individual membership than those published by the party.

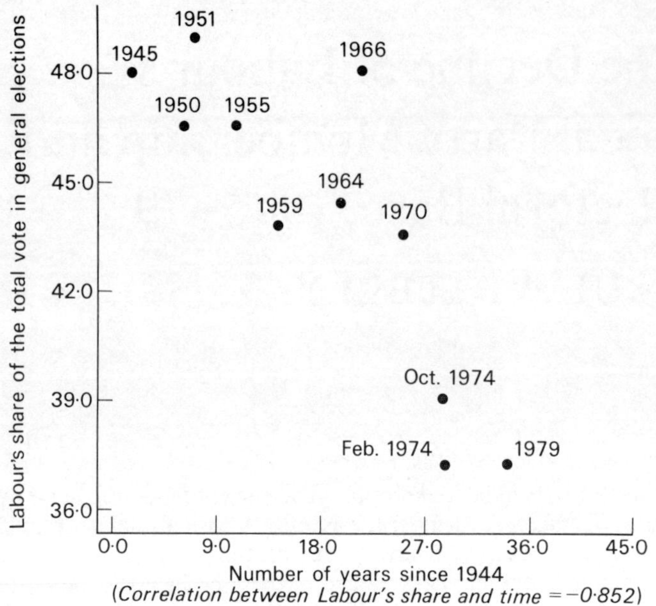

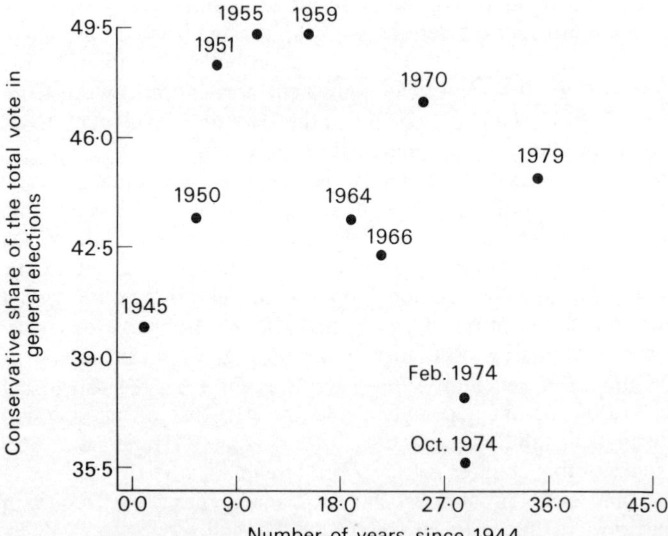

Figure 5.1. *The relationship between the Labour and Conservative shares of the total vote and time, 1945–79.*

Source: D. E. Butler and Anne Sloman, *British Political Facts*, 5th edn (London: Macmillan, 1979).

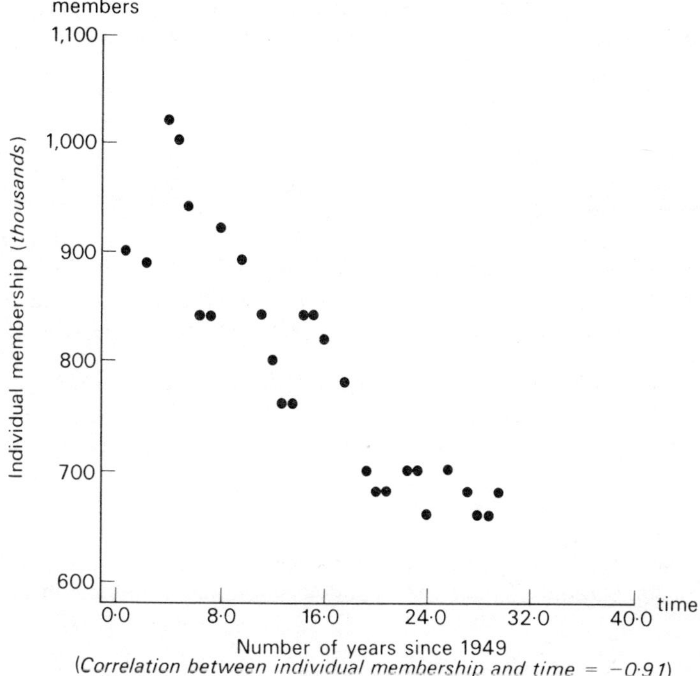

Figure 5.2 *The decline in Labour Party individual membership, 1950–78.*
Sources: Butler and Sloman, op. cit., p. 143, and Labour Party Headquarters.

Individual Membership and Activism in 1979

There are no accurate membership figures held in the party headquarters. Equally the accuracy of local membership figures will vary depending on the efficiency of the local party organisation. In fact, the rule that constituency parties must affiliate with at least 1,000 members which has operated since 1963 was abolished at the 1979 party conference. So the affiliation membership figures for 1980 should be more accurate than in the past. However, the only way to obtain truly accurate estimates of the individual membership of the party is to survey key members of the local constituency parties.

Accordingly, estimates of Labour's membership figures were obtained from a random sample survey of delegates to the 1978 party conference. The survey was part of a Europe-wide study of party activists and was aimed at constituency and trade union delegates to the party conference.[1] The details of the sampling design and response rates appear in the appendix.

Delegates were asked a large number of questions about their backgrounds, political experience, attitudes and beliefs. They were also asked to provide information about levels of membership and activism in constituency parties. There are, of course, difficulties in obtaining accurate estimates from delegates, and it is not easy to verify them. But Conference delegates are for the most part prominent activists in their constituency parties, and as such are likely to be at least as well-informed about the state of the membership as anyone else in the local parties. Thus their responses are taken as accurate measures of the state of the membership.

The responses of constituency party delegates to the questions relating to membership are set out in Table 5.1. Few of the trade union delegates responded to these questions and hence they do not appear in these tables. Delegates were asked to provide an estimate of the total membership, the number of male activists, the number of female activists, and the percentage of active wards in a constituency. It can be seen from Table 5.1 that more than 50 per cent of constituency parties had less than 500 members, and only 13 per cent reported more than 1,000 members, the

Table 5.1 *Individual Membership of the Labour Party, 1978 (average N = 170)*

Number of Members	*Percentage of Parties*
under 100	7
100–499	47
500–999	33
1,000 plus	13
Number of Activists	*Percentage of Parties*
under 25	7
26–50	27
50–100	31
100 plus	35
Percentage of Active Wards	*Percentage of Parties*
all	49
three-quarters	26
half	17
quarter	7
none	1

Source: Survey of party conference delegates, 1978/9.

minimum for affiliation. This last figure provides an independent check of the accuracy of the survey, since it is possible to calculate the percentage of constituencies which affiliate with more than 1,000 members nationally. This turned out to be 14 per cent of constituency parties in 1978, and thus the sample and the population of all constituency parties are roughly the same. This suggests that the sample is representative of the population of constituency parties.

The median number of members of constituency parties in the sample was 400, and median number of activists was 90. Thus approximately 23 per cent of the total membership were reported as active. However, wide variations existed across constituencies in the proportion of total members reported as active. Some 17 per cent of parties reporting less than fifty activists, reported less than a hundred members; whereas 28 per cent of those reporting less than fifty activists, reported more than five hundred members. This highlights the variation in the ratio of activists to members across constituencies. To some extent this will reflect the recruitment policies of local parties, with some parties seeking to maximise membership, and others not wanting a large passive membership which has to be serviced. Another reason lies in the proportion of wards which are active in constituencies. When all wards are active this produces a larger total membership than when only some wards are active, which in turn influences the ratio of the active to total membership.

Given these figures we can extrapolate the same results to the country as a whole. Taking the median number of members and activists as representative of the average constituency, there must have been around 250,000 individual members and 55,000 activists in 1978. This contrasts sharply with the published figure for affiliated membership in 1978 of 675,000.

It is interesting to compare these estimates with the only other national sample survey of local membership available, which was carried out by the Houghton Committee on Financial Aid to Political Parties. Using a sophisticated multi-stage random sample of 100 constituencies, Houghton estimated that constituency Labour parties had an arithmetic mean number of 500 members.[2] A simple extrapolation of this to all constituency parties would give a total membership of around 317,000. However, this is likely to be an overestimate of the true state of Labour's membership for two reasons. First, the arithmetic mean is not an appropriate measure of the average number of members in constituency parties because the distribution of members across all constituencies is markedly skewed. There are a few constituencies with large memberships and a sample arithmetic mean will be inflated by these, so estimating the total membership from the mean number of members will be misleading. Accurate estimates of the membership figures should be calculated from the median number of members in constituencies. A second reason why the Houghton estimates are likely to be inflated derives from their sampling method. They used a multi-stage random sample with varying sampling proportions in England, Wales and Scotland. Their sample is biased in favour of the second two countries compared with England.[3] This is perfectly legitimate since they wanted to increase the number of constituencies in their sample which had active nationalist parties. However, it does bias the estimates of the Labour membership. Labour is markedly more popular in electoral terms in both Scotland and Wales than it is in England. Party membership and voting support are positively correlated,[4] and thus it is likely that the Houghton sample of constituencies have an average level of Labour membership higher than is found in general throughout Great Britain.

I am, of course, concerned with the decline of Labour's membership over the years. A recent article by Seyd and Minkin has suggested that Labour's membership has been increasing rather than declining over the last ten years.[5] They suggest that membership is recovering from the low ebb of the late 1960s, although of course it is still much lower than it was during the 1950s. This is an interesting suggestion but it cannot be verified in the absence of a longitudinal study with a representative sample of constituencies. Their results do, however, highlight the point that the relationship between the affiliated and actual membership of the Labour Party is complex, and one cannot make direct inferences about the latter from the former without taking account of a number of factors which might distort the picture. I shall return to this question later.

If we wish to explain the decline of the party membership over the years, a good way to start is to investigate the reasons activists give for joining the party. Reasons for joining are not, of course, the same as reasons for leaving, but it turns out that in the survey the former threw useful light on the latter. Delegates were asked to explain the main reason they had for joining the party originally. The results of this are discussed next.

Why Join the Labour Party?

In one sense the problem of membership in the Labour Party is to explain why people wish to join at all. This point is not facetious, but is rather rooted in a theoretical analysis of support for voluntary organisations discussed by Olson.[6] He notes that any organisation which seeks to provide public goods will have an acute problem of mobilising support, unless it can use coercion or supply private benefits to members. A public good is a good such that, if it is provided to anyone, it will be available to all. Its characteristics are that no one can be excluded from consuming it once it is provided. Because of this, individuals will have an incentive to 'free ride', and avoid the costs of contributing to the provision of the good. This is likely to produce a sub-optimal provision of the good from the social point of view. Originally the theory was worked out to explain the difficulties of allocating what was thought to be a relatively restricted type of good[7] (e.g. defence provision, lighthouses, etc.). But Olson notes that many types of collective action are concerned with the provision of collective goods, notably interest groups of various kinds.

The relevance of this for the question of Labour's membership is immediately apparent. A political party is a collective-goods-'producing' organisation, *par excellence*. This is because public policies are collective goods (or bads). They seek to implement policy changes at the national level which apply to all. This means that an individual who wants particular Labour policies to be implemented, or alternatively wants Conservative policies not to be implemented, has an incentive to 'free ride' and not become a party member. Thus in so far as individual membership of the party is motivated by instrumental aims, that is, by a desire to see policies implemented, there will be a free rider problem. If membership of the party were solely a matter of instrumental motivation then the party would, according to the theory, have a very restricted membership indeed.

In discussing instrumental motives a distinction must be made between private and public instrumental motives. An individual may want to join the party simply because he is interested in politics for its own sake, and enjoys the intrigue and debate of political life. This is an instrumental motive, but it is private rather than public. This distinction is important in connection with the paradox of collective action, since private instrumental motives are not subject to the free rider problem.

There are also other reasons for joining the party which are not instrumental in the sense described. People join because they are idealistic and want to give expression to these ideals, and we can characterise such motives as expressive motives. An individual who joins the party to end unemployment, or to achieve increased welfare spending, is essentially pursuing instrumental goals or 'public goods'. An individual who joins the party in order to 'build socialism' or achieve 'social justice' is pursuing a private good, or the satisfaction associated with expressing generalised ideological goals. It goes without saying, of course, that the distinction between instrumental and expressive is not absolutely clear-cut; people wishing to build socialism are likely to have strong opinions about policy, and similarly people wanting to pursue particular objectives are not necessarily lacking in ideals. However, there is a meaningful distinction between the pursuit of particular policy objectives or benefits for one's social group or class on the one hand, and idealistic motives such as the construction of a 'better world', or 'building socialism', on the other. Given this, the Olson problem of collective action will apply more readily to people pursuing instrumental goals than to those pursuing idealistic goals.

One of the questions on the survey of Conference delegates asked respondents to cite their main reason for joining the Labour Party. The question had an open-ended coding so individuals were not required to answer in terms of a predefined set of categories, which makes the replies particularly valuable in highlighting motives. The responses to this question appear in Table 5.2, and for reasons which should become clear they are categorised by occupational status. To pursue this distinction between instrumental and expressive motives for joining we might tentatively classify the responses in Table 5.2 as follows.

Table 5.2 *The relationship between Social Class and Motives for Joining the Labour Party (all delegates, percentages)*

Motives for Joining the Party	*Middle Class (N = 131)*	*Intermediate (N = 37)*	*Working Class (N = 62)*
Believes in socialism/Clause 4	35·9	24·3	24·6
Wants a more equal society or social justice	27·5	18·9	21·3
Wants to implement or influence specific policies of the party	12·2	10·8	14·8
Has a generalised loyalty to the Labour Party	3·8	2·7	3·3
Sees Labour as representing and promoting the interests of the working class	3·1	13·5	11·5
Wanted to be involved in politics and is interested in political affairs	3·1	10·8	9·8
Joined because of family background	8·4	5·4	1·6
Involved in local politics or in the social life of the party locally	2·3	5·4	3·3
Joined as a reaction to Tory governments or policies	3·8	5·4	0·0
Involved as an extension of trade union activity	0·0	2·7	9·8

Note: Middle class represents those respondents with a Registrar General's occupational status coding of 1 or 2, intermediate is a coding of 3N, and working class is a coding of 3M, 4, or 5.

Source: Survey of party conference delegates, 1978/9.

A classification of motives for joining the Labour Party

Instrumental reasons	*Expressive reasons*	*Neither instrumental nor expressive*
wants to implement or influence specific policies	believes in socialism/ Clause 4	joined because of family background
sees Labour as promoting the interests of the working class	wants a more equal society or greater social justice	
wants to be involved in politics	has a generalised loyalty to the party	
wants to be involved with the local party		
joined as a reaction to Tory government or policies		
joined as an extension of trade union activities		

The responses in Table 5.2 represent the main categories of response with idiosyncratic replies (e.g. 'I joined because of my girlfriend') excluded. All the responses classified as instrumental have the characteristic that they are concerned with achieving benefits for the individual or social group. Not all of these are concerned with obtaining public goods; individuals who join for social reasons, or because they simply want to be involved in politics, are pursuing private benefits. But those who want to achieve specific policies, want to get benefits for workers, or oppose the Tory government's policies, are pursuing collective goods (or avoiding bads in the latter case). We can illustrate these with some examples of individual responses:

- Unemployment and its effects made me want to join the party. I wanted to do something about it.
- I am committed to the social ownership of the means of production, and to the extension of industrial democracy.
- I joined because I believe Labour is the party which looks after the interests of the working class.
- I joined because of Suez, and because of the Tories' attitude to nationalisation.

Respondents giving expressive reasons tended to reply in much more generalised idealistic terms, not mentioning policies at all. While these are often collective goods, when they are articulated in such general terms they are very much private aims of an expressive nature. For example:

> I support socialism.
>
> I saw it as the best means of achieving a just society.
>
> Clause 4.

Thus while the distinction between expressive and instrumental reasons for joining the party is not watertight, there is a clear distinction between these motives which is readily apparent in the responses of delegates. Moreover, it can be seen in Table 5.2 that respondents were very much more likely to give expressive reasons than instrumental reasons for joining the party. This fits the Olson model, since it implies that individuals tend to join primarily for private reasons rather than for the purpose of producing collective goods. This also tends to throw new light on the old debate about the rights of Conference as a policy-making body in the party.

Conference ostensibly makes policy but it does not control the actions of a Labour government in office. In practice the leadership has been able to pursue policies not accepted by Conference, particularly in the economic field. This is partly a cause and partly a consequence of the fact that delegates are not primarily interested in policy, in the sense of concrete policy outcomes. They are, of course, interested in symbolic or rhetorical issues, and a party leader who pays due deference to this has a wide scope for pursuing policies opposed by Conference. This explains why the most divisive conflict in the Labour Party since the war was over the question of rewriting Clause 4 of the constitution, a purely symbolic question. At the same time policies such as the Labour government's slavish support for the US actions in Vietnam attracted only a rather muffled criticism. This phenomenon is largely explained by the preoccupation of many delegates with expressive issues.

There is a further characteristic of the distinction between expressive and instrumental motives which is particularly important for explaining the decline of the membership. It is clear that important differences exist between middle-class and working-class conference delegates in their reasons for joining the party. Working-class respondents are much more likely to give instrumental reasons for joining than middle-class respondents, who are clearly more expressive. This can be observed in Table 5.2, particularly the first motive in the list, which relates to the ideal of building socialism. Nearly 36 per cent of middle-class respondents cited a belief in socialism as a reason for joining the party, compared with 24·6 per cent of the working-class respondents. Using the classification of instrumental and expressive motives described above, some 49·2 per cent of working-class respondents cited instrumental reasons for joining, compared with 24·5 per cent of middle-class respondents. Similarly, the intermediate occupational status group is also more instrumental than the middle class, with 45·9 per cent of it in this category.

If working-class delegates are more likely than the middle class to cite instrumental reasons for joining, particularly the reason that 'Labour stands for the interests of the working class', what implications could this have for the decline in membership? This is discussed next.

The Decline in Labour Membership

The link between the instrumental orientation of working-class Labour delegates and the decline of party membership is the fact of the decline of working-class activism in the party. The decline of working-class politics was originally discussed by Hindess,[8] and although the idea has been criticised[9] it has aroused a lot of interest. This decline has certainly happened at the elite level in Parliament, and in the National Executive Committee.[10] The present survey confirms that party conference delegates are predominantly middle class, so it has happened at this level too.

Labour councillors also appear to be predominantly middle class.[11] At the level of constituency parties the evidence concerning the changing class compositions of the membership is much less clear-cut than at the elite level. Forrester summarises a number of empirical studies of local Labour parties, and has also carried out a detailed study of one constituency himself.[12] He concludes that most studies indicated that the middle class was disproportionately represented among activists, but not necessarily among members. As to the decline of working-class activists over time, he concludes that the evidence was inadequate to confirm or reject this argument.[13]

However, indirect evidence exists which would support the Hindess thesis. There have been substantial changes in the occupational structure in Britain over the years, leading to a decline in the numbers of manual workers. The survey of occupational mobility by Goldthorpe *et al.* showed that some 43·8 per cent of the occupational structure was made up of manual workers in 1972.[14] Respondents to their survey were asked about their parents' occupation when they were young and their replies indicated that nearly 55 per cent of these parents were manual workers. Thus vast changes in the occupational structure have been taking place, with many manual occupations disappearing altogether and being replaced by white-collar service occupations. One might argue about how 'middle class' some of these service occupations are, but it is clear that they are not the traditional manual occupations and this is bound to have political as well as social repercussions. It would be surprising indeed if the social composition of Labour's local membership had not been affected by these changes in the social structure, making the membership more white collar, and hence up to a point more middle class.

On this basis I shall argue that there has been a decline in working-class activism in the Labour Party, and that this is one of the important reasons for the decline in party membership over time. The changing nature of the occupational structure may partly account for this, but are there any other factors?

One important reason for this decline can be observed in Table 5.2, and was discussed above in relation to the motives for joining. When these are instrumental and relate to the production of public goods they need nurturing or reinforcing by the successful implementation of those policies. Thus the individual who cited the fight against unemployment as the main reason for joining the party would be much more vulnerable to defection than an individual who has diffused and generalised aims at a time when the Labour government presided over increasing unemployment. Similarly, an individual concerned with improved social services would be more likely to leave the party over cuts in these services than someone with a general commitment to greater social justice. Thus, in general, individuals with instrumental motives are more likely to leave the party than individuals with expressive motives at a time of failing policy performance.

In recent years the Labour government has presided over rising unemployment and inflation, and cuts in the welfare state which have increased rather than decreased inequality;[15] and has, as Stuart Holland has put it, 'attempted to run the economy mainly by opposing its own supporters'.[16] Economic performance is a particularly salient issue for the voters as a whole, and it can be inferred that it is also true for Labour Party members. Hence the instrumental members, who are disproportionately working class, are leaving the party as a result of these failures of policy outcomes.[17] Hirschman's analysis of consumer responses to decline in firms, organisations and states is relevant in this context.[18] There are three possible tactics when faced with declining performance: 'exit, voice, or loyalty'. We might crudely summarise the situation in Labour's grass-roots parties in response to the failures of Labour in office as follows: 'nearly everyone voices, but while the middle class remains loyal, the working class exists'. Clearly the Olson paradox tends to make instrumental members more likely to leave than expressive members, regardless of performance, simply because they are pursuing collective goals. But when this inherent vulnerability to defection is coupled with a wide-ranging failure of performance it becomes critical.

Other factors related to the class mix within local parties may also be influential in producing a working-class defection. Hindess shows that for middle-class activists the language of politics and the attitudes towards issues are very different from those of the working class. He argues that in the case of middle-class activists 'politics was seen basically as a matter of general principles, of broad policy outlines. Thereafter, it is a matter of administration, of getting suitably qualified personnel and of setting up the right sort of machinery to execute policy.'[19] On the other hand, for the working-class activists, politics is a question of 'unavoidable personal involvement, in consequence of political decision, to the experience of government . . . as an external or constraining and coercive organisation'.[20] Thus middle-class activists tend to discuss politics in terms of general principles, whereas working-class activists see things in terms of specific events which affect the life of the individual.

These distinctions have been analysed more generally by Bernstein in his examination of the relationship between language and social class.[21] Bernstein distinguishes between the 'elaborated' code of the middle class and the 'restricted' code of the working class. The archetypal elaborated code is characterised by complex sentence structure, a rich vocabulary and the use of abstractions, and it allows subtle distinctions of meaning and fine discrimination between concepts; on the other hand, the restricted code is characterised by simple sentence structure, poor vocabulary, an emphasis on concrete descriptions rather than analytical reasoning and a limited range of expressions.

It is fairly clear that the dominant language code in British politics is the middle-class code, and thus individuals proficient in this are likely to dominate local party meetings. This may well lead to a defection of working-class activists and members, who find themselves either excluded from proceedings or forced to operate in what is very often to them an alien language code. Anyone who has observed the verbosity and circumlocution of a working-class trade unionist giving an interview to the media can appreciate the difficulties of a person socialised in one language code operating in another. Thus a small articulate group of middle-class activists may paradoxically drive out working-class activists. Similar processes may operate at the level of the electorate, where working-class voters hear Labour politicians speaking in an increasingly elaborate language code, replete with phrases like the 'PSBR' and 'monetarism'.

A further reason why middle-class members may remain when working-class members exit relates to their levels of ideological structuring. In the case of Labour councillors, Gordon and Whiteley found that while middle-class councillors were not necessarily more right- or left-wing than working-class councillors, they were more ideologically homogeneous.[22] Their ideological structures were more coherent than those of the working class. If a similar phenomenon exists among Labour activists, then it is likely that individuals with a higher level of ideological structuring will remain active in the face of Labour's record in office in comparison with individuals having a lower level of attitude structuring. This is because their ideology protects them from disillusionment, much as faith sustains the active Christian. Individuals with a weak structuring are not so protected from dissonant messages from the Labour Party in power. This makes them more likely to defect.

Thus there are a number of separate forces acting to increase the likelihood of working-class defection from party membership in comparison with the middle class. However, the discussion concerning the main influence, the performance of Labour in 'delivering the goods', has remained up to this point largely theoretical. Is there any independent evidence to corroborate this performance hypothesis?

If the performance hypothesis is correct there should be a relationship between indicators of Labour's performance in office and the level of membership over time. In other words, the level of individual membership should respond to the policy outputs of a Labour government, and a bad performance should produce an increased rate of defection. There is much poll evidence to suggest that the most salient issues from the point of view of the general public are economic issues.[23] In particular, the rate of inflation and unemployment are always at the top of the list of salient issues in surveys of public opinion.[24] If we assume that these issues are also the most salient for Labour Party members, we can examine the relationship between economic performance and membership of the party over time as a test of the performance hypothesis. Of course, this is only an approximate test; ideally we would require panel data of Labour members over time to examine this proposition fully. But it is a useful preliminary test in the absence of time series, individual-level data.

One obvious problem of examining trends in Labour Party membership over time arises from the fact that we have to use the affiliated membership figures in the absence of an accurate longitudinal measure of true membership. Although the affiliated membership figures are a biased measure of the true membership figures, they can still be used to identify trends, provided such biases are controlled as much as possible. This can be done by incorporating variables into a predictive model of trends in membership which are thought likely to influence this variable. To clarify the point it is useful to consider the relationship between the affiliated or published membership data of Figure 5.2, and the unknown true membership series.

If the factors which cause the affiliated membership series to be a biased measure of the true membership series remain unchanged over time, then the existence of bias is irrelevant for estimating trends. This is because in this case the published and true figures will decline at the same rate over time making it possible to estimate that rate of decline from the published figures alone. More technically, the slope coefficient of the regression of time on the published membership will equal the slope coefficient of the regression of time on the true membership, and only the intercept terms of the two models would differ.

However, it is rather a strong assumption to make, and it is more likely that the published figures and the true figures will systematically vary in relation to each other over time. This is because there are a number of sources of variation in the true membership which might not be fully recorded in the published membership figures. For example, it is well known that the party in opposition tends on average to be more popular in the opinion polls than the party in power. The average lead of the opposition over the incumbent in the Gallup Polls from 1947 to 1975 was 3·6 per cent.[25] On the assumption that trends in membership are influenced by trends in party popularity then incumbency should increase the rate of defection of members. This might or might not be fully recorded in the affiliated membership figures. It is particularly likely that it will not be properly recorded after 1963 when the party introduced the minimum affiliation requirement for constituency parties of 1,000 members. If a local party has to affiliate with 1,000 members or not at all, it is likely to continue affiliation in the face of declining membership producing an ever-increasing bias in the figures over the years.

There are other factors which might possibly produce variations in the true membership figures over time which are not recorded. Faction fighting in public might lose members, although it could be argued that the publicity attendant on disputes like the CND debate of the early 1960s encouraged rather than discouraged a growth in membership. The parliamentary performance and the effectiveness of the leadership might influence the level of individual membership. Clearly there are many influences at work which affect the true level of membership.

With these points in mind I shall investigate the relationship between aggregate economic indicators and the individual affiliated membership over the period 1950–78. An attempt will be made to control the factors which might cause the membership series to fluctuate over time by incorporating three variables into the models. These variables act as controls, that is, it is possible to examine the influence of the economy on the membership while statistically holding constant these sources of variation. These controls are:

(1) the average annual level of popularity of the Labour Party in the Gallup Polls, which should pick up a number of influences including the performance of the party in Parliament, the influence of faction fighting and the success or otherwise of the Conservatives;
(2) a dummy variable scoring 0 up to 1962 and 1 thereafter to measure

the bias in the series introduced by the minimum affiliation rule;
(3) a dummy variable scoring 1 for years when Labour was in power and 0 otherwise, to pick up the influence of incumbency.

The influence of the economy on the level of membership is examined using three economic indicators. These are the rate of unemployment, the value of the index of retail prices, and the change in the index of retail prices in that year. A variety of models and specifications are tested, and the results appear in Table 5.3. It turns out that affiliated party membership and the three economic variables are non-linearly related over time, so it becomes necessary to transform the economic variables to make their relationship with membership linear. This is done by taking the logs of unemployment and changes in prices, and the reciprocal of the level of prices.

Each of the various models in Table 5.3 achieved a high goodness of fit by social science standards, with none of them explaining less than 70 per cent of the variation in membership over time. To consider the economic variables first, both prices variables are statistically significant at the 0·10 level, and the change of prices is variable at the 0·05 level. This means that the probability of obtaining coefficients of those magnitudes due to chance, and not to a genuine effect, is less than 1 in 10. When the prices variables are transformed in order to linearise them, the level of statistical significance is much higher. The statistical significance of the unemployment variable both in the original and in the transformed form is slightly less than prices, but it still approximates the 1·10 level.

Thus when the economic variables are used one at a time they are significant predictors of the level of membership, even after controlling for the confounding influences described earlier. All the signs of the coefficients of the economic variables are as expected. These coefficients have a straightforward interpretation: a 1 per cent increase in the level of the price index decreases the membership by more than 300, and a 1 per cent increase in the rate of unemployment reduces it by 12,600. These figures should be taken only as approximations to the true effects, since strictly we should consider the influence of unemployment and prices increases simultaneously. The difficulty with doing this is that prices and unemployment are highly correlated, and this distorts the results if they are incorporated into the model together. This distortion, due to multicollinearity, can be observed in the model which includes the logs of the price change and unemployment variables.[26] The latter changes sign and becomes statistically non-significant, thus making the model unreliable.

In the case of the three controlling variables, they are all significant at least at the 0·10 level with the exception of one coefficient. Labour popularity in the Gallup Polls is positively related to membership, confirming the hypothesis that the latter is influenced by the former. The 1963

Table 5.3 *Economic Variables as Predictors of Labour's Individual Membership, 1950–78, Controlling for Confounding Influences (dependent variable: individual membership of the Labour Party (thousands); N = 29)*

Predictor							
Labour incumbency dummy	51·6 (1·71)	51·1 (1·71)	40·4 (1·32)	35·2 (1·12)	45·1 (1·52)	14·1 (0·52)	54·5 (1·66)
Labour popularity in the Gallup Polls	11·21 (3·53)	10·96 (3·49)	10·83 (3·21)	10·65 (3·10)	10·42 (3·20)	7·46 (2·50)	11·27 (3·31)
1963 dummy variable	−145·8 (5·41)	−133·0 (4·64)	−141·0 (4·66)	−134·3 (3·98)	−134·4 (4·59)	−56·9 (1·56)	−137·8 (4·04)
Index retail prices (100 = 1963)					−0·32 (1·80)		
Change in index retail prices	−1·59 (1·68)						
Rate of unemployment			−12·62 (1·30)				
Reciprocal of index of retail prices						16829 (3·57)	
Log of change in index of retail prices		−27·6 (2·13)					−31·2 (1·68)
Log of rate of unemployment				−37·7 (1·26)			11·4 (0·27)
Constant term	370	406	403	407	427	330	391
Coefficient of determination (R^2)	75·8	77·2	74·7	74·6	76·2	82·3	77·3
R^2 adjusted for sample size	71·7	73·2	70·5	70·4	72·2	79·4	72·1

Note: t ratios in parenthesis; t ratio ⩾ 1·71 significant at 0·05 level and ⩾ 1·32 significant at 0·10 level.

Sources:

Membership and price variables: D. Butler & A. Sloman *British Political Facts 1900–1979* (London: Macmillan 1980) pp. 143, 349, and *Annual Abstract of Statistics* (various years).

Unemployment variable: calculated by dividing the June unemployment figure by the total number of employees, using various issues of the *Department of Employment Gazette,* 1950–79.

Labour popularity: the average annual level of popularity in the Gallup Polls, calculated using various issues of the Gallup political index, 1950–78.

dummy variable is highly significant with a negative sign which means that membership fell dramatically after this year despite the minimum affiliation rule. In the 1950s many parties affiliated with more than 1,000 members in comparison with today, so the affiliation rule will not have influenced their membership figures, until they reached the minimum figure. This dummy variable measures the extent to which affiliation fell *despite* the minimum rule, and as we can see it is quite substantial. In the first model which uses the rate of change of prices affiliation was reduced by nearly 149,000 after 1963. The incumbency dummy variable is positive, so that incumbency appears to increase membership rather than decrease it as mentioned earlier. However, this result is produced by controlling for Labour popularity. The bivariate correlation between incumbency and membership is –0·47 which is consistent with the earlier point about opposition being more popular than governments. However, if we control for the level of popularity it makes incumbency marginally more satisfactory for retaining membership than opposition.

These results indicate that economic policy outcomes have influenced the decline in the affiliated membership of the Labour Party. These findings are consistent with the previous analysis which attributes the decline of membership to the performance of the Labour Party in power. This relationship is not confined to the years when Labour is incumbent, but also influences membership when Labour is in opposition. The historical experience of electoral defeats leading to post-mortems on the previous Labour government, which in turn produce faction fighting and internal wrangling, would explain this. When the shortcomings of Labour in office are aired more in opposition than in power, then the decline in membership should be greater when Labour is out of office, which is exactly what we observe.

Aggregate analysis of this type has its limitations. Thus while we can observe the broad trends we cannot probe the detailed processes which operate to detach individuals from membership of the party. The previous discussion has tended to discuss members and activists together without differentiating between them. However, it is obviously necessary to do this, and it seems likely that the decline in membership is primarily caused by the decline in activists, since it is the latter who service and maintain the former. But other psychological processes may be at work to detach members from the party than the performance of the party in power. Changes in symbolic outputs are likely to be influences affecting the membership; wider cultural changes in society such as the decline of public meetings and the increasing dominance of the media in determining the nature of political debates are also influential. The rise of the issue-based pressure groups, particularly in the social welfare field, may have attracted formerly active Labour members who see more future in pursuing narrowly defined campaigns than broad policy strategies. The decline in the influence and status of the party conference in the 1970s undoubtedly transmitted signals to the constituency parties about their relevance in the scheme of things, although this has changed in the late

1970s.[27] But having said all this, it is clear that performance in office plays an important role in explaining the decline in membership.

It was suggested earlier that the decline in membership and the decline in the Labour vote were related, which implies that the performance hypothesis also partly explains the decline of the Labour vote in the successive five general elections since the war. This is examined next.

The Decline of the Labour Vote

We can examine the performance hypothesis in relation to the decline in the Labour vote using methods similar to those used for the previous section. If the decline in the vote is similarly influenced by policy outcomes, then there should be a relationship between economic indicators and the Labour vote for the eleven general elections since the war. Obviously inferences about the Labour vote are more tentative than inferences about the membership, since there are not enough cases to test models with complete confidence. But it is interesting to see if the analysis confirms or rejects the performance hypothesis.

The decline of partisanship in Britain has been examined using individual level panel data from the British election study by Crewe *et al.*[28] They showed that a significant decline in the percentage of panel respondents having strong party identification occured between 1964 and 1974. Some 40 per cent of those asked in 1964 claimed to identify strongly with the Labour or Conservative parties, and this was reduced to 24 per cent by 1974. This decline took place mainly after 1970, and was attributed to three separate influences. First, there had been an erosion in the strength of the relationship between partisanship and social class, such that by October 1974 barely half the electorate identified with its 'natural' class party. Secondly, there were short-term factors associated with the crisis election of February 1974 which particularly eroded the Conservative vote. Finally, there was a growing rejection of many of the basic tenets of the Labour Party by Labour voters, and in particular a growing hostility in these voters towards the trade union movement.

In terms of the aggregate election statistics in Figure 5.1, it is evident that for Labour this process of dealignment continued up to the May 1979 election, since that result was very much on trend. My hypothesis is that a relationship should exist between the Labour percentage share of the vote and economic performance over time. However, as before, a number of intervening factors need to be controlled before this relationship can be estimated accurately. First, incumbency is likely to influence the vote, since voters are passing judgement on a Labour administration when the party is in office. Secondly, changes in turnout over the years

Table 5.4 *Economic Variables as Predictors of the Labour Share of the Vote, 1945–79, Controlling for Confounding Influences (dependent variable: Labour percentage share of the total vote; N = 11)*

Predictor				*
Turnout	–0·179 (0·83)	–0·187 (0·90)	–0·116 (0·58)	–0·113 (0·69)
Labour incumbency dummy	0·955 (1·27)	1·18 (1·57)	1·13 (1·62)	1·46 (2·47)
Years since 1944	–0·376 (4·89)	–0·339 (4·22)	–0·24 (2·14)	–0·16 (1·63)
Rate of unemployment			–1·2 (1·54)	–1·47 (2·26)
Rate of change of retail price index		–0·205 (1·21)		–0·27 (2·00)
Constant term	64·0	65·5	59·3	60·1
Coefficient of determination (R^2)	78·7	82·9	84·8	91·5
R^2 adjusted for sample size	69·6	71·5	74·6	83·0

Notes: t ratios 1·94 significant at 0·05 level, 2·02 for * model; 1·44 significant at 0·10 level, 1·48 for * model. Incumbency variable = +1 if Labour was in office at time of election, –1 if not.

Sources: See Figure 5.1 and Table 5.3 for all variables except incumbency.

might be expected to influence the Labour vote share and thus this needs to be controlled. Finally, we can also include a third variable, the number of years since 1944 to act as a composite index of all the political influences acting on the vote over time. Some of these were discussed by Crewe *et al.* but one might also note the influence of socioeconomic changes, the gradual rise of the Liberal vote, and perhaps generalised cynicism about the efficacy of British society in general, and the political system in particular. This time variable does not explain anything in itself, but rather acts as a summary measure of many long-term trends.

Thus we examine the relationship between the economy and Labour voting controlling for incumbency, turnout and time. The relationship between the economic variables and the Labour share of the vote is examined with four regression models in Table 5.4. To consider the control variables first, they alone explain nearly 70 per cent of the adjusted variation in the Labour vote share for these general elections.

The statistical significance of the coefficients is, as before, measured by the t statistics and the tests are particularly stringent with such a small sample. On this criterion, turnout is not significantly related to the vote share in these models. Incumbency, controlling for these other variables, is positively related to the Labour vote so it helps the party to have been in office at the time of the election. This is the same as the membership model. The time trend variable is highly significant, representing as it does a composite of many factors. These factors collectively operate to reduce the Labour share of the vote over time, regardless of which model is examined.

The economic predictors perform much better jointly than individually in these models. Thus the model which includes both the rate of unemployment and the rate of change of prices explains 83 per cent of the adjusted variation in the vote share. Both economic variables are highly statistically significant, and the model is not distorted by multicollinearity since the correlation between unemployment and inflation in this sample of postwar years was only 0·30. The models suggests that a 1 per cent increase in the rate of change of retail prices reduced the Labour vote share by 0·27 per cent, and 1 per cent increase in unemployment decreased it by 1·47 per cent. These effects are, of course, independent of the influence of incumbency, turnout and time, which are controlled. Clearly a poor economic performance reduces Labour's vote in the same way that it reduces membership. In addition to the economic variables the vote share has been reduced by 0·16 per cent each year since 1944, but incumbency has tended to increase the share by 1·43 per cent.

These findings are provisional in view of the small sample size. With eleven cases we are operating at the limits of statistical model-building, but the results do underline the vulnerability of Labour's electoral base. There is also survey evidence to suggest that the fragmentation of the working class brought about by changes in the occupational structure is a significant factor in explaining this decline.[29] This implies that the fall in Labour membership and in the Labour vote have similar historical origins.

Conclusions

It is readily apparent that as a matter of urgency Labour must take action to revitalise itself both electorally and in membership terms. Part of this will involve rebuilding the party machine, and recruiting new members and activists. It is too early to estimate the impact of recent changes in the party constitution, in particular the mandatory reselection of MPs, on the state of the local parties. It is instructive that the growth in the electoral fortunes of the Parti Socialiste in France has been in part attributed to the revitalisation of the party machine, and the recruitment of new cadres.[30] There may be a lesson for Labour in this.

The most important conclusion which can be drawn from this analysis relates closely to long-running debates between the left and the right in the party. The right has often argued, with the backing of a certain amount of survey evidence, that the left is wrong to advocate radical socialist policies since such policies are unpopular with the electorate and would be likely to produce electoral defeat. There is an idea implicit in this analysis that the electorate will vote against a party which advocates anything falling outside the mainstream consensus view in British politics. The present analysis changes the focus of this debate by emphasising the importance of performance in office, and the nature of the policy outcomes at the end of the day. Solemn declarations in the party manifesto and resounding speeches during elections may influence some voters, but for most the Labour party performance in office is what counts. If radical socialist policies were to bring performance successes, particularly in the economic field, they would become electorally popular. If centrist policies fail, as they have done for the most part during Labour's tenure in office, no amount of moderation will bring electoral success. Butskellism in practice has been tried and found wanting, and it remains to be seen whether the alternative strategy of the left, if given a chance, can bring the success the party needs if it is to survive.

Appendix: The Sample of Labour Conference Delegates

The population consisted of 623 constituency party delegates in Britain, and approximately 550 trade union delegates. Two big unions with 120 delegates refused to co-operate, so there were 430 possible trade unionists in the target population.

A random sample of 1 in 2 of these populations was selected. A sampling approach was used purely to reduce coding costs. From a mailing of 311 questionnaires to delegates we received 183 responses (including 5 non-delegates), giving a response rate of 58·8 per cent. From the mailing of 200 questionnaires to trade union delegates we received 78 responses, giving a response rate of 39 per cent.

The analysis of constituency party membership excludes the great majority of trade union respondents, because they did not reply to those questions.

A test of statistical significance of the difference between the mean Labour vote for the respondent constituencies and the mean Labour vote nationally in 1974 showed no significant difference. This suggests that the sample is representative of the population of constituencies in Britain.

Notes: Chapter 5

1 See P. Whiteley and I. Gordon, 'Middle class, militant and male', *New Statesman*, 6 January 1980, pp. 40–1.
2 *Report of the Committee on Financial Aid to Political Parties* (Chairman: Lord Houghton), Cmnd 6601 (London: HMSO, 1976), pp. 30–9.
3 *ibid.*, pp. 153–5.
4 See Whiteley and Gordon, op. cit., p. 41.
5 P. Seyd and L. Minkin, 'The Labour Party and its members', *New Society*, 20 September 1979, pp. 613–15.
6 M. Olson, *The Logic of Collective Action* (New York: Schocken Books, 1968).
7 See P. Samuelson, 'The pure theory of public expenditure', *Review of Economics and Statistics*, vol. 36 (1954), pp. 387–9.
8 B. Hindess, *The Decline of Working Class Politics* (London: MacGibbon & Kee, 1971).
9 See R. Baxter, 'The working class and Labour politics', *Political Studies*, vol. 20 (1972), pp. 97–107, and R. Dowse, 'The decline of working class politics', *British Journal of Sociology*, vol. 24 (1973), pp. 264–5.
10 For a discussion of the thesis at the parliamentary level, see R. W. Johnson, 'The British political elite 1955–72', *European Journal of Sociology*, vol. 14 (1973), pp. 35–77; at the level of Labour's National Executive Committee, see V. T. Hanby, 'A changing Labour elite: the National Executive of the Labour Party 1900–72', in I. Crewe (ed.), *British Political Sociology Yearbook*, vol. 1 (London: Croom Helm, 1974), pp. 126–58.
11 See J. Brand, 'Party organisation and the recruitment of councillors', *British Journal of Political Science*, vol. 3 (1973), pp. 473–86; L. J. Sharpe, 'Elected representatives in local government', *British Journal of Sociology*, vol. 13 (1964), pp. 169–209.
12 T. Forrester, *The Labour Party and the Working Class* (London: Heinemann, 1976).
13 *ibid.*, p. 93.
14 J. H. Goldthorpe, *Social Mobility and Class Structure in Modern Britain* (Oxford: Clarendon Press, 1980), table 2.1, p. 44.
15 See N. Bosanquet and P. Townsend, *Labour and Equality* (London: Heinemann, 1980), particularly pt III.
16 S. Holland, *The Socialist Challenge* (London: Quartet Books, 1975), p. 144.
17 The classic study by Goldthorpe on affluent workers showed that although many of them retained their traditional allegiance to the Labour Party they were more instrumental than other workers and more likely to be influenced by the performance of the party in power. This parallels the conclusions about working-class activists being more instrumental. See J. H. Goldthorpe, D. Lockwood, F. Bechhofer and J. Platt, *The Affluent Worker in the Class Structure* (Cambridge: Cambridge University Press, 1969).
18 A. O. Hirschman, *Exit, Voice and Loyalty* (Cambridge, Mass.: Harvard University Press, 1970).
19 See Hindess, op. cit., p. 136.
20 loc. cit.
21 See B. Bernstein 'Language and social class', *British Journal of Sociology*, vol. 11, no. 3 (1960), pp. 271–6; see also A. D. Edwards, *Language in Culture and Class* (London: Heinemann, 1976).
22 See I. Gordon and P. Whiteley, 'Social class and political attitudes: the case of Labour councillors', *Political Studies*, vol. 28 (1979), pp. 99–113.
23 See D. Butler and D. Stokes, *Political Change in Britain* (London: Macmillan, 1974), particularly ch. 18.
24 This can be seen by examining any of the Gallup political index reports and the questions

on issues. Unemployment and inflation are nearly always the most salient issues mentioned by the public.

25 See P. Whiteley, 'Electoral forecasting from poll data: the British case', *British Journal of Political Science*, vol. 9 (1979), pp. 219–36.

26 For a discussion of the problems of multicollinearity, see A. Koutsoyiannis, *Theory of Econometrics* (London: Macmillan, 1973), ch. 11.

27 For a full discussion of this, see L. Minkin, *The Labour Party Conference* (London: Allen Lane, 1978).

28 See I. Crewe, B. Sarlvik and J. Alt, 'Partisan dealignment in Britain 1964–74', *British Journal of Political Science*, vol. 7 (1977), pp. 129–90.

29 See particularly K. Roberts, F. Cook and E. Semeonoff, *The Fragmentary Class Structure* (London: Heinemann, 1977), ch. 9.

30 Byron Criddle, 'The French Parti Socialiste', in W. Patterson and A. H. Thomas (eds), *Social Democratic Parties in Western Europe* (London: Croom Helm, 1977), pp. 25–66.

6 The Labour Party and the Geography of Inequality: a Puzzle

L. J. SHARPE

> Nowhere, indeed, within the labour movement can one see any influential sections able or willing to resist the corroding influence of centralisation which has infected the whole party. One looks in vain in the Labour Party for political leaders who are ardent guardians of local liberties. (William Robson)

Introduction: The Geography of Inequality

The thesis of this chapter may be briefly stated: as the party of the underdog the Labour Party ought also to be the party of the periphery and of the localities. This is because Britain, like France, Norway and Denmark, has a single overwhelming dominant centre – London and the South East. But in Britain such concentration has also meant that the hierarchy of power, wealth and status has a spatial or horizontal as well as a class or vertical dimension. We will call this spatial distribution the geography of inequality. It may in very general terms be viewed as a cone with London and its penumbra as its summit and the periphery, the Celtic fringe, as its base. As we move from the London region, so at the same time we descend the hierarchy of power, wealth and status. Occasionally the gradient of the cone is smooth, at other points it is distorted and bumpy; sometimes markedly so as we encounter outliers of the metropolitan society – Cambridge, say, or Cowes – or independent but always secondary centres of wealth and prestige – North Cheshire, Edinburgh – or, where the periphery nestles close to the centre – West Ham or Battersea.

Bumpy or not, however, the overall inclination from the London centre will always be socially and economically downward, for the London region is the overwhelmingly dominant centre for almost all the productive processes other than those of primary production. It is also the governmental, financial, managerial and cultural nub of the country. No other centre comes remotely near to rivalling its pre-eminence. In a very real sense the whole of the UK is the London region's hinterland. As one foreign observer has remarked: 'London is so clearly at the centre of things in Britain that its dominance is simply taken for granted'.[1] As the 'centre of things' the London region shapes not only the economic structure of Britain but also its social structure. This is, naturally enough, most clearly perceived by those with the best vantage point at the top of the cone for whom, according to W. J. M. Mackenzie, 'the provinces are outside their ken entirely, since they include (from this point of view) only Thirsk, Aintree and some grouse moors'.[2]

The pre-eminence of the London region is maintained and reinforced in all manner of ways. One which is of crucial importance and at the same time powerfully illustrates the geography of inequality is the elite sector of the education system. At its most exalted level are the top public schools which are, in every sense, national institutions designed to prepare their charges for entry to the national London-centred community. These schools have few or no roots in their local community, and are mostly situated in the South East in any case. Raymond Williams has described this as 'a network of ruling class schools' for whose products 'England is an act not so much of membership as of conscious attitudes ... the definition of "England", its myths and its ideology, has been for more than a century in just their hands'. Entering the top strata of British society for the son if not the parent entails entering this system.[3] Further down the pecking order come the high prestige, semi-private and now mostly private provincial grammar schools. These have real local roots but are linked to the most vital of all metropolitanising conduits, Oxbridge, which siphons off to the London region the brightest and most ambitious of each generation in each locality.

In few countries can there be such a clearly defined status system where the upper levels of all the various occupational and social hierarchies converge and intermingle in one geographical location. Every road leads to the London penumbra:

> It has been the lamentable fact that anyone in Britain who sought success made straight for London, and, within our social structure, it has never been fashionable to live anywhere else – except in the country.[4]

Provided domicile *is* the country then, like the metropolitan outliers mentioned earlier, it may be acceptable and remain spiritually part of the South East heartland. It need not be in any sense a domicile that is linked in any fundamental way with the life of the locality in which it exists. Even if it is, the local paper remains *The Times*, the children's school will be in the South East, major shopping is done in central London. The higher the social status of the individual, the more his parish will tend to be the South East, which as well as being the fount of status is also the national heartland: all the emblems and symbols of nationhood are ineffably South Eastern.

Before explaining the lineaments of this geography of inequality further, it is important to emphasise that we have included in the initial thesis not only the concept of the periphery in relation to the dominant centre but also that of the localities in general in relation to the centre as well. Combining the two requires some explanation since their relationships to the centre are not necessarily congruent. For example, it is possible for the Labour Party to combat the geography of inequality by increased centralisation, to the detriment of the localities in terms of their capacity to govern themselves. It is, however, important to include both since Labour-controlled local authorities may be as important agents for promoting equality as Labour-controlled national governments. For although all left parties in Western democracies have a nationalising and centralising bias[5], the politicisation of local government, which is especially evident in the UK, means that those localities in greatest need will tend to have Labour majorities. By acting individually or collectively, such authorities can also combat their own unequal position even when the Labour Party is out of power nationally. Given this situation, greater centralisation will also be sought by the Conservatives when in power nationally in order to resist such strategies by Labour-controlled localities. This tendency has been strongly evident since 1970, and now seems to be a firmly entrenched fact of political life such that the Labour Party is confronted with a major dilemma. Which promotes the ultimate egalitarian aim best? Is it an outright commitment to centralisation on the assumption that all that matters is to gain power nationally, or is it some sort of balance between central control and local autonomy? Such a balance would be designed to ensure that, whatever the loss of control over these local authorities in the hands of the opposition, the party is able to promote its egalitarian aims in at least some of the localities (and those moreover which may need it most) even when the party is out of power nationally. We shall return to the relationship between centralisation and equality later. Enough has been said so far to show that combating the geography of inequality is not necessarily in conflict with a decentralist disposition towards local government as well.

To return to the geography of inequality, in Table 6.1 are set out nine indicators of relative affluence by region. The regional columns have been placed very broadly in terms of their nearness to the South East – the farther to the right on the table, the farther from the South East. This is necessarily a somewhat crude ordering since in the first place for those regions bordering the South East the placing has to be arbitrary. Secondly, some of the regions are quite extensive. Thus the South West borders on the South East, buts its western extremity is as far away from

Table 6.1 *Selected Indicators of the Geography of Inequality by Region*

	South East	*West Midlands*	*East Anglia*	*South West*	*East Midlands*	*Wales*	*North West*	*Yorks & Humberside*	*North*	*Scotland*	*Northern Ireland*
Av. personal weekly income per head (1977–8)	41·93	35·65	33·79	34·13	34·27	34·12	33·39	33·72	32·98	35·66	26·94
Av. weekly household expenditure (1977–8)	84·11	76·56	68·48	70·43	71·35	74·55	72·21	71·20	71·74	74·49	71·31
Net output in manufactures, £m. (1976)	120,483	54,441	12,737	23,972	32,502	20,545	64,305	40,971	28,269	38,415	7,703
% households with telephone (1977–8)	70·3	57·1	53·5	54·5	52·7	49·7	56·1	54·3	45·4	66·0	41·2
% 2-car-household ownership (1978)	12·0	11·7	11·6	12·2	9·5	13·5	9·0	7·2	6·7	7·9	7·0
Unemployment rate, % (1978)	4·2	5·6	4·9	6·5	5·0	8·4	7·5	6·0	8·8	8·2	11·5
Infant mortality rate (1978)	12·8	13·6	10·8	12·4	13·4	13·2	13·7	13·3	13·9	12·9	16·1
Pupils in private schools, thousands (1978)	222·5	33·4	14·3	56·4	21·1	10·6	28·9	18·6	12·9	17·0	0·4
% pupils staying at school to 18 (1976–7)	8·3	6·3	5·2	5·8	6·2	8·3	5·2	6·3	5·7	1·7	5·4

Source: Regional Statistics: Vol. 15 (London: HMSO, 1980).

London as parts of the North region. Bearing the arbitrary element and the lumpiness problem in mind, plus the fact that the degree of urbanisation has an independent effect on the indicators, Table 6.1 does bear out the claim made initially that the spatial dimension to the distribution of socioeconomic inequality in the UK is related to London and the South East. The downward or upward progression of the indicators from left to right is not perfectly regular for any of them, possibly for the reasons given earlier about the placing of each region in the table, but the overall decline in some of the more fundmental measures of life chances from the South East to Northern Ireland is unmistakable. Moreover, the South East predominates for all indicators, sometimes by a striking margin. Only for two indicators (two-car ownership and infant mortality) is the South East not better off than all the other regions. Equally, if not more consistently, Northern Ireland is worst off, often by an even more striking margin.[6]

The extent of the geography of inequality needs no further emphasis. It is clearly a reality and one which has been with us for a very long time.[7] Yet despite its existence the Labour Party has been curiously reluctant to make its elimination a central plank in its programme. This is puzzling in itself, but becomes even more puzzling when viewed in relation to the growth of the party's support in the periphery. With the exception of Northern Ireland, this has grown steadily over the postwar period and the party is now more a party of the periphery than it has ever been in the past. At the 1979 general election it won 62 per cent of the seats in Scotland and 58·3 per cent of the Welsh seats, compared with only 39·3 per cent of the English seats. In each of the three most distant English regions from London – the North, North West, and Yorks and Humberside – it won a higher percentage of seats than in Scotland, in the North region over 80 per cent. Curtice and Stead have summarised this pattern at the 1979 general election as follows:

> we have witnessed at each election since 1959, stages in a long-term shift in the regional voting behaviour . . . The peripheral areas of Britain, with their higher unemployment, and the decline in the inner part of conurbations have become steadily more Labour; while the expanding more prosperous areas have become more Conservative.[8]

If the party were dependent on the seats it can win in England, its chances of achieving power would be slim indeed for it has not won 50 per cent of the English seats since 1951 except for 1966. Since the late 1960s, moreover, it has been under threat from the two nationalist parties in Scotland and in Wales. Thus the motivation for pursuing policies that are deliberately designed to woo the periphery has been particularly strong. In its apparent reluctance to do so, the Labour Party provides an interesting contrast to the socialist parties in two of the other three single-centre-dominant states in Western Europe. In France the Socialists have yet to form a majority government on their own in the postwar era, but in Norway the Labour Party has always maintained a very strong peripheral dimension to its policies when in power, in its successful pursuit of the support of small-scale farmers, agrarian and forestry workers and fishermen.[9] In Denmark the main social democratic party, although not so peripherally oriented, has given full support for the 'unbalanced Denmark' policy. This underlies the reorganisation of Danish local government in the late 1960s, giving it a wider range of powers and resisting the extension of the boundaries of the city of Copenhagen.[10] The main Danish social democrats have also favoured a new decentralised regional policy.[11]

In comparative terms, then, the British Labour Party may appear surprisingly centralist. This centralism is perhaps even more surprising when viewed against the consequences, already noted, of the centralising tendencies of the Conservatives as they seek to block the equalising policies of Labour-controlled local authorities. This tendency has become increasingly apparent in the policies of successive Conservative administrations beginning with the 1958 Local Government Act. This sought in its financial provisions to reduce percentage grants (which increased central aid as local authorities increased their expenditure) in favour of the block grant which placed a fixed limit on central aid for each year. The Heath administration greatly accelerated this form of Conservative centralism in the 1972 Housing Finance Act and in the shift in the rate support grant in favour of the counties.

Under Mrs Thatcher the Conservative centralist attack on Labour-controlled areas, covering as it does almost all the major services, has reached an almost frenzied level of intensity, with Part VI of the 1979 Local Government and Planning Act constituting probably the greatest diminution in the financial autonomy of local government ever achieved in one single legislative enactment.[12]

The Labour Party appears not yet to have evolved a policy to cope with this sea change in Conservative policy. Indeed, viewing the postwar period as a whole, the two major parties have outbidden each other in new centralist measures in order to achieve precisely the opposite result! The Labour Party's instincts seem to be still as firmly centralist as they have been for the past forty years. Christopher Price has claimed: 'The besetting sin of the Labour Party is an obsessive desire to impose socialism from above by Act of Parliament, combined with a chronic insensitivity to the needs of the community at the local level.' The party strategy for change has therefore, so Price argues, always been 'first to make policy through the National Executive and the Party Conference; then to fight a general election and gain parliamentary power; and finally to carry out policy by central government action and parliamentary legislation'.[13]

Another View of Party Policies

It may be countered that this is an unfair portrayal, if not a gross distortion, of the Labour Party's attitudes to the periphery and to local government generally. To take the former first, it may be claimed that the party has pursued a whole battery of industrial and office location policies, as well as other forms of intervention, that have sought to redirect industry to the poorer regions and to the periphery in particular. During its period of office from 1964 to 1970 it set up the regional planning system and in addition so extended regional aid policies that virtually all the regions outside the South East and West Midlands regions were to a greater or lesser degree net recipients of government largesse designed to combat their economic weakness relative to the two high-growth regions. Financial assistance to the depressed regions increased tenfold between 1964/5 and 1969/70.[14]

It could also be claimed in defence of the party's attitude towards the provinces that it has inaugurated other redistributive policies and structures. The purposes of these may not have been directly spatial in intent, but they have had the effect of benefiting the periphery as compared with the centre simply because the population in the periphery has been in greater need. This effect is well illustrated by Table 6.2, taken from the Kilbrandon Commission Report,[15] which shows the considerable extent to which the periphery was favoured in per capita public expenditure terms compared with England during the period of the first two Wilson governments.

Table 6.2 *Public Expenditure Per Head Expressed as % of Public Expenditure in England*

Year	*England*	*Wales*	*Scotland*	*N. Ireland*
1963–64	100	116	118	103
1964–65	100	117	116	102
1965–66	100	114	114	108
1966–67	100	116	115	108
1967–68	100	113	121	109
1968–69	100	117	128	114
1969–70	100	116	131	118

Source: Kilbrandon Commission Report, Vol. 1, p. 178.

None of this can be denied, and Table 6.2 shows clearly that the Labour government certainly increased expenditure for Scotland and Northern Ireland. It must be noted, however, that the Labour Party did indeed make major amplifications in both the 1940s and the 1960s to old-style industrial location policies and, later, to the more elaborate regional policies. But both types of policy were inaugurated by its opponents: the National government in 1934, with the Distressed Areas Act, and the Conservatives in 1963 when regional plans were promulgated for Scotland and the North East and Mr Heath was made Secretary of State for Trade, Industry *and* Regional Planning.

It is also easy to inflate the importance of these various regional and industrial location policies. We do not know what the effect of regional policy was in terms of actually changing the distribution of factors from what they would have been had there been no policy. This was the firm conclusion of the House of Commons Expenditure Committee when it examined the matter.[16] This lacuna is partly, no doubt, the consequence of the techniques that are available for the measurement of policy outcomes. In so far as such techniques can tell us the direct effect of regional policies for the period 1963–71, the two studies that have attempted to measure them, in terms of jobs, both seem to agree that the policies generated about 100,000 jobs,[17] that is, about 12,000 on average per year. In terms of the impact of regional policies on investment, various estimates have been made, the most comprehensive of which attributes 4–8 per cent of total UK investment over the period to regional policies.[18] All things considered, these findings do not suggest a major equalisation role for regional policies. Moreover during the Labour Party's last spell in office, 1974–9, the effectiveness of regional policy was almost certainly declining. The tighter labour market conditions in the growth regions during that period, especially in London and the South East, and the fact that there was a significant proportion of growth industry to be relocated, added to the disincentive element of regional policies.

However, even if the redistributive effects of Labour's regional policies had been more significant than they seem to have been, it would still be true that the party has shown much less interest in the provinces, given the geography of inequality. This is because only part, possibly not even the main part, of the motivation for such policies was redistributive. One of the most authoritative policy reports ever issued by the party on its regional planning policy summarises the case for regional policy under four broad headings, of which only (2) could be said to be redistributive:

(1) to stimulate national economic growth;
(2) to foster the development of the less productive regions;
(3) to achieve a better allocation of public investment;
(4) to plan, in economic and physical terms, for an increasing population.[19]

Moreover, whatever the precise extent of Labour's redistributive intentions, the primary motive has not been to change the geography of inequality of the country, but rather to stop it getting worse. With the possible exception of Belgium, peripheral economic decline in the UK (as opposed to peripheral economic difference as is found, say, in Italy and Spain, or France) since the 1920s is probably greater than in any other advanced industrial democracy. Even at the height of the postwar boom in the Western economies between 1963 and 1970, the North region lost 100,000 male jobs. In the North West region employment in cotton textiles halved between 1956 and 1966. Taking Scotland, Wales and the North together, more than 300,000 jobs were lost in mining, agriculture and shipbuilding in the decade from 1956 to 1966. Between 1964 and 1970, 100,000 coal-mining jobs were lost in the development areas alone.[20]

A further reason for not accepting the arguments that the Labour Party has been active in altering the geography of inequality to any significant extent is that I am concerned more with motivation than with effect. Redistributive welfare policies designed to combat general inequality will have the effect of redistributing resources territorially if inequalities are geographically concentrated. This is certainly part of the explanation for the rise in public expenditure in Scotland and Northern Ireland during Labour's period of office in the 1960s (Table 6.2). Some was also certainly due to the Labour Cabinet's concern for the periphery, in the sense that it wanted to outflank the SNP in Scotland and to ameliorate social conditions in Northern Ireland following the recrudescence of nationalist versus unionist conflict. It shared both sentiments with Conservative Cabinets. In short, the party was less directly concerned with the geography of inequality than with short-term political problems. The argument still stands that the party is relatively uninterested in the periphery.

It may be further argued on behalf of the Labour Party as a champion of the provinces that it has been much more willing to respond to peripheral aspirations in relation to devolution than the Conservatives. Whatever the truth of this claim in the past when the party was committed to home rule, it is difficult to sustain it for the period since 1945. For, despite its authorship of the Devolution Acts, they were very much a product of the party's need to preserve its majority in the House of Commons, where for three of its five years in office it lacked an overall majority. The Devolution Acts were clearly not a product of its own ideological dissatisfaction with the geography of inequality. It is true that sections of the party were committed to it, and to 'an effective devolution of decision-making and functions from Whitehall'.[21]. An impressive list of discussion documents and White Papers on the theme of decentralisation and devolution issued from Whitehall and Transport House, each pledging the government's wholehearted commitment to the policy in hand. Yet even the most charitable observer would be hard put to describe the way in which the parliamentary party got the Devolution Acts on to the statute book in any way other than 'with a heavy heart'.

Most of the government's prolonged agonies in steering the legislation through the House, from the first White Paper in June 1974 to the two Acts of July 1978, arose not from the opposition or the nationalist MPs but from its own supporters. Three White Papers were necessary before the Bill could be safely launched and even after the mandatory referendum was conceded to its own backbenchers, no less than forty-five Labour MPs failed to vote for it, twenty-two voting against and twenty-three abstaining. A further concession, again to Labour backbenchers, had to be made in the form of the 40 per cent rule before the Bills became law, and the Labour government's strict adherence to the 40 per cent rule led directly, as we know, to its enforced dissolution in 1979. The Devolution Acts were merely part of the Labour government's tactics of survival.

A New Decentralist Ideology?

John Gyford has noted the emergence of the makings of a broad decentralist movement within the party on both the right and the left. It embraces not only political decentralisation and community action but also the decentralisation of power in the workplace, the latter drawing upon concepts of workers' control and workers' co-operatives. He cites fifteen publications by party members, including four former ministers (J. Bray, A. Benn, E. Luard and D. Owen), published between 1968 and 1980, as examples of the trend. He concludes: 'Without overestimating its present impact on the party at large it thus seems plausible to argue that a certain head of steam has begun to build up in recent years behind the movement for a more decentralised socialism.'[22]

It is also possible to discern a change in the party's official attitudes since the early 1970s for, as Gyford notes, during its 1974–9 period of office the Labour government introduced the Industrial Common Ownership Act and created the Co-operative Development Agency. Also its plans for 'organic change' in local government would have involved a degree of decentralisation from larger to smaller local authorities.[23] Since the 1979 election defeat, decentralisation also seems to have become part of the day-to-day coinage of Labour Party debate and discussion. This plea for decentralisation seems to crop up in newspaper articles by ex-ministers and party luminaries, including Tony Benn, Shirley Williams and, most consistently of all, David Owen. References to decentralisation also occur in the famous 'letter' to the *Guardian* in August 1980 by David Owen, William Rogers and Shirley Williams; 'bureaucratic centralism and state control' were attacked and pleas were made for the party in its future programme to 'begin the process of devolving power and decision-making to smaller units'.[24]

It is impossible to forecast just how far these tendencies and hints will blossom into a fully developed decentralist philosophy that will have a bearing on the programme of a future Labour government. But there are certain features of the trend that suggest caution. In the first place, all parties in opposition tend to appreciate the grass roots more and ex-ministers keep their ears closer to the ground than those in office. With rare exceptions,[25] once back in the comfortable embrace of the back seat of the official Rover, red box on knee, things look altogether different. During the first two years at least, solicitude for the provinces, for the localities, for the periphery, tends to give way to the beady-eyed statesman anxious to reassure his department or the *Times* leader-writers – both strong bastions of the London-dominated society – by demonstrating, as quickly as decorum will allow, his unswerving belief in the firm smack of government. Perhaps this form of backsliding is more strongly felt in the Labour Party because a curious distance and mutual hostility between members of the ministerial corps and Labour Party rank and file seems to arise very quickly after the party assumes office. One reason for this deterioration probably has to do with the rank and file's dislike of all governments, even when their own side is in power. It also has something to do with what Minkin has called the 'curious neurosis' that overcomes Labour ministers, who feel that they have to show '"responsibility" in all policy decisions', which means among other things 'making a public display of independence of the Labour Party in the country'.[26] His Wykehamist, New College and Garrick Club connections, the house in Vincent Square and a taste for metropolitan night-life may have made Richard Crossman particularly susceptible to this distancing and alienating effect. Also, like all good journalists, he knew exactly the kind of slightly heightened frankness which attracts the reader. None the less, on this subject, his *Diaries* may not be very untypical and they reek of both his sense of alienation from his local party and its undisguised hostility to him.[27] The *Diaries* also reveal a mild despair with most of the local leaders and bureaucrats that he was required to meet during his frequent forays up and down the country when he was Minister of Housing and Local Government.

In relation to commitments made now about decentralist intentions when in office, ministerial backsliding may be all the more likely since it is possible that for some of the decentralism school this newfound interest is performing the largely negative function of providing a stick to beat some other proposal – in this case further old-style nationalisation – rather than a positive commitment to the issue. In fact it is difficult to envisage a future Labour Cabinet engaging in any major decentralisation policies for two reasons. On the right there is still the unshakeable commitment to the belief that one of the primary tasks of the Treasury is to manage the economy. Although this belief has its origins in the adoption of Keynesian theories of demand management in the 1940s, it probably matters little whether this is now mixed with a strong dash of monetarism as in the later phases of the Callaghan government, since the latter, if anything, requires an even greater role for the Treasury as economic manager. The Treasury's abject failure during the postwar period even to get its own forecasts of government expenditure right has in no way diminished this deeply held belief. On the contrary, as the Treasury's failure persists, so the conviction seems to grow that if only greater control can be brought to bear on the public sector at least, especially on its more 'open-ended' elements like local government, the hitherto elusive management function will be achieved. For this reason it would be mistaken to see the 1979 Local Government and Planning Act, which empowers the Secretary of State for the Environment to set norms for local authority budgets, as simply the brainchild of Mrs Thatcher's monetarism. Despite the fact that the Act constitutes a degree of central encroachment that in other countries would be an issue of constitutional importance, it will be interesting to see how far it will be dismantled by a future Labour Government. The Labour Party's attitude to the Act will be an acid test of the real status of the new decentralism.

The second reason for some scepticism about whether the decentralist posture will affect the behaviour of future Labour Cabinets has to do more with the left's predispositions, especially on what may be called the 'permanent revolution' assumption. Broadly speaking, this is the assumption that every time the Labour Party wins a general election it is in power for ever. On this view, pockets of decentralised power in the hands of the Conservatives, who retain grammar schools, say, or sell off council houses at knock-down prices, become intolerable. Legislation must be passed immediately to stop such subversion of the socialist programme. The proposition that a future Conservative government could use the same legislation to increase the number of selective secondary schools or enforce the sale of council houses at even more knock-down prices becomes almost subversive, since it admits of the possibility that the party is not in power for ever.

Another set of reasons for sceptism as to whether the new interest in decentralisation will have any permanent effect on Labour Party policies in office has to do with the age-old problem of the difference between aspiration and action. It is, of course, easy and relatively costless for us all to devise new structures and procedures on paper and to add to their appeal by decking them out with attacks on bureaucracy and an encomium or two to democracy. But perhaps in no other sector of the political system is the disparity between these paper constructs and what the average Labour parliamentarian is willing to tolerate in reality sharper than in that concerning proposals for greater decentralisation.

Let us look at political decentralisation first; it is odd to argue, as Williams, Owen and Rodgers did in their *Guardian* letter, against the growth of centralised bureaucracy while at the same time advocating an increase in the powers of the EEC. Even the most agnostic observer is forced to inquire how it is that the Berlaymont Building is somehow immune from the virus that apparently infests, say, the National Coal Board or the Department of Industry. Equally, it is one thing to argue for elected regions with a wide range of powers, at present exercised directly by central government or by public corporations and quangos, as Mackintosh,[28] Crowther-Hunt[29] and Luard[30] have done. But it is something quite different to countenance the most populous of those regions and the most important one by almost every politically significant measure – the South East – being permanently under the control of the Conservative Party, as assuredly it would be.

The same disparity between abstract aspirations and cold reality is discernible in the long-drawn-out battles that seem to have taken place in the Callaghan Cabinet over the changes in the local government system entailed in 'organic change'.[31] This would have involved an amendment to the 1972 Local Government Act which the party had fiercely resisted, perhaps more so than most of the legislation of the Heath government, and which would have merely partly restored the *status quo ante* by decentralising powers from the counties to the ten bigger cities. It is impossible to discover precisely who (in the Cabinet) was resisting this, possibly one of the more obvious policy changes open to the Callaghan government. But it would be illuminating to discover who, among the new decentralists, actually favoured organic change, or even perhaps actually resisted it.

The disparity between decentralist thought and decentralist action is if anything even more acute in relation to the decentralisation of power at the workplace. When Evan Luard makes a plea for greater control rather than ownership of economic enterprises by workers,[32] and Giles Radice advocates 'a meaningful system of industrial democracy . . . based on the work group and trade union organisation',[33] they both have in mind systems of worker participation that exist in other countries such as West Germany and Sweden, where such systems may also have increased industrial efficiency. Such a happy conjunction may be the main attraction for some advocates of more industrial democracy. What Luard and Radice are unlikely to mean by 'greater democracy on the shop floor' is the kind of decentralised power that is already exercised by workers in this country via their trade union organisation at plant level. For Britain has possibly the most decentralised trade union structure in the Western world, whether we measure it by the degree of specialisation among unions or the independent power exercised by shop stewards.

It is this very decentralised character of British industrial relations that is usually seen as one of its great failings. It may be, then, that the workers' control advocated by the new decentralisers is required not so much to combat centralisation, bureaucracy and alienation as to replace other forms of decentralisation. Such a sceptical thought is strengthened by the equivocal reaction of the 1974–9 Labour government to the Bullock Report which, whatever defects it may have had, did at least attempt to reconcile the decentralised facts of British industrial relations with the more conventional modes of industrial democracy.

The shrinking from the Bullock Report may be in essence another example of the difference between advocacy of decentralisation in the abstract and the decentralisation of power in a concrete situation. But it is also something more which goes even deeper and which offers further grounds for scepticism about the probabilities of any major shift in Labour policies in a decentralist direction. These are, first, the strong commitment of all wings of the party to strengthen the capacity of government to plan the economy, whether the objective is to mount a full-blown incomes policy, the strengthening of bi-partism, the adoption of the alternative economic strategy, or the resurrection of the National Plan. At this stage in the discussion we must note that any decentralisation on the industrial front is always likely to be a potential lion in the path of the central planning function.

Secondly, enhancing shop-floor democracy is potentially in conflict with the Labour Party's role as champion of the consumer, in particular those consumers who are not also producers in the conventional sense. This category includes old age pensioners, children, the unemployed, the long-term sick, the badly disabled and those producers who for various reasons are completely unorganised. The growing interest in industrial democracy, especially on the left of the party, does not seem to have given much recognition to the possibility that there is a producer versus non-producer conflict. It is notably absent, for example, from Tony Benn's writings.[34]

To sum up so far: despite clear evidence of a new interest in decentralisation, it is unlikely to become a sufficiently large plank in Labour policy to reshape the party's normal but puzzling indifference to both the periphery and the localities generally. This still leaves the question as to why the self-proclaimed party of those of low incomes and status, and increasingly the *de facto* party of the periphery itself, remains so steadfastly centralist and metropolitan-minded. It is towards providing a tentative and what must be a rudimentary answer that we now turn.

II Structural Factors

There seem to be several reasons for the Labour Party's disinclination to make a frontal assault on the geography of inequality and to show a greater sympathy to the needs, attitudes and aspirations of provincial Britain. There is inevitably some overlap between them, but for the sake of clarity of exposition they will be treated separately. They fall into two groups. The first are those which may be attributed to the setting in which the party has to operate, that is, the basic structure and modes of British government. The second group are ideological in the sense that they may be regarded as being broadly consistent with the party's egalitarian ideology. But it is clear that these reasons do not fully explain the party's centralism, for there remain aspects of it that appear to have little to do with structure or party ideology, and which therefore may be justifiably described as puzzling.

The first of the structural factors is the absence of an intermediate level of either government or administration between central government and local government in the British political system. With the exception of New Zealand, the UK seems to be unique in this respect among the advanced industrial democracies since it is neither a federal system, where an intermediate level of government is essential, nor, except for the Scottish, Welsh and Northern Ireland Offices, does it follow some form of the prefectoral model which entails an intermediate level of decentralised central administration. One of the effects of this peculiarity of the British system and one which makes it highly relevant to the present discussion is that central government is seen in functional terms by its principal practitioners – the ministerial cadre and the civil service.

The predominant governmental mode is seen as the provision of state services by specialised departments to client groups, families, or individuals, who are, implicitly at least, uniformly distributed throughout the country and living in a society which is equally uniform in character throughout the country. With the exception of the variations in expenditure wrought by the Scottish, Welsh and Northern Ireland Secretaries of State, or where it is sanctioned by a separate statute, variation in service delivery to meet spatial differentiation is seen as the role of local government. Viewed in this way, each UK citizen has not only uniform rights but also uniform needs and any variation from them becomes an 'accident of geography'.

A very different, but possibly even more influential, structural characteristic which has encouraged the Labour Party to have less concern for the periphery is the absence of a formally constituted executive in local government. There is no indirectly elected executive committee nor is there an elected commission or board. Above all, there is no directly elected mayor or burgermeister combining symbolic and executive functions. There is an extra-constitutional executive in most Labour-controlled local authorities, usually comprising the leader and the party officers. Neither he nor his colleagues, however, have any institutional strength or the power that separately elected status gives to the mayors and burgermeisters, both in the localities in which they are elected *vis-à-vis* their national parties. In short, in the British Labour Party there is no automatic local leadership. Local leaders do emerge from time to time by sheer force of personality, luck, or length of council service – a Heycock, a Braddock, a Watton, or a Henig. But they do not constitute a permanent feature of the internal power structure of the party with which the central party institutions have to contend. According to Donoughue and Jones, Herbert Morrison is the 'only Labour figure in British politics who reached the top ranks of his party through local government'.[35] This absence of local leaders arises, it must be remembered, in a party that derives its support almost solely from urban areas. Prominent provincial leaders backed by major city parties which in other countries would constitute crucial blocks of power within national labour or socialist parties hardly exist. In consequence, the national leadership is again curiously insulated and those local leaders who, for the reasons noted earlier, do try to punch their weight are viewed as anomalies to be rendered quietly harmless by the application of a little patronage from that veritable cornucopia that British party leaders always have to hand once they are in office. In this way the model of the party is preserved as a national entity, pyramidal in structure with its base organisation consisting not of local government units but of parliamentary constituencies.

Another structural factor that helps to explain the Labour Party's centralist character is the fundamental constitutional fact of parliamentary supremacy. The whole apparatus of British politics is tributary to the House of Commons, the majority within it, the Cabinet that heads the majority and finally the Prime Minister, who is more than *primus inter pares* within that Cabinet. No other Western democratic system perhaps (with the possible exception of New Zealand) concentrates power so sharply and so decisively. No written constitution, no second chamber of any consequence, indeed no real legislature at all, obscures the symmetry of this pyramid of power at the apex of the British political system, and the framework that supports it is the party. Thus the party is the beginning and end of the British system of government. Not only does any party which takes part in that system have to fashion its internal arrangements to suit the system, but the system's highly centralised character in turn fashions and shapes the way the party goes about its business and how it views the world: a centralised party for a centralised system.

III Ideological Factors

I now come to the ideological reasons for Labour centralist attitudes, that is, those which may reasonably be interpreted as being broadly consistent with socialist ideology, or at the very least as being not entirely inconsistent with it. The first of these, and the one which it must be admitted barely qualifies as a 'consistent' factor, is the centralist tendencies of the trade unions. This anti-localist posture has expressed itself in a number of ways, but it is a subject about which evidence is decidedly scanty; partly no doubt because the unions have seldom expressed themselves on the subject in public and still less on paper. In short, it is an influence on the centralism of the Labour Party that still awaits proper investigation and research, so its treatment here is necessarily sketchy. However, there can be little doubt that British trade union leaders have always been centralisers.[36] In the first place, because the union structure has been overwhelmingly occupational rather than industrial, it has tended to have its membership spread throughout the country rather than geographically concentrated. The focus of the union has therefore always been national. Secondly, trade union leaders are only too aware of the problems, as they see them, of too much local autonomy. British unions remain today, as we noted earlier, some of the most decentralised in the world, and the tension between the local branch or the shop stewards and national HQ is one of the dominant characteristics of the trade union movement.

Since it was the trade union leaders who were highly influential architects of the modern Labour Party, it is hardly surprising that the party should bear the strong imprint of their organisational preoccupation. By the mid-1920s, when the main foundations of the present-day party had been laid, McKibbin had summarised the trade union influence on the distribution of power within the party thus:

> Like the unions the Labour Party was national in its organisation and centralised in its institutions. It deliberately over-rode regional boundaries and local interests . . . In its formal organisation the Party had consistently imitated the great unions. With its national executive, secretariat and pyramidal structure it was (and is) quite unlike any other British party . . . Throughout the period [i.e. 1910–24] increasing centralisation of the Party was accompanied by growing dependence on the unions.[37]

During the party's formative period that McKibbin was summarising, there occurred an episode revealing another aspect of the unions' anti-localism, their dislike of local government autonomy where it would weaken the unions' own role in wage bargaining. This happened during the prolonged battle in the early 1920s in London over, among other things, the appropriate wage rates for the employees of the Poplar Poor Law Union. The Labour-controlled guardians of the union were paying wages above the norm and the district auditor proclaimed that these were 'unreasonable'.[38] The Poplar guardians persisted in pursuing what they regarded as a central plank in the socialist programme and were surcharged and, when they failed to pay, imprisoned. The London Labour Party, led by Herbert Morrison, was against the guardians for understandable electoral reasons since the auditor's decision was upheld by the House of Lords. But so were the trade unions, led by Ernest Bevin who was organising Poor Law Union workers.[39] Bevin in fact was as firmly against what came to be called 'Poplarism' as the district auditor, the Conservative Party and the middle-class ratepayers. For the implication of Poplarism in its wage rate aspect was that if Labour-controlled guardians were free to pay a high wage rate, Tory guardians could pay something less. Equally the unions, and Bevin in particular, did not want their primary role as the champions of higher wages to be usurped by local politicians, whether or not they were Labour.[40] Rowett has summarised this attitude up to the early 1930s in the following terms: 'The subsidiary position of local government was reinforced by the preponderant influence exercised within the national party by the overwhelming centralist trade union leaders.'[41] The unions, as national organisations themselves, wanted above all an ordered, disciplined and predictable national system of wage bargaining very much more than they wanted socialist-controlled segments of the national polity. Later, during the nationalisation process between 1945 and 1951, there is the same union insistence on centralisation – the one big board – as an essential prerequisite for effective bargaining over wages and conditions of work.[42]

The unions' desire for centralised public corporations as the appropriate form of nationalisation was also influenced by the experience of those unions which operated in the public sector or in potentially nationalised industries. These were principally the mineworkers and post office workers, but included others too.[43] In the earliest period and particularly immediately following the First World War, when the unions were both under the influence of G. D. H. Cole and flushed with the power they had won in the favourable conditions of the war, they favoured some form of workers' control with union representation on the nationalised boards.

The miners wanted representation on local boards of management, down to individual pit level. With the gradual weakening of the unions during the prolonged slump of the 1920s, the debilitating effects of the General Strike and the financial crisis from 1929 onwards, interest in the decentralist approach to nationalisation tailed off, as did the demand for direct representation on the board.[44] Instead, the unions increasingly backed the Morrisonian public corporation idea which put effective and efficient management as the key consideration and which it was thought would avoid the worst excesses of civil service bureaucracy. This last advantage had a particular appeal to the post office workers who had had a long and disillusioning experience of the benefits of nationalisation in its departmental form via the cold hand of the Treasury. Moreover, for many trade unions the departmental forms were anathema because of their conviction that higher civil servants were likely to be convert Tories.[45]

So much for the trade union effect on the party's centralist predilections. Linked to the Poplarism issue was another reason for Labour's abandonment during the interwar period of alternative decentralised roads to socialism of the kind, for example, adumbrated in 1920 by the Webbs in their *A Constitution for the Socialist Commonwealth of Great Britain.*[46] This was the treatment Labour-controlled councils and boards of guardians such as Bedwellty and Chester le Street received at the hands of the district auditor and Neville Chamberlain at the Ministry of Health. They found, like their Poplar colleagues, that *ultra vires* was a perfectly adequate instrument for ensuring that local government was not used as a vehicle for socialism. Yet the alternative – a Private Bill – was equally hazardous not only because of the high cost, but also because the Conservative majority in the Commons that existed throughout most of the period would vote such a Bill down if they thought it smacked of municipal socialism.[47] Perhaps even more decisive in weakening the resolve of local Labour strongholds was the parliamentary leadership's own retreat from its stated policy. *Labour and the Nation*, the party's major policy statement in 1928, said:

> In contrast with the distrust apparently felt in some quarters for the democratic machinery of Local Government, the Labour Party holds that the inhabitants of London and Manchester of Leeds and Sheffield and of other great cities of the country, are the best judges of their own affairs, and it desires to see an extension of the activities of Local Authorities into new spheres. It proposes, therefore, as indicated in the Local Authorities (Enabling) Bill, already introduced by it, to untie hands, to encourage them to expand their functions and, subject to due safeguards in respect of efficiency and capital expenditure. to empower them to undertake such services as their citizens may desire, including the compulsory acquisition of land by the cheapest procedure without unnecessary formalities, and the conduct of economic enterprises from which at present they are debarred.[48]

When the party became the government in 1929, the responsible minister, Greenwood, who had promoted an Enabling Bill when in opposition, reversed his position and persuaded a group of Labour backbenchers to withdraw the very measure extolled in *Labour and the Nation* and summarised in the quotation from it just given. Greenwood's action marks in effect the final demise of the Labour Party's dabbling with the local road to socialism.

As Keith-Lucas and Richards have noted:

> The election in 1945 of a Labour Government with a secure majority might have been expected to revive the issue of municipal socialism. By this time, however, the Labour movement was interested in nationalisation rather than municipalisation.[49]

There are a number of reasons why the parliamentary leaders ceased to see local government as an important vehicle for the socialist revolution. Having tasted office twice in five years, they were, no doubt, already adherents of the belief in central omnipotence that the British political tradition rarely fails to imprint on all who reach Cabinet rank. Secondly, office had also changed their perspective: more autonomous local government meant that Conservative local councils could all the better thwart Labour's national policies.

It would be an error to assume, however, that the abandonment of localism was only the result of a change of heart at the top of the party. As Rowett has noted, despite the bold party pronouncements, it was only in a minority of areas where the party was very well entrenched that the localist road became an article of faith. The speed with which the party won national power focused attention on the centre and undermined the need to establish the socialist society by the local route.[50]

Another centralising factor that is consistent with Labour ideology is the belief that it must be one of the primary tasks of government to manage the economy. As we have already noted, this view is shared by all wings of the party and is apparently in no way diminished by the planning failures of successive postwar British governments, of whatever colour. The objective sought may be different – Keynesian demand management, quasi-monetarism, another National Plan, or just plain socialisation; nevertheless the result is broadly the same, the centralisation of government. In practice if not on paper, decentralised institutions exercising independent power, whether they be territorial or functional, will be seen as just as big an obstacle to the achievement of the planning function as the market sector itself. Although the objective of managerial flexibility clashes with the national economic planning function, there can be little doubt that it was this planning function that also influenced the peculiarly concentrated and centralised character of the one-big-corporation approach to nationalisation.

The last, but probably the most important reason for the Labour Party's centralist proclivity that is consistent with this ideology, is the relatively high priority it has always given to combating inequality. As in other Western states, it is this aspect of the Labour Party's legislative output when in power that has made a major contribution to the growth of central government. Simply stated, this centralising trend is based on the assumption that only by extending the jurisdiction for public service delivery to the whole state is it possible to ensure adequate conditions for equality in that delivery. Decentralised forms of government, it is thought, cannot achieve the necessary degree of uniformity unless under close central supervision, partly because of the maldistribution of needs and resources up and down the country, and partly because decentralised delivery makes it much more difficult to ensure equality of standards. Where decentralised delivery is retained then a considerable increase in central government, to provide adequate supervision and inspection, still occurs so as to ensure that equality of standards is achieved throughout the state. Also, centralisation will occur because the centre has to make good the tendency for resources to be in an inverse relationship with need by the provision of grants. In brief, so this argument runs, he who says equality says centralisation.[51] The strength of this belief in the equalising capacity of centralisation in the Labour Party is underlined by a brief account of the enormous scale of the NHS, which is perhaps the greatest monument to that belief.[52]

The NHS is the largest single organisation in the UK. Employing over 800,000 people, it is also the tenth largest employer in the world. In financial terms it is the largest single spender, absorbing more than 10 per cent of public sector expenditure.

Whether the equality-entails-centralisation assumption always holds is open to some doubt, once we look at the striking degree of variation in standards of service in the health service that still persist after over thirty years of centralised administration. We rarely get the equivalent of laboratory tests in politics, but the results of a survey by the 1974 Resource Allocation Working Party place an enormous question mark against the redistributive capacity of centralisation. They suggest that in the ninety area health authorities and their coterminous personal social service authorities there was a greater discrepancy in minimum standards of health care in the health authority areas than there was in the health functions transferred from local authorities. Further, in 1948 when the NHS was created, the spread of provision around the national average was about 50 per cent and this degree of variance was precisely the same in 1973.[53] As one Labour Health Minister, David Owen, has remarked,

> the responsibility for redressing inequalities has been woefully neglected ... Resource allocation, minimum standards, quality assessment and even inspection are all legitimate central government responsibilities. Yet these important central functions have been neglected often because of the sheer scale of the intervention and involvement of central government in other more detailed areas of day-to-day management and control.[54]

This is not the place to pursue this aspect of the party's centralism any further, but it must be emphasised that whether or not the party has been mistaken in its assumption that equality is always better achieved by centralisation, there can be little doubt about is intentions, for it has always given the pursuit of equality a very high priority. Despite its largely non-ideological origins as a vehicle for increasing the number of trade union MPs, its long-standing tendency to welcome members of the upper-middle class in its senior echelons[55] and its often vehemently asserted reputation for opportunism, Labourism and class betrayal generally,[56] on the question of egalitarianism the Labour Party can hold its head reasonably high in comparison with other Western parties of the left. It was the first government, for example, to create a comprehensive health care service for all, irrespective of income. It was the first to introduce universal flat rate pensions, and it has made no less than three attempts to socialize land values. It has also been part instigator and staunch defender of a pattern of housing tenure in which one-third of all housing is publicly owned or, broadly speaking, subsidised and allocated according to need. With the New Towns Act it established experiments in classic socialism. Finally, although there is still some way to go before anything like a fair and just system is established, the party has conducted a long and somewhat bitter campaign to equalise what was probably one of the most unequal secondary education systems in the Western world.

In these examples of the party's relative egalitarian zeal the wholly centralised approach has not been attempted in all cases, but where it has not, in housing and education, there has been a considerable increase in central controls. Since the party has never made any attempt to change the local taxation base, which seems to be unique in being wholly dependent on a property tax, the potential for central control has been enhanced, as continous inflation makes the localities increasingly dependent on central grants. This refusal to alter the local tax base so as to give it a direct link to the general level of prices persisted even when such an alteration was strongly recommended by the Layfield Committee.[57] The party centralised the property valuation process in 1948, and yet when in power it has never fulfilled the obligation that such centralisation placed on the Cabinet to have regular revaluations, especially in the hyper-inflationary conditions of the mid-1970s.

This leads us to a subject of enduring importance, namely, the party's attitude to bureaucracy. No discussion of the party's centralist predisposition, especially when it is rooted in the egalitarian ideal, can fail to note that one reason why it is so readily misled into assuming that a major change in society can be effected simply by an Act of Parliament is that it does not seem ever to have spent much time thinking about the character of modern state bureaucracy.[58]

To say this is not to rehearse the old propaganda favourite of the right that socialism because it leads to more state action, must always be a threat to the liberty of the individual. There is no doubt that, like all socialist parties, the Labour Party will always be ambivalent about the dangers of increased state power.[59] Freedom can never be viewed as a zero sum game, since one of the primary effects of the expansion of the state in the twentieth century has been a palpable extension of individual autonomy. This is so whether that extension takes the form of unemployment pay, social security and subsidised housing, which enables the unemployed worker, say, to exercise choice as a consumer, or whether it takes the form of providing electric and television power lines, motorways and airports, which enables the businessman to live in the country and still communicate with the outside world.

Ambivalent about bureaucracy or not, the party has in any case an impeccable record on the question of individual rights against the state. It was responsible for the Crown Proceedings Act and the Legal Aid and Advice Act, and set up the Ombudsman, unquestionably three of the most important safeguards of individual liberty in relation to central government in the postwar era. It is clearly not this aspect of bureaucracy which the party has neglected, and which inclines it to centralist solutions. It is rather the extent to which it assumes that an agency of government will undertake fundamental change in society that cuts across the grain of existing spatial inequality – like the equalisation of health services without requiring any change in the bureaucracy itself and without any political input other than the minister ensconced in Whitehall. I shall return to this subject later.

There remains a further aspect of the party's aim of equality and its centralising consequences that merits our attention. It is the assumption that equality is solely related to attributes that can be measured in personal terms. This is a conception of equality that is quite consistent with the centralist model of government which, we noted earlier, assumes a spatially undifferentiated value system in which a given quantity of governmental output will be of equal value throughout the state. Such a model assumes that 'if no individual is discriminated against then no group can be'.[60] It thus leaves out of account the possibility of sub-national communal values that see such governmental outputs as a threat rather than an aid to equality. If such sub-national variations in values do exist, and the resurgence of Celtic nationalism is perhaps only the most drastic confirmation that they do, then the pursuit of equality can only be achieved, not by centralisation, but by decentralisation.

IV Puzzling Factors

We now come to what, in terms of the arguments presented at the outset, may be thought to be the most interesting aspects of the Labour Party's relative lack of interest in the geography of inequality. They are the more interesting because they do not seem to be related to either the structural characteristics of the political and governmental system in which the party operates, or the party's broad ideology. They are in this sense the puzzling aspects of the party's centralism.

Although they are obviously linked in the sense that they both derive from the parliamentary party, I am going to assume that there are two, separate, puzzling factors. The first we may call backbench anti-localism; the second, the bourgeois party model. Both have manifold aspects but, given the limits of space, I will be able to sketch in only their salient features.

Let me begin with perhaps the less important of the two, the anti-localist predisposition of the average Labour Party backbencher. At first blush this may be thought to be an unlikely characteristic since various studies going back to the early 1950s have shown that the Parliamentary Labour Party tends to contain more members with local government experience than the Conservatives.[61] Over the period 1945–79 about 45 per cent of all Labour MPs, as opposed to about an average of a quarter of Conservative MPs (in aggregate about one-third of all MPs), have been councillors before election to Parliament.[62] Not only is there a higher proportion of Labour MPs with local government experience, but Labour MPs with that experience tend to have served longer as councillors than Conservatives.

High as these proportions may seem, when compared with other countries they are on the low side.[63] What is much more important anyway is that MPs with local government experience tend to sever their links with local government fairly soon after entering Parliament. Once in the government or on the shadow front bench they almost always do. This also distinguishes British practice sharply from many other Western legislatures. Herbert Morrison, who did retain his links with London local government even after becoming a minister and was regularly accused of being a Tammany Hall boss, may have lost his chance of the leadership because of the link.[64]

One reason for British MPs' relative indifference to local government is almost certainly that the British electoral system is, and during the modern era always has been, a carpetbagger's paradise. Because there is no locality rule, of either a statutory or a conventional kind, candidates can be adopted and elected without having any connection at all with their constituency. There is no compulsion for them to develop one beyond the usual minimum requirement of a weekly surgery in the constituency. This tradition is all part of the parliamentary supremacy rule noted earlier, since it reflects the fact that the primary objective of the representative system is to produce a government and a shadow government. Ambitious and talented politicians can be slotted in, whenever a vacancy occurs, and the highly favoured and lucky found in a constituency not too far from Westminster. What is puzzling is why the carpetbagger tradition is as acceptable to the Labour Party as it is to the Conservative and Liberal Parties.

It may be assumed that carpetbaggers are scarce among the 45 per cent of Labour MPs who have local government experience; nearly two-thirds of these MPs actually represented a district 'which was related to that which they had formerly represented on a local authority'.[65] There is also some evidence that selection committees are becoming more and more reluctant to take absolute outsiders, particularly if they appear to be being promoted by the party HQ.[66]

Despite both these trends, however, the ethos of the Parliamentary Labour Party still seems to be remarkably cold and remote from local government, including the local council in the MP's own constituency. Examples of this indifference include the relative lack of backbench opposition to the Wilson government's plans for local government reorganisation in 1970.[67] This would have involved an even more drastic holocaust of the existing units than was actually carried out in 1972 by the Heath government, itself probably the most drastic ever carried out by any Western country.[68] More pertinently, the 1970 Labour proposals would have been as damaging to Labour Party interests in the localities, possibly more so, than the Heath Cabinet's 1972 Act. The parliamentary party fought that Act fiercely, yet, as we have already noted, did nothing beyond producing a White Paper during its four years of office to change the system, despite the entreaties of its own supporters in the party's provincial bastions for the relatively modest proposals for 'organic change'.

A broadly similar attitude of indifference is clearly evident in relation to the Layfield Committee's equally modest recommendations for bringing the financial basis of local government into line with practically every other Western system by allowing local authorities to have some share of the income tax.[69] This committee was set up by a Labour minister and its recommendations had the broad support of the party in the localities, yet they were mainly ignored and the party's backbenchers remained largely acquiescent.

There seems to be an unwritten code that disinclines MPs, whether Labour or Conservative, to form the kind of alliance with local government, often involving the retention of a local elective office, which is common among MPs in other democracies. These links play a crucial role in amplifying the formal, legal relationship between local and central government in such countries, most notably in the USA and France.

Almost thirty years ago W. J. M. Mackenzie compared the interrelationship between Britain and other states in terms of the differences between the *de jure* power of the localities and their *de facto* power derived partly from the operation of locality rules on members of the legislature, and partly on the members' linkages with local government. Mackenzie was discussing all MPs, not just Labour, but in this respect there is little difference between the parties and it is also likely that the conclusions of his study still stand: 'forms of British law give local government a status of exceptional freedom, but that legal autonomy is overriden in practice by party discipline and the prevalence of the "carpet baggers"'.[70]

There are two reasons which go some way to explaining backbench indifference to local government. The first has to do with the extraordinary frustrations of the backbench British MP, especially a Labour one who is less likely to have another form of employment in which to exercise his or her talents in the City or in the Inns of Court. In a representative assembly of over 600, which lacks any legislative powers, his chances of shining are severely limited. Even his opportunity for speaking is very restricted if he is not an ex-minister or in that small group of backbenchers accorded special status by the Speaker. He may be able to carve a public niche for himself with a bit of luck and a willingness to devote a great deal of his life to a special issue which happens to interest the media or one of the select committees. An alternative route to media interest is a willingness to criticise his own party in public. The majority of Labour backbenchers, however, have in the end to content themselves with making their primary task in life looking after their constituencies and, if they are energetic, harrying the government front bench. Yet they find that, apart from the usually very complex and tedious complaints about pensions, taxation and compensation, which now can, thankfully, be passed on to the Ombudsman, their constituents tend to bring them complaints about housing, planning and education, all of which are local government matters. Local government, however, is unlikely to accord him any special status unless he is a minister or ex-minister, and as a representative institution itself may perhaps give him less recognition than he feels is his due. In short, the backbencher is very much aware that in carrying out one of his main jobs he is in direct competition with local government. And yet he has the strong feeling that the majority of the public seem to be indifferent to local government. Why did they bring their problems to him and not to the body responsible in the first place?

A second, perhaps more decisive reason for backbench indifference to local government is that in another of his roles, as watch-dog of the executive, the member has, paradoxically, a vested interest in the centralisation of power. For the more clear-cut the lines of accountability are, and the more responsibility is concentrated on the minister, the more easily the latter can be held responsible. Any ambiguities surrounding the minister's 'answerability', any power-sharing between him and external bodies such as local authorities, is therefore anathema to the backbencher, for such ambiguities enable the minister to evade responsibility. It may be claimed that this last centralist attitude of the party is structural rather than puzzling. However, it is difficult to see what is structural about an attitude that views local government as being no different from a public corporation, or a quango. Whatever their defects, local authorities are still elected bodies with the right to tax and in this sense can never be creatures of the centre. Ministers can therefore never be made answerable for them.

That this fundamental difference between local government and other non-central governmental institutions is only hazily perceived by most of the party's parliamentarians was neatly revealed during the Clay Cross saga in the early 1970s. This involved the refusal of a Labour-controlled urban district council to implement the Conservatives' Housing Finance Act which sought, among other things, to raise council rents.[71] Without delving too deeply into the rights and wrongs of the issues, Clay Cross Council's refusal to implement the Act, although in breach of the law, could not be classed in its unlawfulness with robbing a bank or coshing old age pensioners. The council was a publicly elected body which had, moreover, fought an election on the non-implementation of the Act and won. That gave its actions a status in relation to the minister and to Parliament that had to be recognised, if not necessarily condoned. In this case they were highly elaborate because the Conservative Cabinet knew that the Act represented a fundamental attack on what hitherto had been regarded as an exclusive right of local government – to set the rents of its own housing. Yet the Labour Party's shadow front bench, when discussing the subject in public, never faltered in its public condemnation of Clay Cross's action and was only marginally less critical than the Conservative Cabinet itself.

The Clay Cross episode reflects in one sense a very important feature not only of the parliamentary party's coolness to local government but also of its uncritical embrace of the status implications of the principle of parliamentary supremacy. By fixing the one fount of power in such a highly centralised way in a society which is itself so unequally concentrated geographically by all the conventional measures of wealth and status, such geographical inequality is reinforced. Reinforcement of this kind holds no terrors for the Conservative Party, indeed it is for it a logical relationship. But for the Labour Party, accepting unchanged Cabinet hegemony has meant cutting itself off from its origins and, in a curious way, from its provincial, distinctly unglossy, and sometimes proletarian self. At the risk of romanticising the past, it must be emphasised that the Labour Party was not born amidst the polished mahogany of the ministerial suite, or in the smoking rooms of the House of Commons, or even at a Fabian weekend school. The party's creation was part of a wider democratic awakening in the bowels of unrestricted capitalism, which its subsequent embrace of centralism has obscured. As Halsey has it:

> Democracy came to Britain from the bottom upwards. The urban working classes of the nineteenth century were uprooted newcomers to the growing provincial industrial towns who responded to their circumstances with extraordinary social inventiveness to give Britain in the first half of the twentieth century its most characteristic popular organisations – the Co-operative store, the trade union, and the Labour Party, as well as the dance hall, the football club, and the friendly society. The first and the greatest three of these were experiments in democracy. This urban proletariat created its own local, communal welfare societies. Nothing could have been more democratic than the constitution of the Co-op, nothing more fraternal than the Miners' Lodge. Nowhere could we find a more sturdy institutional protection for individuals against becoming a mass to be manipulated. Then, with political organisation as its instrument, the Labour movement set out to nationalise democracy and welfare; to translate fraternity, equality, and liberty from the local community to the national state ... So the movement which had invented the social forms of modern participatory democracy and practised them in union branch and Co-op meeting, thereby laying a Tocquevillian foundation for democracy, was ironically fated to develop through its political party the threat of a bureaucratic state.[72]

We now come to the last puzzling aspect of the party's centralism, an aspect that did not emanate from the constraints of the political system or its own ideology. This is its acceptance of what may be called the bourgeois party model, and it is closely linked to the parliamentary party's anti-localism just discussed.

By the bourgeois party model is meant a conception of the national party as the handmaiden of the parliamentary; its primary task being to produce and support the parliamentary team. The local party organisations are conceived as being mainly election machines and its members are assumed to be 'devoted primarily to the national party's goals, its organisation and its leadership'.[73] R. T. McKenzie has described the bourgeois model thus:

> No emphasis on the auxiliary functions of the mass organisation outside Parliament can be allowed to obscure the basic proposition that the mass parties are primarily the servants of their respective parliamentary parties; that their principal function is to sustain teams of parliamentary leaders between whom the electorate is periodically invited to choose.[74]

The leader thus produced becomes the leader of the whole party, although the party outside Parliament will have played no part in this election. The only major adaptations to this model by the party, other than the major adjustments that have been necessary in recognition of the special place of affiliated trade unions, have been the election of the leader by the parliamentary party (now copied by the Conservatives), according *de jure* but not necessarily *de facto* powers of policy-making to the annual conference and the National Executive and, finally, the creation of the NEC, the supreme authority for the national party elected by the annual conference. The reforms of 1980 should in due course greatly weaken the model.

The quote from McKenzie refers to both of the major parties in the British system, but there can be little doubt that there is a significally greater degree of centralisation in the Conservative Party than in the Labour Party. The former is, as may be expected, a purer example of the model. In his insistence that the two parties are similar in their internal power structure, McKenzie leaves out of account the impact of the trade unions in moderating the centralising tendencies of the bourgeois model. Above all, he tends to cast the whole of his analysis of where power lies in terms of horizontal levels of the party, whereas major conflicts within the party, which may or may not be overtly about power, are almost always vertical, cutting across the horizontal layers of the party.[75] There is, in short, within the party as a whole, a shadow party system. Each shadow party contains elements from each level,[76] but the right shadow party always contains a larger proportion of the higher echelons of the party. However, the accuracy of McKenzie's claims is not germane, since it seems probable that in comparative terms the Labour Party's adhesion to the bourgeois model has meant that it is more centralised than most parties of the non-communist left. This is partly reflected in the relative insulation of the parliamentary party, both collectively and individually. In the latter aspect it has meant that MPs for safe seats usually have security of tenure for life provided the party whips are not regularly flouted. Adherence to party doctrine is of little or no consequence and on the fringes of the parliamentary party there have always been Tories in all but name, fellow travellers, supporters of Franco's Spain, and of the Greek Colonels. Nor have MPs ever been required to contribute from their parliamentary salaries to party funds, a practice which is common in other Western socialist parties.

An even better indication of the party's centralist character that is derived from the adoption of the bourgeois model is the extent to which the parliamentary party has, until very recently, been able to exclude the rest of the party from participating in the election of the leader. In this respect it has been able to lag behind even one of the bourgeois parties – the Liberals, who since 1976 have opened up the leadership election to their constituency parties. In a survey of the methods for electing the equivalent to the British party leader in nineteen socialist and labour parties, only one, the Australian party, restricted the election solely to the legislative caucus party after the British pattern.[77]

Further discussion of the extent to which the party has adopted the bourgeois model, or how far in doing so it is more centralised than comparable parties in other countries, need not detain us further. What is primarily at issue is, after all, not so much the distribution of power between the party's main organs – leader, parliamentary party, national executive, or annual conference – since all of them are already central institutions of the party, though in varying degrees. Since national politicians or trade unionists now always dominate the elections to the NEC,[78] only the annual conference provides entry for the rank and file into the policy-making process. But the shadow party system always tends to nationalise this input, for although the typical constituency activist tends to be suspicious of all governments and inclined to border on the paranoid about the party leadership when in office, he is, nevertheless, somewhat parsimonious in the number of alternative modes he entertains for achieving socialism. The minister and his department reign supreme:

> for many Labour people the 'menace of bureacracy' is an invention of the conservatives to scare the timid away from socialism and to make the administration of a welfare state more difficult. They feel that as long as the departments of state and other governmental agencies are controlled, immediately or ultimately, by ministers, who are responsible to Parliament, which is responsible to a democratic electorate, no harm can come of giving more and more power to the official.[79]

This profound faith in the existing governmental system is not merely a reflection of that rather narrow view of modern bureaucracy which we have already discussed; at bottom it also gives government the capacity for action, and provides very clear lines of accountability between government and electorate. This concentration of power and of responsibility is in marked contrast to the USA, for example, where, as I have argued elsewhere, the fragmentation of government makes concerted governmental action very difficult, thus undermining the quality of representative democracy.[80] But the possible deficiencies of the American system do not in any sense justify the Labour Party's uncritical acceptance of the bourgeois model for if the American governmental system errs on the side of fragmentation the British errs on the side of concentration. Moreover, the fragmentation of the American system is not solely, or even mainly, derived from its undoubtedly spatial decentralisation but from too much fragmentation at the centre itself. One final defence of the party's adoption of the internal organisation of its rivals we have already encountered. This argues that the constraints of the system were such that it had no choice. It follows that its acceptance of the bourgeois party model is not a puzzle, but is simply due to structural constraints. There can be little doubt that those constraints are very powerful. They reside not only in the tangible world of institutions, their procedures and statutes, but also in one of those deeply and widely held tacit understandings that underpins British politics and government. This is the implicit assumption of the 'profoundly unitary nature of the United Kingdom, as expressed in the supremacy of Parliament'.[81] According to Bogdanor, this is possibly the strongest of all the tacit understandings:

> We find it difficult to think in terms of a separation of powers, and difficult also to think of government as a series of interdependent layers, each with its own rights and responsibilities. Britain is, amongst democracies, the largest of the unitary states, apart from Japan; for other democracies do not seek to manage the affairs of so large a population through a single parliament.[82]

The answer to this claim must be that no one can know what the role of this constraint was because the bourgeois model was adopted before any other model, that might have been more appropriate to the party of the underdog and therefore of the provinces and the localities, was ever tried. If anything, after some initial hiccoughs, the parliamentary party settled down to the procedures and accoutrements of the Westminster nexus with appparent relish. We have already noted the insulation of the leader's election and the security of tenure of backbenchers. Both demonstrate the relative independence of the parliamentarians from the grass roots. We must also note the party's almost complete failure to do much about the House of Lords after almost twenty years in power, which on any view is an affront to the most limited definition of democracy. It will be interesting to see if the constitutional reforms adopted in 1980–1 will shatter that bourgeois model. At a more trivial but symbolically revealing level there is the party's disinclination to reflect in the fabric of the Palace of Westminster any indication of the democratic revolution and the arrival of the bulk of the population to some form of common citizenship. This is a transformation of our society which the party has played no mean part in achieving. The decorations of the Palace remain, however, almost wholly devoted to the glorious dead of our pre-democratic past.

Summary

The retention of the bourgeois model, in short, was not inevitable and, together with the anti-localism of the parliamentary party generally, it constitutes a genuinely puzzling characteristic of the British Labour Party. When viewed against the peculiar spatial distribution of power, wealth and status in this country – the geography of inequality – so too do some of the party's other characteristics and attitudes. Neither its coolness to local government nor its belief in ministerial accountability can be explained wholly in terms of its desire for equalisation and the national minimum. Finally, its strong preference for the one big corporation cannot be attributed wholly to the trade unions. In sum, the British Labour Party's centralism is, in part at least, an enigma.

Notes: Chapter 6

A number of people have been kind enough to comment on an earlier version of this chapter and I am most grateful for their help. I would like to especially thank Knut Heidar, G. W. Jones, Franco Kjellberg, Roger Liddle and Ken Newton. I also want to thank Dennis Kavanagh, who was a most helpful editor.

1 Donald L. Foley, *Governing the London Region* (Berkeley, Calif.: University of California Press, 1972), p. 7.

2 W. J. M. MacKenzie, *Theories of Local Government* (London: LSE, 1961), p. 16.

3 Raymond Williams, *Orwell* (London: Fontana/Collins, 1971), pp. 8, 16, 17, 18, and A. H. Halsey, *Change in British Society* (Oxford: Oxford University Press, 1978), p. 46.

4 Ronald Butt, 'The basis of reform', *The Times*, 12 June 1969.

5 Stefano Bartolini, 'The membership of mass parties: the social democratic experience 1889–1978', in H. Daalder and P. Mair (eds), *Working Papers on Western European Party Systems* (forthcoming).

6 See J. C. Banks, *Federal Britain?* (London: Harrap, 1971), ch. 2, for further voluminous evidence of the geography of inequality; and A. H. Birch, *Political Integration and Disintegration in the British Isles* (London: Allen & Unwin, 1977), ch. 3.

7 Michael Hechter, *Internal Colonialism* (Berkeley, Calif.: University of California Press, 1975), provides useful statistical evidence of its extent over the past century.

8 John Curtice and Michael Stead, 'An analysis of the voting', in David Butler and Dennis Kavanagh, *The British General Election of 1979* (London: Macmillan, 1979), p. 402.

9 Knut Heidar, 'The Norwegian Labour Party: social democracy in a periphery of Europe', in W. Paterson and A. Thomas (eds), *Social Democracy in Western Europe* (London: Croom Helm, 1977), p. 295. Also see Stein Rokkan, 'Geography, religion and social class: cross-cutting cleavages in Norwegian politics' in Seymour M. Lipset

and Stein Rokkan, *Party Systems and Voter Alignments* (New York: The Free Press, 1967).

10 Finn Brunn and Carl-Johan Skovsgaard, 'Local determinants and central control of municipal finance: the affluent local authorities of Denmark', in L. J. Sharpe (ed.), *Is There a Local Fiscal Crisis in Western Europe? Myths and Realities* (London: Sage, 1981).

11 Letter to the author from Finn Brunn.

12 Restricting the egalitarian policies of Labour-controlled local authorities by centralising functional and financial responsibility is not the only technique open to Conservative governments. There is the institutional reorganisation strategy which via the extension of local government boundaries reduces the possibility of Labour control at the local level. This was one of the motivations of the London reorganisation in 1963 as it was of the massive reorganisation of the rest of the country in 1972–3.

13 Christopher Price, 'Labour and the town halls', *New Statesman*, 2 July 1971, p. 6.

14 Maurice Wright and Stephen Young, 'Regional planning in Britain', in Jack Hayward and Michael Watson (eds), *Planning, Politics and Public Policy* (London: Cambridge University Press, 1975), p. 261.

15 *Report of The Royal Commission on the Constitution* (Kilbrandon Report), Cmnd 5460 (London: HMSO, 1973), Vol. 1, p. 178.

16 House of Commons Expenditure Committee, *Regional Development Incentives: Report*, HC 85 (London: HMSO, 1973), see esp. para. 116.

17 Bill Nicol and Douglas Yuill, *Regional Problems and Policies in Europe: The Post War Experience*, Studies in Public Policy No. 53 (Glasgow: University of Strathclyde, 1980), p. 31.

18 loc. cit.

19 *Report of the Study Group on Regional Planning Policy* (London: Labour Party, 1970), pp. 15–16.

20 ibid. p. 18.

21 Quoted in *Devolution and Regional Government in England* (London: Labour Party, 1975), p. 4.

22 John Gyford, 'Socialism and decentralisation: dilemmas and ambiguities', unpublished mimeo., September 1980, p. 2. The publications he cites are:
A. Benn, *Arguments for Socialism* (1980)
J. Bray and N. Falk, *Towards a Worker-Managed Economy* (1974)
K. Coates (ed.), *Can the Workers Run Industry?* (1968)
K. Coates (ed.), *The New Worker Co-operatives* (1976)
A. Fox, *Socialism and Shop-Floor Power* (1978)
M. Goyder, *Socialism Tomorrow: Fresh Thinking for the Labour Party*
P. Hain, *On Reviving the Labour Party* (1980)
P. Hain and S. Hebditch, *Radicals and Socialism* (1978)
P. Jay, *The Workers' Co-operative Economy* (1977)
Labour Party, *Workers Co-operatives* (1980)
E. Luard, *Socialism without the State* (1979) and *Socialism at the Grass Roots* (1980)
D. Owen, *Human Rights* (1978) and *Co-operative Ownership* (1980)
G. Radice, *Community Socialism* (1979)
D. Watkins, *Industrial Common Ownership* (1978).

23 White Paper, *Organic Change in Local Government*, Cmnd 7457 (London: HMSO, 1979).

24 *Guardian*, 1 August 1980, p. 11.

25 Both Tony Benn and David Owen have written articles and pamphlets advocating decentralisation and Owen wrote an article arguing unequivocally that decentralisation ought to be a central plank of Labour policy. See his 'The fatal stranglehold of the state', *Guardian*, 28 September 1976.

26 Lewis Minkin, *The Labour Party Conference* (Manchester: Manchester University Press, 1978), p. 292.
27 For example, see *The Diaries of a Cabinet Minister* (London: Hamilton and Cape, 1975), Vol. 2, p. 591, and Vol. 3, p. 45.
28 John Mackintosh, *The Devolution of Power* (London: Chatto & Windus and Charles Knight, 1968).
29 *Report of the Royal Commission on the Constitution* (Kilbrandon Report), *Vol. II: Memorandum of Dissent,* Cmnd 5460 (London: HMSO, 1973).
30 Evan Luard, *Socialism at the Grassroots,* Fabian Society Tract No. 468 (London: Fabian Society, 1980).
31 White Paper, *Industrial Democracy,* Cmnd 7231 (London: HMSO, 1978).
32 Evan Luard, *Socialism Without the State* (London: Macmillan, 1979), ch. 7.
33 G. Radice, *Community Socialism,* Fabian Tract No. 464 (London: Fabian Society, 1979), p. 14; also see C. Mullin (ed.), *The Industrial Democrats* (London: Allen & Unwin, 1978).
34 See, for example, Tony Benn, in C. Mullin (ed.), *Arguments for Socialism* (London: Cape, 1979), or A. Wedgwood Benn, *The New Politics,* Fabian Society Tract No. 402 (London: Fabian Society, 1970).
35 Bernard Donoughue and G. W. Jones, *Herbert Morrison: Portrait of a Politician* (London: Weidenfeld & Nicolson, 1973), p. 63.
36 *Kilbrandon Report,* Vol. 1, p. 91.
37 Ross McKibbin, *The Evolution of the Labour Party 1910–1924* (London: Oxford University Press, 1974), pp. 241–2.
38 For a detailed discussion of this affair and 'Poplarism' in general, see Bryan Keith-Lucas and Peter G. Richards, *A History of Local Government in the Twentieth Century* (London: Allen & Unwin, 1978), ch. IV.
39 G. W. Jones, 'Herbert Morrison and Poplarism', *Public Law,* Spring 1973, pp. 11–31.
40 ibid., pp. 25, 27.
41 J. S. Rowett, 'The local government policies of the Labour governments of 1924 and 1929–31', paper to the SSRC Urban Politics History Seminar, York, April 1980.
42 Sir Norman Chester, *The Nationalisation of British Industry 1945–57* (London: HMSO, 1975), p. 1029.
43 See D. N. Chester, 'Management and accountability in the nationalised industries', *Public Administration,* vol. 2, no. 30 (1952), pp. 27–47, for a discussion of the changes in trade union attitudes towards nationalisation from 1912. Also H. R. G. Greaves, *Democratic Participation and Public Enterprise,* Hobhouse Memorial Lecture No. 34 (London: Athlone Press, 1964).
44 Chester, 'Management and accountability', p. 34.
45 H. R. G. Greaves, 'Post-war machinery of government. VII: Public boards and corporations', *Political Quarterly,* vol. 16, no. 1 (1945), pp. 67–77.
46 It would be an exaggeration to imply that the Webbs' solution dominated the intellectual debate in the party and some would argue that the Fabians, or at least those associated with the New Heptarchy proposals, had already abandoned local government as commonly understood before the First World War. See Andrew Sancton, 'British socialist theory of the division of power by area', *Political Studies,* vol. XXIV, no. 2 (1976), pp. 158–70.
47 Keith-Lucas and Richards, op. cit., ch. III
48 Quoted in Rowett, op. cit., pp. 2–3.
49 Keith-Lucas and Richards, op. cit., p. 40.
50 Rowett, op. cit., p. 32.
51 For a discussion of egalitarianism as a source of government growth, see L. J. Sharpe, 'Decentralist trends in Western democracies: a first appraisal' in L. J. Sharpe (ed.). *Decentralist Trends in Western Democracies* (London: Sage, 1979).

52 I do not wish to imply that the only reason for creating the NHS as a centralised system was due to Labour's desire for equality, but it was the main reason. Its sheer cost ensured that the Treasury would demand central control and the medical profession too demanded centralisation.
53 D. Owen, *In Sickness and in Health* (London: Quartet Books, 1976), ch. 4.
54 Owen, 'The fatal stranglehold of the state'.
55 Egon Wertheimer, *Portrait of the Labour Party* (New York: Putnam, 1929); W. L. Guttsman, *The British Political Elite* (London: MacGibbon & Kee, 1963); C. A. Cline, *Recruits to Labour, the British Labour Party 1914–31* (Syracuse: University of Syracuse Press, 1963).
56 For example, R. Miliband, *Parliamentary Socialism* (London: Allen & Unwin, 1961); Leo Panitch, *Social Democracy and Industrial Militancy* (Cambridge: Cambridge University Press, 1976); David Coates, *The Labour Party and the Struggle for Socialism* (Cambridge: Cambridge University Press, 1975).
57 *Report of the Committee of Inquiry into Local Government Finance*, Cmnd 6453 (London: HMSO, 1976).
58 A. H. Hanson, *Parliament and Public Ownership* (London: Cassell, 1961), ch. 1.
59 William B. Gwyn, 'The Labour Party and the threat of bureaucracy', *Political Studies,* vol. XIX, no. 4 (1971), pp. 383–402.
60 Brian Barry, 'Reflections on conflict', *Sociology*, vol. VI (1972), p. 5.
61 See, for example, W. J. M. Mackenzie, 'The conventions of local government', *Public Administration*, vol. XXIX (Winter 1951), pp. 345–56; D. E. Butler, 'Local government and Parliament', *Public Administration,* vol. XXI (Spring 1953), pp. 46–7; W. J. M. Mackenzie, 'Local government and Parliament', *Public Administration,* vol. XXXII (Winter 1954), pp. 409–23.
62 Colin Mellors, *The British MP* (Farnborough: Saxon House, 1978), p. 90. I am grateful to John Gyford for supplying figures for the 1979 House of Commons which show that the proportion of MPs with local government experience is very similar to that for the earlier period covered by Mellors.
63 Mackenzie, 'Local government and Parliament'.
64 Donoughue and Jones, op. cit., p. 242.
65 Mellors, op. cit., p. 97.
66 The difficulties that Mr McNally and Mr Harris, both senior apparatchiks in Transport House, experienced in being selected for a seat – in Mr Harris's case complete failure, in Mr McNally's success only after seven rejections – are probably examples of this trend. It also underlies, of course, the current debate about compulsory reselection.
67 White Paper, *Reform of Local Government in England*, Cmnd 4276 (London: HMSO, 1970).
68 See L. J. Sharpe, '"Reforming" the grass roots: an alternative analysis', in David Butler and A. H. Halsey (eds), *Policy and Politics* (London: Macmillan, 1978), p. 95.
69 See note 57.
70 Mackenzie, 'Local government and Parliament', p. 418.
71 See D. Skinner and J. Langdon, *The Story of Clay Cross* (Nottingham: Spokesman Books, 1974).
72 A. H. Halsey, *Change in British Society* (Oxford: Oxford University Press, 1978), pp. 84–5.
73 M. Parkinson, 'Central–local relations in British parties: a local view', *Political Studies,* vol. XIX, no. 4 (1971), p. 440.
74 Quoted loc. cit.
75 S. H. Beer, *Modern British Politics* (London: Faber, 1969), ch. VIII.
76 L. J. Sharpe, 'How Labour evolves policy', *New Society*, 13 July 1972, p. 511.
77 Ken Coates, *Democracy in the Labour Party* (Nottingham: Spokesman Books, 1977), ch. V.

78 W. Guttsman, *The British Political Elite*, (London: MacGibbon & Kee, 1968), p. 272. Also see Chapter 9 below.
79 Hanson, op. cit., p. 6.
80 L. J. Sharpe, 'American democracy re-considered: part II', *British Journal of Political Science*, vol. 3, pt 2 (1973), pp. 129–68.
81 Bogdanor, *Devolution*, (Oxford: Oxford University Press, 1979), p. 7.
82 loc. cit.

7 The Peculiar Relationship: The Party and the Unions

COLIN CROUCH

Britain is the only industrial country in which a labour movement political party has had a substantial share in government alongside a trade union movement which has remained highly decentralised. By itself this fact proves nothing, and many may regard it as irrelevant. But I believe it takes us closer to understanding the problems of the relationship between the unions and the Labour Party than do the more obvious peculiarities, such as the block vote or the party's dependence on union financial support. Perhaps the significance of the point will become more apparent if it is recalled that during periods of Labour government the unions have sometimes acquired a temporarily powerful centre, and that these have been spells of relatively 'successful' Labour government: 1945–50, 1975–8.

My contention is that party–union relations are most usefully discussed in terms of the structure of the unions and the part they play in the political economy, rather than by concentrating on immediate intra-party politics. I am also taking the fact of some kind of relationship between party and union for granted. However, these other issues are important and are at the centre of the public debate over the subject. I shall therefore discuss, first, the general question of a political party with some kind of close links to organised labour; secondly, the peculiar form taken by that relationship in Britain; and thirdly, the issue of union decentralisation to which I wish to draw attention.

The Case for a Union-Related Party

The proportion of union members who automatically support the Labour Party is declining. This is not just a result of manual worker disaffection, it also follows the changing social composition of union membership – a factor which also explains the declining proportion of members in unions affiliated to the party. The great increase in unionisation of the past decade has occurred primarily in white-collar and professional unions, most of which are not affiliated, while unions in decline as a result of a shrinkage in their occupational base (e.g. mining, railways, shipbuilding) have been Labour strongholds.[1] But whatever the cause, this decline is enough to raise questions about the party–union relationship. Meanwhile, the now well-established tendency for Labour governments to demand income restraint has caused acute strains in the relationship. The party is discomfited when the unions incur public hostility through unpopular strikes and similar occurrences, while the unions find the appeals to loyalty launched at them by Labour ministers a millstone around their necks. Not surprisingly, within the ranks of the union movement there is a considerable response to the call for 'pure and simple unionism', uncluttered by political ties which seem anyway to belong to the past, or at best to the remote and aloof circles of ministers and national union leaders. Syndicalists and Conservatives unite in opposing union involvement in politics and support 'free collective bargaining' – provided the former are shouting so loud that they do not hear the Conservatives adding, *sotto voce:* 'so long as you don't expect full employment as well'.

In many unions the social reality of the link is that a few people, largely officers but also some lay activists, sustain a web of personal contacts and various kinds of mutual aid with officers and activists of the party, thanks to the apathy and ignorance of the mass of the union membership.[2] Is this anything more than a house of cards which could be blown down at will by, say, a Conservative government sufficiently ruthless to reintroduce contracting-in? The case for answering 'no' rests on the unreality of the claim that union business need have little or nothing to do with politics.

While there are gains to be won for organised labour at a purely industrial level which have no negative economic consequences (e.g. certain wage claims against oligopolistic firms, individual grievance-handling), the point must eventually be reached where improvements in the pay and conditions of labour which go beyond the increase in productivity can be won only at the expense of higher unemployment. If labour is to do anything about this it must act at the level of the political economy, seeking changes in demand-management policies, in manpower policy, in government intervention in industry, and in legal measures to improve conditions across the board at either national or international levels.

In addition, in a society organised on the assumptions of a free market economy (or on any other basis which subordinates labour, such as state socialism), the very right of unions to exist and to increase or defend their rights to operate will require repeated action at the political level, to create and maintain a legal framework in which unions can overcome the legal handicaps imposed on autonomous collective action by labour. The incident which finally drove British unions to form the Labour Party, the Taff Vale case, sometimes appears as a fortuitous event, the avoidance of which might have prevented the unions' entry into party politics from ever occurring. But the question of union rights within the laws safeguarding the capitalist economy is so inherently political that sooner or later some other event of the same kind would have been certain to occur. Indeed, legal cases raising similar principles have continued to appear, with increasing frequency in very recent years.[3]

It may be argued that the search for political or any collective action to improve labour's position is futile because anything which interferes with the free market is doomed to failure. But that is merely to assert the essentially contested position which is at the heart of the conflict over labour's political participation. The available evidence is not such as to allow the proponents of the unimpeded market to claim that their cause is a simple matter of knowledge against error, beyond conflicts of interest. So long as these issues are contested, it will be open to the organisations of labour to see what improvements in the parameters of their economic activity can be secured at the political level. The apparent irrelevance of this level to what takes place in shop-floor or company-level conflict is simply a result of the myopia of the small scale, the political manipulation of which is crude populism.

This could all be conceded, but it could still be argued that unions would do better to enter politics by making demands on whatever is the government of the day, rather than by tying themselves to one party. There is some truth in this. Unions have to remain willing to do business with Conservative governments; and they have to tell Labour governments that they cannot be regarded as simply the industrial arm of the party. But there is another, larger question at stake: that of the social bases which can support the heterogeneity of parties necessary to a competitive political system; support in the sense of the provision of blocs of loyalty, of cadres of activists and policy-proposers, of supportive propaganda, possibly also of a press and finance. Whatever may be the attitude of manual and routine non-manual workers to the unions and to their link with the Labour Party, the fact remains that no other organisations have appeared in British society which emerged from the lives of these people and try actively to prosecute an interpretation of their interests where these conflict with others in the society. To advocate the end of all links between the Labour Party and the unions is nothing less than to advocate the end of political pluralism in Britain, for there is no social cleavage within the society to support a major degree of party competition other than that which is represented by the conflict between organised labour and capital. Further, there is little evidence that this conflict is merely a historical legacy, for the past decade has seen a revival of several of the issues at the heart of the conflict. In the face of the country's economic decline and the international recession such issues as full employment, the welfare state and the nature of managerial prerogatives are again at the top of the political agenda.

It is possible for other major cleavages to exist in societies, when there are deep cultural (including racial, linguistic, religious and national) divisions which provide a more salient basis for social allegiance than class and which are able to generate their own organisations and social networks. In such societies organised labour may indeed play a subsidiary part in forging the major political divide. However, even then it is rarely if ever altogether absent. For example, while there is no labour party as such in the USA, and American labour unions remain less political than most, it is nevertheless clear that, apart from a temporary lapse in the early 1970s, the unions form part of the Democratic Party coalition. In the Netherlands, a society primarily divided on cultural-religious lines, there is both an orthodox Labour Party and important union-based wings to some of the Christian parties, with the result that in several areas of policy these parties behave rather like labour parties.

However fragile the unions' political involvement sometimes seems, this is partly because it can be taken for granted. Were action taken to sever the link as it now exists it would re-form, though probably through different means. A useful example of how this occurs may be found in the history of Germany. A re-establishment of the old Weimar party–union relationships was prohibited by the *Grundgesetz* of the Federal Republic which, as part of de-Nazification, prevented the formal affiliation of economic interest groups to political parties and also provided state subsidies for parties to render them independent of interest group support. The unions also wished to avoid the appalling factionalism which had left them divided before the Nazi onslaught in 1933. Today they continue to stress their political independence. However, in everyday relations it is clear that their relations with the Social Democratic Party are close. Union officers and activists provide an important source of party members and activists; policy platforms are similar; union leaders regard an SPD-led government as 'their' government; even more SPD parliamentarians are union members than are British Labour MPs; and Social Democratic cabinets have contained more former union leaders and senior union officers than have recent British Labour cabinets.[4]

The fact that union links with political parties are not unique to Britain but exist in nearly all democratic societies is itself evidence that one is not here dealing with some historical oddity, but with a central characteristic of advanced capitalist societies. Certain white-collar unions or minor confederations may maintain indifference, but this is never true of the bulk of the movement, and even in these exceptional cases one often finds that union officials and activists are in fact strongly involved in labour movement parties. A notable case is that of the Confédération Française Démocratique de Travail (CFDT) which, after cutting itself off from the Catholic rump of the Confédération Française de Travailleurs Chrétiens (CFTC) in the mid-1960s, found itself as the only significant manual union confederation in Europe without some party connection. After a few years experimenting with a return to early French syndicalist traditions, by the early 1970s the confederation had aligned itself fairly closely to the French Socialist Party.[5]

The Peculiar Relationship

Discussion has so far been in terms of some kind of general link between labour movement parties and trade unions. It is now necessary to consider the specific form taken by the relationship in Britain; at this point one ceases to move comfortably through generalities that apply to a broad range of liberal democracies. In comparative perspective the relationship between the political and industrial wings of the labour movement in this country appears distinctly odd, an oddness that may be summarised in terms of the dependence of the party on the unions. This dependence can be related to another striking characteristic of the British Labour Party: while, in terms of its capacity to win elections, it is among the most impressive labour movement parties in the world,[6] it is, in comparison with many others, organisationally weak. It is poor, has few staff and a low and declining individual membership. The party 'solves' this weakness by its extreme dependence on the unions; but this raises the question: to what extent has this dependence caused, perpetuated, or extended the weakness, by inhibiting the search for more imaginative solutions?

Some of the dependence can be traced to early history. In only two European countries, the first two European industrial nations, Britain and Belgium, did the union movements found their respective political parties.[7] Elsewhere socialist parties forged trade union movements out of the congeries of craft societies and similar bodies which were springing up with industrialisation. (An extreme case are the Scandinavian Social Democratic and Labour parties, which acted as their countries' first trade union confederations.) Much of the constitutional domination of the Labour Party by the unions dates back to these origins. Today the relationship has three aspects: (1) the web of informal ties and mutual dependencies; (2) the party's financial dependence on the unions; and (3) the unions' constitutional dominance of the party's decision-making organs. The first of these is similar to that found in most labour movements, but points (2) and (3) form the core of the unusual dependency relationship, and are indeed closely linked.

The party depends on the unions for something over 80 per cent of its money.[8] Union support comes partly from affiliation fees; partly from special donations to election funds, nationally and locally; and partly from a mass of instances of help with facilities, premises and personnel. Until 1980 the national party was a tenant, on favourable terms, of the Transport and General Workers' Union, and throughout the country local party headquarters are often situated within union premises. The extent of this dependence is unique among the major labour movement parties of Europe, for two reasons. First, in other countries there is often substantial state aid for political parties, something which does not exist here.[9] Secondly, and more curiously, individual membership of the Labour Party is considerably lower than that of the Conservative Party, while elsewhere in Europe the membership of major socialist and communist parties is almost universally higher than that of their right-wing rivals.[10] This is even true in France, where the membership base of the Socialist Party has usually been stronger than that of the Gaullist and other parties of the right, even though the latter have monopolised government since the mid-1950s. In Germany the SPD has always had a larger membership than the two Christian parties, even though the latter have obtained a higher share of the popular vote in all federal elections except one since the founding of the Federal Republic.[11] This membership weakness of right-wing parties outside the UK helps explain why state finance for political parties is accepted as uncontroversial by many of them but fiercely opposed by British Conservatives.

How is the membership weakness of British Labour to be explained? One cannot seek an explanation in terms of general national characteristics because the Conservative Party has such an extraordinarily high membership. Of course, if one includes the collective membership of the party affiliated via union membership, Labour's membership is enormous. But one cannot legitimately do so since all comparable labour movement parties elsewhere[12] depend on individual membership. Indeed, if a union member wants to be active in his local Labour Party he is expected to become an individual member; it cannot be claimed that millions of workers do not bother with individual membership because they regard themselves as already members through their union. But does the fact of collective membership provide a consoling myth of a mass membership of 6 million, and the revenue to go with it, which relieves the party of the necessity of working hard to build a genuine mass membership?

The financial dependence is closely related to the constitutional one. The formal expressions of this are the extremely high proportion of votes at the party conference which are cast by union delegates, and union domination of the National Executive Committee (the unions directly elect twelve of the twenty-eight members, and through the strength of their Conference vote control the choice of the further six members who are elected by Conference as a whole). Between 1955 and 1977 the union share of Conference votes grew from 82 to 89 per cent, the change reflecting both a rise in union membership and a decline in individual membership of constituency labour parties (CLPs).[13] Unions can affiliate for any number of members they like, up to a ceiling of the number of their members who have not elected to contract out of the political levy proportion of their union subscription. Many unions affiliate for less than their potential, either in order to save money, or (in the case of the very biggest unions) so as not to appear to be throwing their weight around. The number of affiliations bears no necessary relation to the number of members who even vote for the Labour Party in elections.

The millions of votes cast by union delegations at Conference do not therefore represent millions of persons, and the conference cannot be regarded as an exercise in mass democracy. The nearest analogy is that of shareholder voting in limited liability companies. A union's vote depends, not on the views of a particular number of its members, but on the size of the financial stake, in terms of membership affiliations (shares), which it has decided to put into the party. The position of CLPs is not very different; whatever their membership they are required to affiliate for, and receive Conference votes in respect of, a minimum of 1,000 members. The majority of CLPs have considerably fewer than this,[14] so their votes too do not represent persons, but financial stakes. The fact that by convention all votes are cast as blocks, irrespective of the balance of opinion within the group deciding policy for the CLP or union, only strengthens the analogy with share-holding voting. This analogy is helpful in making sense of an apparently unique procedure,[15] but it is rarely discussed in such terms. It is obviously embarrassing for socialists to acknowledge that they have based their internal procedures, not on democracy, but on financial stake; but Conservatives, who enjoy drawing attention to the oddness and lack of democracy in Labour procedures, may not like to recognise that they bear a distinct similarity to those of their own favourite form of organisation!

The main point for our present purpose is that the Labour Party is an organisation responsible, not to a mass membership, but to a group of other organisations, and this is because of the union connection. But does it matter? Would the Labour Party behave any differently if its relations with unions more closely resembled those of labour movement parties elsewhere?

Assessing the Record

The aspect of the peculiar relationship which excites the most interest is the most trivial: the presentational point that it *looks* bad for a party to be the creature of a particular interest group, especially one which is often unpopular. Trivial though the point may be in substance, it may well have hurt Labour in several recent general elections: 1959, 1970, February 1974 and 1979.[16] The Australian Labour Party has suffered similarly in the past from the even more direct control exercised over its policies by the unions.

It is far more difficult to judge whether the unions actually use their power to shift the policy of the party in directions it would not have followed if the unions had not had such power. Would Labour policies look very different if the party's relations with the unions were, say, similar to those of the SPD? Observers seem agreed that union financial contributions have never been made an issue in disputes between unions and party, such as that over the 1969 Industrial Relations Bill.[17] Unions have rarely used their financial sponsorship of individual MPs as a means of trying to dictate their conduct, and on occasions when local branches have tried to do so they have usually been repudiated by the national leadership.[18] Members of the trade union group (TUG) of Labour MPs are expected to raise, as individuals, questions of interest to their unions, but that is part of a far more widespread system of MPs acting as spokesmen for outside interests, and in many of the commercial arrangements far more money changes hands than in union sponsorship of a candidature each general election. On only one recent occasion has the TUG acted in concert on a political issue, over the 1969 Industrial Relations Bill. However, the initiative to do so came, not from the unions, who rather ignored the group and preferred to lobby through their direct line to ministers, but from the MPs themselves, and there has been no suggestion that they acted other than from their own convictions. The case illustrated a general point, and one which has more to do with the practice of British government than with party–union connections: an interest group will usually make more progress working through its extensive links with ministries than through backbench MPs.

While it would be folly to deny that union leaders appreciate the value to them of close ties with a major party, there is occasionally evidence of their embarrassment at their potentially all-powerful role in a field that is, after all, not their speciality. Thus, during the debates over state financing for political parties surrounding the Houghton Report, party-affiliated unions strongly supported state financing, fully conscious that this would have reduced the party's dependence on them. At the time of writing, the party's constitutional tangle over the formation of an electoral college to replace Labour MPs as the sole constituency electing the party leader has demonstrated an interesting paradox: of all the proposals for the structure of a college, the ones that give the least role to the unions are those coming from the big unions themselves.

We might have evidence of union power were we to find cases of the union block vote imposing a policy on the party which directly contradicted the votes of GLP delegates at Conference, or of similar clashes between union and other representatives on the NEC. Some such instances will be considered below. But some methodological problems arise here. The unions loom so large within the party that we cannot, as it were, assume them out of existence, examine how everyone else was acting and conclude that that was how the party would have acted in the absence of the unions. It may be that, were the unions not to play their present role, much of the activity that is now conducted through union channels would be diverted to the CLPs. On the other hand, it is conceivable that, in a party less tied to trade unions, activists in the rest of the party would feel less committed to union interests than do people in the British Labour Party.

With these cautionary points in mind we may turn to the historical record of party–union relations. On this basis the following conclusions may be drawn.

(1) *The form taken by the union connection may have inhibited Labour's growth as a mass membership party;* partly by providing a false sense of large size and by reducing the need for members as a source of revenue; and partly by reducing the CLPs to a marginal role in decision making. This speculative conclusion is based on the discussion above.

(2) *If the union vote at Conference and in the NEC has pulled the party in a different direction from that sought by the CLPs, it has (with one important exception) been in order to support a centre-right leadership against the left.* That this has been so should not be surprising. While CLP policy stands are decided by activists, those of unions are usually determined by leaders and officers, who are more likely to share the caution and pragmatism characteristic of party leaders. Leading figures of the right within the party, for example, Sidney Webb and Hugh Gaitskell, have been grateful for the stability and moderation they felt was represented by the union presence.[19] For most of the party's history, and especially during the 1940s and 1950s, the majority of union leaders provided what McKenzie termed the Praetorian guard for the party leadership, sometimes in defiance of occasional left-wing majorities among the CLPs.[20] The majority of NEC representatives elected on union votes have tended to be from the right and centre of the party, while the CLPs have often elected left-wingers. During this period the socialist left, which was relatively uninterested in union affairs anyway, was the party faction which opposed the block vote. The important exception concerned the only major occasion when the parliamentary leadership suffered a temporary defeat at the hands of the party outside Parliament; at the Scarborough conference in 1960, when the party adopted unilateral nuclear disarmament, over 60 per cent of CLPs voted with Gaitskell against unilateralism, while a majority of unions voted in favour.[21]

But in general the majorities within the unions and the CLPs have stood together: until the mid-1960s they did so on the right;[22] but since the late 1960s increasingly on the left. But the leftward movement has been more pronounced within the CLPs than within the unions.[23] The now right-of-centre minority within the NEC depends on union as opposed to CLP votes, and bigger minorities of the unions have supported the parliamentary leadership than of the constituencies.

(3) *The nature of union participation in the party at national level is such as to make the party vulnerable to almost random shifts in policy that do not necessarily reflect broad trends in opinion among the party's supporters.* In addition to the oddities of the unions' constitutional role in the party already discussed, two further points are relevant: first, a union's Conference vote is a block vote; secondly, since the unions' main business is industrial relations, their political positions may change as unintended by-products of industrial factors. Thus a slight change in leading personnel, determined by internal and often non-political criteria, can lead to a shift in several hundreds of thousands of votes at party conference. A striking instance of this occurred in 1956. Arthur Deakin, the right-wing leader of the TGWU, retired in 1955, having ensured the succession of a man of similar views. However, this man died unexpectedly within a few months, and left-winger Frank Cousins stood next in line for the post. On several issues he was able to move the union's million votes from the right to the left, the most dramatic case being the 1960 vote on unilateral disarmament which shifted the majority within the entire conference.

In fact, a change could come about with no changes in personnel or even in the opinions of individuals at all. Let us assume that in a particular year union A with 100,000 members, which adopts line *(a)* at Conference, amalgamates, for purely industrial reasons, with union B, with 500,000 members, which adopts line *(b)*. If the addition of the smaller union's leaders to the executive of the larger union is insufficient to shift the balance of opinion within that union, line *(b)* will have gained 100,000 votes at the expense of *(a)* at the next Labour Party conference without a single opinion being altered.[24] Alternatively, if the addition of union A leaders to union B's executive turns a minority within the latter supporting *(a)* into a majority, line *(a)* will have gained half a million votes, and line *(b)* lost half a million, again without any change of personnel or opinion! Somewhat differently, unions which have affiliated below their maximum may make sudden changes in their membership level. In the late 1960s the emergence of left-wing in place of right-wing leaders in just four unions was decisive in shifting the position of the entire party.[25]

The move of two of these figures, Jack Jones and Hugh Scanlon, towards the centre of the party in 1975 swung the movement temporarily away from the left, until their retirement. Jones's union, the TGWU, then moved to the left again. (Scanlon's union, the Amalgamated Union of Engineering Workers, AUEW, shifted further to the right on the election of his successor, though Conference voting by the AUEW, the second biggest union within the party, has always been unpredictable.) To a certain extent it can be claimed, however, that these changes did reflect changes taking place in the positions of political activists within the unions, though questions remain as to the representativeness of these activists of Labour voters as a whole. Since union membership is not limited to Labour Party supporters, there is no guarantee that the election of individuals who then wield hundreds of thousands of votes at Conference and in elections to the NEC has not been secured by Conservatives, Liberals, or Communists.

Similar points affect union conduct on the NEC. The deals among unions which lead to a particular pattern of representation often have little to do with politics, but concern inter-union industrial relationships. The political complexion of the committee is therefore to some extent the chance outcome of a series of extra-political decisions.

These oddities would not be important were there to be a large number of unions each wielding a small proportion of the total vote; in that situation random changes would, in the medium and long term, cancel each other out. But that is not the case. Not only does a small number of very large unions control a very high proportion of the total vote, but their share has been growing. This growth has, again, been for reasons quite unconnected with politics: a general growth in union membership and, in particular, union amalgamations. In 1955 the two largest unions held 25 per cent of the total conference vote, the three largest 34 per cent and the six largest 53 per cent. By 1977 this had risen to 32, 42 and 58 per cent respectively.[26]

(4) *The formula which once ensured a certain stability in the unions' party role has been destroyed by the politicisation of industrial relations and incomes issues which has occurred since the 1960s.* The 'formula' in question was that the union leadership would support the parliamentary leadership, while the latter would ensure that a Labour government would respect the unions' sacred preserve of free collective bargaining.[27] In other words, each group of leaders would respect and protect the autonomy of the other. With temporary interruptions, this formula worked until 1967. From that point onwards the deteriorating position of the British economy and the role of union wage and manning practices within it led successive governments to intervene increasingly in industrial relations and collective bargaining in ways which most unions regarded as hostile.[28] The detailed history of incomes policy, industrial relations legislation and tripartite policy bargaining will be found elsewhere.[29]

Where party–union relations have been concerned the important points have been: (1) that waves of intervention by Labour governments have destroyed the terms of the formula, and thus the basis on which most union leaders offered support to the parliamentary leadership; but ironically (2) that the party leadership, when comprising the government, has leaned ever harder on that support to secure union co-operation on income restraint and industrial relations reform.

This process and its built-in tensions reached their apogee during the 'social contract' period of the 1974–9 government. On the 'positive' side the peculiar relationship showed its capacity when, between 1974 and 1977, Britain moved from virtually unrestrained wage militancy to union co-operation in securing a temporary reduction in working-class living standards in response to economic crisis. While this shift was 'helped' by widespread fear of economic catastrophe, the union–party connection (personified in the figure of Jack Jones) was very heavily used indeed.[30] Despite the fact that the connection is increasingly limited to the level of leaderships, it appeared for a time the only rallying point for a minimal consensus in the country as a whole. Further, in the process the unions also gained major improvements in their own legal position and that of individual workers *vis-à-vis* their employers, these agreements all stemming from an intensified form of party–union collaboration through the TUC/Party Liaison Committee established in 1972.[31]

But this co-operation had shallow roots. It was a temporary departure from a more pronounced tendency for union leaders to desert their Praetorian guard role as Labour governments intervened in industrial relations. By 1978 the underlying tensions burst through and it proved impossible to maintain collaboration. The terms of the old formula have now disappeared. It is not possible to envisage a Labour government which can promise to respect free collective bargaining, unless it is willing to jettison an even more central plank of Labour politics: the pursuit of full employment. Is there any possibility of a new formula, which would concern the terms on which a Labour government and a union leadership would co-operate on incomes policy and industrial relations reform? The claim that such a formula existed was embodied in the social contract idea, was central to Labour's platform in 1974, and was intended to be the party's platform again in 1979 until its credibility was damaged by the strikes of the winter. The matter is therefore not one of abstract speculation, but has been at the heart of politics since the mid-1970s.

Union Decentralisation

The question of the viability of any 'new formula' will be partly determined by the peculiarities of British party–union relations. Since long spells of labour movement party government in other countries have been associated with precisely such a formula,[32] there are good grounds for explaining some of the difficulties of the British case in terms of the fact that the party–union *modus vivendi* has always been concerned with regulating the unions' potential domination of the party, rather than with the requirements of unions and party in the pursuit of the economic policies of a Labour government. But this is only part of the answer. To complete it we need to look beyond the essentially political world of the unions as actors within the Labour Party, and turn to the day-to-day conduct of industrial relations.

Here two major facts stand out. First, British unions have been uniquely successful in securing their goals at the industrial level alone. Where unions in other countries have often needed political action to win, say, a legal right to recognition by employers, British unions have, in general, achieved this through their own industrial strength. At the same time, and perhaps as a result of this fact, British unions have been more willing than some Continental ones to be content with those goals which can be achieved industrially and require little political initiative.[33] Meanwhile, the conditions that helped determine this characteristic – Britain's position as the first industrial country and its concomitant world economic supremacy – have disappeared. What, therefore, beyond inertia, sustains the strength of the union commitment to unfettered collective bargaining? For the answer we must look to the second outstanding fact about British unions: their considerable decentralisation.

There is no other country in which an autonomous union strength has been concentrated at shop-floor level with such power, for so long, and across so broad a range of industries. And over the past fifteen years or so decentralisation has spread to many sectors previously regarded as centralised. Many of the gains made by British workers in recent years must be attributed to this phenomenon. But this very same feature has led to such a poor record on other aspects of policy of importance to the labour movement. For example, the commitment to full employment runs the constant risk of provoking inflation unless there is some artificial restraint on earnings exercised by organised labour. But that implies a union leadership capable of making strategic decisions and taking macroeconomic considerations into account when formulating wage policy. This is forestalled by union decentralisation. It is this association between full employment and wage restraint which begins to make sense of the observed association between labour movement party participation in government and union centralisation in several other countries.

Similarly, decentralisation inhibits the capacity of unions to make deals which stick. If unions are to use their strength at the national political level, they have to be capable of guaranteeing some kind of restraint in the exercise of that strength in exchange for concessions; otherwise there is little to be gained for governments in making agreements with them. The period during which the unions made significant gains in this kind of political bargaining, the mid-1970s, was also the period of temporary centralisation. When that centralisation collapses it is difficult to see on what grounds the national leadership can invite its bargaining partners to continue to treat with it, while by definition the shop-floor movement itself is incapable of acting on a national political stage.

British unions are caught by their own structure in a position where, in order to make gains, they strike ever harder at the shop-floor level where their power is usually concentrated, thereby increasing the damage done to the labour movement's overall political position. Decentralised local groups are incapable of taking into account the impact which their combined actions will have upon the whole, because the actions of any one group do not have a discernible effect at the macro level.[34] For example, a mass of competing wage claims may stimulate or perpetuate an inflation from which no one gains, making it rational for everyone to accept restraint. But if there is no means of co-ordinating restraint, any one group must fear that restraint by it alone will lead to its being left behind. It is therefore rational for it to achieve whatever it can. Similarly, a number of incidents during strikes which cause public outcry (as occurred during winter 1979) may result in a political attack on the unions which might weaken their powers. If so, it would be rational for the movement to exercise restraint over the conduct of disputes, as indeed the TUC tried to do in arrangements reached with the government in the wake of the 1979 strikes. But if there is no real means of co-ordinating restraint, any one local group must fear that restraint by it alone will lead to its being left behind, while it will still suffer from the political attack consequent on the lack of restraint of others.

But advocating greater centralisation is not by itself very helpful. How is it to be achieved? Would it not lead to an unhealthy substitution of bureaucracy for rank-and-file participation? Would it not undermine the labour movement's most impressive achievement, shop-floor strength?

Union activists will not exchange the real strength they have won on the shop floor for the often shadowy talking-shops that comprise national tripartite activity. While unions have been well represented on forums for discussing national economic policy, the outcome of such deliberations has always enjoyed lower priority than the economic measures deemed necessary by the Treasury. In its turn the Treasury has been guided by the need to maintain a high parity for the pound sterling, a need dictated by the importance of the City of London, which always lies beyond the reach of the tripartite forums. The most complete example of this was the collapse of the National Plan and failure to devalue sterling in 1966. During the mid-1970s the place of the strong pound was temporarily taken by the first experiments with monetary policy, but since then monetarism has in turn become wedded to a high sterling strategy, and the pattern of the financial sector pursuing its interests at the expense of industry has been resumed, now aided by the economic impact of North Sea oil. Most industrialists favour the retention of an autonomous and powerful financial sector, despite the damage this does to their immediate concerns, because through it they can escape from the declining industrial sector into more profitable outlets. Labour, on the other hand, is wedded to the interests of domestic industry, partly because the ranks of organised labour are concentrated there, and partly because the industrial sector appears to be the best source of high levels of employment. The failure of all three periods of Labour government to do anything to adjust this balance is one of the factors which render unrealistic the hope that unions would find their main role in overall national economic policy-making alongside a Labour government, on the Scandinavian model.[35]

Setting such problems aside, what would be the future of the shop-floor movement in a trade unionism more concerned with economic development than with free collective bargaining within individual sectors? Is there no channel for that extraordinary fund of energy and activism other than the pursuit of wage claims and the defence of working practices which in the long run increase inflation, reduce employment and spoil competitiveness? There is no easy solution to that problem, but one possible approach was started and promptly dropped by the last Labour government. The Bullock Report, *Industrial Democracy,* raised the possibility of a form of participation that (1) might express itself more constructively than present shop steward power; (2) would probably have appealed to the same activists as does shop-floor bargaining; and (3) might have tied company-level representatives more closely to overall union policy because of their dependence on the union for technical advice. There was indeed a case for arguing that shop-floor power could only advance further if it did so through participative channels, because of the increasing complexity of company decision-making.

So the outline emerges of a union leadership which, at the national level, might acquire some real capacity to share in determining the parameters of economic policy, and which as a result and in exchange would be prepared to secure a wage policy consistent with economic objectives. The limits on shop-floor autonomy implied would be partly compensated for by worker participation in company management. This would be a very different union movement from that with which we are familiar, but it would look more like those which have proved compatible with lengthy spells of social democratic government in Scandinavia, Austria and, to a certain extent, West Germany. But how likely is it that a Labour government would pursue the kinds of policies necessary to establish such a situation?

Let us examine the positions of the factions whose rivalry currently dominates internal party debate. The left, as at present dominating the NEC, is alert to the problem of industrial strategy and, without entering the question of whether its particular economic policies would be effective, it is probable that it could engage union cadres in national policy-making more thoroughly than in the past. On the question of industrial democracy the left within party and unions is as undecided as the rest of the Labour movement. Certainly some members of the left (such as Bullock Committee members Lord Wedderburn and Jack Jones) saw the possibilities, but many were suspicious of its potentiality for incorporating and blunting the edge of shop-floor conflict. There were few signs of a campaign to save Bullock from the savaging it was receiving from the CBI and the Labour right.

On a third relevant issue, unfettered collective bargaining, the position of the left is hypocritical. Its strategy of rapid reflation based on increased public spending behind a shelter of import controls would run the risk of very rapid inflation were workers to use the economic recovery to recoup living standards that had declined during the recession. The inflationary forces would be particularly strong as import controls limited supply, at least in the short run. It is difficult to avoid the conclusion that the left's economic strategy requires, even implies, conscious wage restraint in at least the early stages, and it is highly relevant that the calculations of the effect of a protectionist policy made by the Cambridge Economic Policy Group assume income restraint, enforced by controls,[37] while political advocates of the policy are offering it as an alternative to income restraint!

It will be argued by the left that pursuit of its policies by a government would attract the spontaneous co-operation of shop stewards and other activists. This is the kind of egocentric optimism often sincerely believed by politicians which an outside observer must leave out of account: 'So long as our friends see us there in office, carrying out our promises, they will automatically rally round . . .' The truth is that the left has become hopelessly committed to the cause of decentralised free collective bargaining, so that it is unable to spell out the unfortunate consequences for that cause of its own preferred economic strategy. The reasons for this take us back to the relatively recent association of the socialist left with trade unionism which helped break up the earlier pattern of the unions' right-wing role within the party.

The rise of shop-floor power produced union activists who were politically conscious but who could not identify with the policies of the Labour leadership in the 1965–9 period. The established left embraced this new radical element within the movement, the first fruits of the new alliance being the strong opposition of Tribune Group MPs to the prices and incomes legislation of the government. At the same time the old left was becoming increasingly dependent for support within the CLPs from small groups on the far, formerly extra-party, left. These groups, previously excluded from political influence by their own insignificance and by the Labour Party's now abandoned proscription rules, had grown during the various social disturbances of the late 1960s. While primarily recruited from student and young professional classes, several such groups have achieved considerable support from union activists seeking to locate their shop-floor work in some kind of political framework but finding official social democracy unresponsive to their problems. Here, their main power base lay in the espousal of unrestricted union militancy. Acceptance of this doctrine by the established left, together with the relaxation of the proscription rules, enabled many of these people to enter the party. Support for free collective bargaining is thus now a lynch-pin of the strength of the whole Labour left, despite its uncomfortable implications for policies of economic planning and full employment. Thus, Tony Benn, writing on union wage policy, acknowledges that the unrestrained pursuit of wage claims may cause problems, but skirts the problem of restraint by suggesting that unions therefore need to extend their goals beyond wages by further developing free collective bargaining on other issues. He does not say whether these issues might still involve problems of rising unit labour costs.[38]

Turning to the social democrats within the party, who may be broadly identified as the faction which has dominated the policies of recent Labour governments, one finds a very different but also flawed policy. The right is acutely aware of problems posed by free collective bargaining. In office it has used both voluntary and statutory incomes policies and in doing so has leaned heavily on support by union leaders. It has left to them the problem of rank-and-file activism, with which it has itself made no attempt to come to terms as part of the same labour movement. Instead it treats it with unconcealed hostility, confident of its wider electoral unpopularity. While offering considerable participation in national forums to union leaders, the right has done little about the problem noted above of the inefficacy of much of this activity and has failed to make good Labour's claim to be the 'producers' party'.[39] The right must also bear much of the responsibility for the failure of Bullock. Right-wing unions were as divided on the issue as were the left, but it was a group of centrally placed social democratic ministers (in particular Edmund Dell and Shirley Williams) who were responsible for watering down the Bullock proposals to the point where they stood no chance of union acceptance.[40] This showed an extraordinary failure of imagination. There could be little sense in a Labour government simply setting its face against shop-floor power, or trying to divert it into very weak forms of participation, since this underestimates the value placed by many union and party activists on the achievements in pushing back for frontier of managerial control which shop-floor militancy has won. The Labour right must still confront the question: how does it propose to coexist with shop-floor power?

In conclusion, one should draw attention to the changed context within which these questions will have to be resolved. An important consequence of the current recession, indeed a conscious intention of recessionary policies, is likely to be a decline in shop-floor power. Workers fearing redundancy are less willing to take opportunistic action; lay-offs provide employers with a chance to shed 'troublesome' workers and ensure that they do not find work elsewhere; many workers will blame militants for the problems being experienced by their companies; and unemployment always reduces the pressure of workers' demands and the viability of the strike threat. There are therefore certain to be setbacks for decentralised union strength, though it may well prove partial and temporary. Shop-floor power has over the past two decades spread to an increasing range of occupations, and it must be expected that when an economic recovery eventually occurs, shop-floor power will also recover its strength. Meanwhile, the hiatus could provide an opportunity for the various factions in the Labour Party to adjust their response to it; will any of them do so?

Notes: Chapter 7

1 L. Minkin, 'Left-wing trade unionism and the tensions of British Labour politics', in B. E. Brown (ed.), *Eurocommunism and Eurosocialism: The Left Confronts Modernity* (New York: Cyrco Press, 1979), p. 238.

2 M. Moran, *The Union of Post Office Workers* (London: Macmillan, 1974), and B. Roberts *et al.*, *Reluctant Militants* (London: LSE, 1972).

3 K. W. Wedderburn (ed.), *Labour Relations Statutes and Materials* (London: Sweet & Maxwell, 1979).

4 H. W. Schmollinger, 'Zur politisch-gesellschaftlichen Bedeutung von Gewerkschaftsmitgliedern: Gewerkschafter in Parteien, Kirchen und Vereinen', U. Borsdorf *et al.* (eds), *Gewerkschaftliche Politik: Reform aus Solidarität* (Cologne: Bund-Verlag, 1977).

5 J. D. Reynaud, 'Trade unions and political parties in France: some recent trends', *Industrial and Labour Relations Review*, vol. 28, no. 2 (1975), pp. 208–25.

6 I have used labour parties, socialist parties and social democratic parties as interchangeable terms when speaking comparatively, as the different names have no consistently distinctive meanings between countries.

7 Between 1945 and 1976 the British Labour Party had held 46 per cent of Cabinet seats, a level exceeded by labour movement parties only in Sweden (94 per cent), Norway (79 per cent), Denmark (60 per cent) and Austria (51 per cent) among the eighteen main capitalist democracies – and in some of the other countries the figure represents occasional coalitions between more than one labour party. See W. Korpi and M. Shalev, 'Strikes, industrial relations and class conflict in capitalist societies', *British Journal of Sociology*, vol. 30, no. 2 (1969), pp. 164–87.

8 Outside Europe, the Australian and New Zealand labour movements developed somewhat similarly to the British, of which they were in any case descendants.

9 Lord Houghton, *Financial Aid to Political Parties*, Cmnd 6601 (London: HMSO, 1977).

10 Trade union affiliation fees account for 90 per cent of the total income of the national Labour Party, but that is not the full extent of financial help afforded at that level. CLPs have their own sources of income, within which local union donations will be included, but probably at a far lower level than the national party; unions do not affiliate on a block vote basis to CLPs.

11 In 1977 the combined membership of the CDU/CSU was 824,641, compared with 1,006,316 for the SPD. See B. Schäfers, *Sozialstruktur und Wandel der Bundesrepublik Deutschland* (Stuttgart: Enke, 1979).

12 In Norway and Sweden unions are able to affiliate their members to the labour movement political parties, but they do so by taking decisions at the local branches, and affiliate at the local level. Actual membership is then limited to those workers choosing to take advantage of the facility. The ability of a small number of national decision-makers to define large numbers of union members as party members characteristic of the UK is therefore wholly lacking, and there is no such thing as a union block vote.

13 L. Minkin, 'The party connection: divergence and convergence in the British labour movement', *Government and Opposition*, vol. 13, no. 4 (1979), pp. 458–84.

14 In 1979 only 85 out of 623 CLPs affiliated for more than 1,000 members, according to the Conference Report (p. 23). It can be assumed therefore that in the great majority of cases the number of conference votes bears little relation to the size of the membership.

15 Not all union or other donations are reflected in affiliations; in that sense, affiliation fees constitute shares in the equity, while other contributions are the equivalent of non-voting shares.

16 During the year preceding the 1959 general election the party was widely considered to have damaged its reputation by supporting the TGWU in an unpopular and prolonged bus strike in London. The 1970 election followed the conflict between unions and government over *In Place of Strife,* and the Conservatives made an issue of Labour's capitulation to the union position on this. In February 1974, while the Conservative government's handling of the mining dispute obviously dissatisfied many voters, Labour's support for the miners was not popular either. The party polled fewer votes than the Conservatives, and achieved its smallest share of the electorate since 1935. In the 1979 election, which followed the 'winter of discontent', Labour did even worse than in February 1974. While election results cannot be immediately attributed to particular industrial relations events, there is direct evidence of increasing public hostility to trade unions; see Chapter 1 above.

17 J. Ellis and R. W. Johnson, *Members from the Unions,* Research Series No. 316 (London: Fabian Society, 1974).

18 Minkin, 'The party connection'.

19 R. T. McKenzie, *British Political Parties,* 2nd rev. edn. (London: Heinemann, 1964), p. 505, and P. Williams, *Hugh Gaitskell* (London: Cape, 1979), p. 541.

20 M. Harrison, *Trade Unions and the Labour Party since 1945* (London: Allen & Unwin, 1960), and D. Howell, *British Social Democracy* (London: Croom Helm, 1976).

21 K. Hindell and P. Williams, 'Scarborough and Blackpool', *Political Quarterly*, vol. 33, no. 3 (July 1962), pp. 306–20.

22 McKenzie, op. cit., p. 562.

23 L. Minkin, *The Labour Party Conference* (London: Allen Lane, 1978).

24 However, in some cases unions which amalgamate keep their own executives and continue their own political line.

25 Minkin, 'The party connection', p. 470.

26 ibid., pp. 483–4.
27 I. Richter, *Political Purpose in Trade Unions* (London: Allen & Unwin, 1973).
28 It should be noted that a minority of union leaders has long supported more or less permanent incomes policy, e.g., the postal and telecommunications unions and the National Union of Railwaymen.
29 L. Panitch, *Social Democracy and Industrial Militancy* (Cambridge: Cambridge University Press, 1976), and C. Crouch, *The Politics of Industrial Relations* (London: Fontana, 1979).
30 Crouch, op. cit., ch. 4.
31 It is difficult to estimate the extent to which the exceptionally important role of the unions in that period can be attributed to the particular form of the British union–party link. Against such an attribution are the facts (1) that the process of taking union leaders deep into national economic discussions as an inducement to wage restraint had in fact begun under the Conservative government of Edward Heath; and (2) that major improvements in union law as part of a general understanding between unions and state were undertaken in most European countries at around the same time.
32 C. Crouch, 'The conditions for trade-union wage restraint', in L. N. Lindberg and C. S. Maier (eds), *The Politics and Sociology of Global Inflation* (Washington, DC: Brookings Institution, forthcoming).
33 F. Leijnse, 'Workplace bargaining and trade union power', *Industrial Relations Journal*, vol. 11, no. 2 (1980).
34 This reasoning is based on the theory of collective action. See M. Olson, *The Logic of Collective Action* (Cambridge, Mass.: Harvard University Press, 1965).
35 C. Crouch, 'Varieties of trade union weakness: organised labour and capital formation in Britain, Federal Germany and Sweden', *West European Politics*, vol. 3, no. 1 (1980), pp. 87–106.
36 Lord Bullock, *Industrial Democracy*, Cmnd 6706 (London: HMSO, 1977).
37 A. Singh, 'North Sea oil', in F. Blackaby (ed.), *De-industrialisation* (London: Heinemann, 1978), p. 209.
38 A. Benn, *Arguments for Socialism* (London: Cape, 1980), pp. 153–5.
39 F. Longstreth, 'The City, industry and the state', in C. Crouch (ed.), *State and Economy in Contemporary Capitalism* (London: Croom Helm, 1979).
40 J. Elliott, *Conflict or Co-operation? The Growth of Industrial Democracy* (London: Kogan Page, 1978).

8 Power in the Labour Party: the Issue of Intra-Party Democracy

ROBERT McKENZIE

The struggle within the Labour Party during 1980/1, the most serious internal crisis the party had faced since 1931, saw the re-emergence of an intractable problem which had been repeatedly fought over, and never decisively resolved, since the formation of the party at the turn of the century: the problem of intra-party democracy. In the recriminations which followed the party's defeat at the election of May 1979, the left argued that a principal explanation of what it considered to be the party's mediocre, if not disastrous, record in office during 1964–70 and 1974–9 was that the party's leaders and representatives in Parliament had wholly escaped the control of the party membership outside Parliament; and in addition, that successive Labour prime ministers and cabinets had ridden roughshod over the decisions of the NEC and, even more important, those of the party's annual conference. Hence the left-wing campaign spearheaded by Tony Benn to transform the internal machinery of the party. At the party conference in Blackpool in the autumn of 1980[1] Mr Benn and his associates won two of their three initial objectives. The conference confirmed that henceforth all Labour MPs would be subject to reselection; and it voted to 'widen the franchise' for election of the leader of the party. (A special conference of the party held in January 1981 at Wembley proceeded to adopt a form of electoral college which provided that in future elections for the leadership of the party, 70 per cent of the vote would be cast by extra-parliamentary groups – the trade unions 40 per cent and the constituency parties 30 per cent – while the members of the PLP would cast 30 per cent of the vote.) On only one issue, the attempt to transfer final control of the election manifesto to the NEC, were Mr Benn and his allies defeated; but they promised to renew the struggle for this objective at the party conference in the autumn of 1981. These changes were denounced as a threat to parliamentary democracy by those who were to set up the Council for Social Democracy in early 1981 under the leadership of Roy Jenkins, Shirley Williams, David Owen and William Rodgers, all of whom had been senior ministers in recent Labour governments.

Clearly the endemic confusion over intra-party democracy (along most major policy differences in the party) now seems likely to lead to a major schism in the party which could affect its fate for decades to come.

The first part of this chapter provides a brief reminder of the differing views of leading members of the Labour Party on the issue of intra-party democracy over the past eighty years and the second part attempts an explanation of why parties of the left and, for that matter, political theorists of the left, have tended to find it so difficult to comprehend the relationship between 'intra-party democracy' and the democratic institutions in the broader polity.

I

Writing in 1937, Clement Attlee gave what could be considered the classical definition of intra-party democracy in the Labour Party. 'Conservative conferences', Attlee wrote, '. . . simply pass resolutions which may or may not be acted upon . . . [They] are generally more like demonstrations than conferences. Leaders come down and make speeches, but they do not really depend on these gatherings to lay down lines of policy, far less do they in any way feel bound to follow them.' And to emphasise the contrast between the Conservative and Labour Party organisations in this regard, Attlee added that the Labour Party Conference 'lays down the policy of the Party and *issues instructions* which must be carried out by the Executive, the affiliated organisations and its representatives in Parliament and on local authorities . . . the Labour Party Conference is in fact a Parliament of the movement' (my italics).[2]

It may seem astonishing that Attlee should have offered this flatfooted statement about the right of the Labour Party Conference to issue instructions to its representatives in Parliament when, from the earliest days of the Parliamentary Labour Party after 1906, the parliamentary leaders had on a number of occasions made clear their resistance to the idea that they should be required to accept instructions from the annual conference. For example, when the 1907 conference passed a resolution on women's suffrage with which Hardie, then chairman of the PLP, did not agree, he startled the conference by saying that 'if the motion they had carried that morning was intended to limit the action of the Party in the House of Commons, he would have seriously to consider whether he remained a member of the Parliamentary Party' and a few years later he wrote: 'in the House of Commons the membership of the Party decide their own policy without interference from the Executive or any outside authority. This is the right which the Parliamentary Party has always claimed, and which has never been seriously challenged.'[3]

Yet despite Hardie's insistence on the ultimate autonomy of the PLP, the party has never since managed to clear its mind on the subject and Attlee's insistence in 1937 on the right of Conference to issue instructions to the PLP has repeatedly cropped up in the great policy debates which have surfaced within the party until our own day. No better illustration can be provided than the struggle over unilateralism in 1960/1. After it was clear that Gaitskell had won the battle, *The Times* remarked:

> Mr Gaitskell and his loyalist majority in the Parliamentary Party have surely exploded the theory that the Party Conference is the policy-making body which issues orders to the MPs and their chosen leader. None of last year's exaggerated claims for the powers of the Conference can be seriously made for years to come – until, in fact, the Labour rank-and-file have a total lapse of memory.[4]

But *The Times* underestimated the almost infinite capacity for wilful self-deception in even the higher reaches of the party. Within a month after it had become clear that Conference would reverse itself and fall in line with the majority of the PLP, the chairman of the NEC, R. H. S. Crossman, could write, in the light of these events, that it was clear that 'the extra-parliamentary party . . . [is] the final authority on policy issues . . .'.[5] And after presiding over the actual conference that reversed itself, he declared in an interview that this proved 'yet again' that Conference had final authority in matters of policy.

Interestingly enough, it is doubtful if Hugh Gaitskell himself had thought through the nature of the problem of intra-party democracy until he found himself caught in the trap over unilateralism in 1960. In the previous year (on 17 July 1959) when there seemed to be no real prospect that the Labour Party Conference would 'go unilateralist', Gaitskell had been asked in an interview with the present writer about his views on the powers of the conference. He had said that the conference should not try to 'dictate to a future Labour government exactly what it should do' but he added: 'of course, the great issues of principle must be settled by the conference'. The transcript of this interview continues as follows:[6]

> *Interviewer:* Well, if it can settle great issues of policy, suppose the conference carried a resolution in favour of unilateral nuclear disarmament . . . would that not bind a future Labour government?
> *Gaitskell:* I think that would, yes.
> *Interviewer:* And therefore that would be [a great issue of principle]?
> *Gaitskell:* Yes, I would certainly accept that.

Yet at Scarborough a year later Gaitskell was advancing the argument that it was precisely on the great issues of principle that a major parliamentary party cannot be forced to reverse itself at the behest of its extra-parliamentary organisation, unless that parliamentary party is prepared to surrender all claims to electoral respect. This was the very core of Gaitskell's argument in his famous speech to the 1960 conference; and it was, in effect, the basis of his claim to the loyalty and support of the PLP in the successful struggle to reverse the conference decision in 1960/1.

But there is, of course, another strand in the debate over intra-party democracy within the Labour Party. In 1930 Beatrice Webb quoted Sidney as saying that 'the constituency parties were frequently unrepresentative groups of nonentities dominated by fanatics and cranks, and extremists, and that *if* the block vote of the Trade Unions were eliminated it would be impracticable to continue to vest the control of policy in Labour Party Conference'.[7] And ironically, after his strange claims about unilateralist debate of 1960/1 having demonstrated the final authority of the party conference, Crossman, only two years later, picked up Sidney Webb's theme in his introduction to a new edition of Walter Bagehot's *The English Constitution:*

> since it could not afford, like its opponents, to maintain a large army of paid party workers, the Labour Party required militants – politically conscious socialists to do the work of organizing the constituencies. But since these militants tended to be 'extremists', a constitution was needed which maintained their enthusiasm by apparently creating a full party democracy while excluding them from effective power. Hence the concessions in principle of sovereign powers to the delegates at the Annual Conference, and the removal in practice of most of this sovereignty through the trade union block vote on the one hand, and the complete independence of the Parliamentary Labour Party on the other.[8]

II

Why has the Labour Party, like many other parties of the left, and so many political theorists concerned with the role of parties in democracy, found it so difficult to grasp the relationship between intra-*party* democracy and the formal democratic institutions of the polity?

Much confusion has arisen from the fact the Michels, in his study of the oligarchical tendencies within organisations, and most of those who have followed in his footsteps, have grouped together political parties on the one hand, and trade unions and all other forms of voluntary associations on the other, as if they fulfilled broadly comparable functions in the political system and, in effect, constituted a single species of social aggregate. But, in fact, in a democratic political system political parties fulfil a fundamentally different function from that of all other forms of organisation. And this difference in function, which will be examined below, is of critical importance in discussing the problem of oligarchy. In the case of interest groups and all other forms of organisation except political parties, the trend toward oligarchical control may hinder the fulfilment of their appropriate functions in the political system. But in the case of political parties oligarchical control by the party leaders of their party organisation is indispensable for the well-being of a democratic polity. To restate the position in another way: it may be desirable to maximise intra-organisational 'democracy' (which, borrowing Robert Dahl's phrase, I shall take to mean 'a relatively high degree of control of leaders by their followers') within interest groups and voluntary associations; but intra-*party* democracy, strictly interpreted, is incompatible with democratic government.

The all-important distinction between political parties and interest groups lies, of course, in the fact that the primary function of the former is to sustain groups of political leaders who offer themselves as potential governors of a political community, while the function of the latter is, in Eldersveld's phrase, to 'aggregate, articulate and transmit group demands' (these demands are transmitted to, among others, the particular group of party leaders who constitute the government).

If a political party is successful in an election and its leaders form a government then, whatever the party's internal arrangements – whether in theory the leaders are subject to control of their followers or not – the party leaders, under whatever label, become the chief decision-makers within the political system. And almost every political system has rules which provide that the government and ruling party in the legislature cannot be subject to the direction of any body of political decision-makers outside the legislature.

In arriving at their decisions the leaders of a party who have formed a government will be subject to an enormous variety of pressures and demands. These will include the views of foreign governments, the claims and promptings of their followers (and their opponents) within the legislature, the advice of their permanent officials, an enormous array of (often conflicting) group demands, the pressure of public opinion, of press comment, and so forth. Above all, of course, they must contend with the 'hard facts of the situation' (which may range from a balance-of-payments crisis to a crop failure and food shortage). The party leaders *qua* government must determine public policy in the face of these pressures, problems and demands. In doing so they will take into account – to a greater or lesser degree – the ideology of their party (if it can be said to have one), their electoral programme (which is rarely explicit enough to act as a continuing guide to government policy making) and the *ad hoc* pressures from their supporters outside the legislature on particular issues as they arise.

But these party pressures, taken together, can be only one factor to be taken into account by the leaders of a governing party in a pluralistic society. If they were at every point to be given an over-riding importance, and in particular if the party leaders *qua* government were to hold themselves responsible to the organs of the party outside the legislature – as a strict theory of intra-party democracy would imply, then these party organs would supplant the legislature and the executive as the ultimate decision-making bodies in the polity. The organs of party would transcend in importance the organs of government, as is usually the case in totalitarian political systems.

Although members of the party organisation outside the legislature cannot formally, in any strict sense, control the activities of their leaders who constitute a government, they can often exert very considerable influence over them. The activists among the party members play, in many systems, a very important role in nominating and renominating candidates; they constitute the vital nucleus of the party's electioneering organisation; and they often play a predominant role in drafting the resolutions which are debated at party congresses. The party leaders, therefore, even when they are in government, will take great pains to retain the confidence of their followers and, so far as is consonant with their other responsibilities, will try to fulfil their expectations.

Between elections the party organisation outside the legislature becomes, in a sense, yet another interest group, with which the party leaders *qua* government must contend. But they constitute an interest group with a special channel of communication with the government (the party machinery) and with special sanctions which they can apply if they are dissatisfied with the government's performance. While interest groups proper can do no more than threaten, more or less openly, to persuade their members to vote in the next election against the government which has failed to meet their demands, the party activists by withdrawing their labour, can, in effect, dismantle the governing party's electoral machine.

For a variety of reasons, the mass of party members are most unlikely to attempt to take advantage of the opportunities they theoretically enjoy to bring over-riding pressure to bear on their leaders who are in government. (For the most part these are the psychological and 'technical' reasons for oligarchy which Michels has so brilliantly analysed.) But it is surprising that students of oligarchy in organisations have not recognised more clearly that political parties are unique among organisations in that their leaders must *escape* control of their followers if they are to fulfil their broader role as the principal decision-makers in the political community. And it is even more surprising that lip service is still paid to the 'ideal' (albeit the 'unattainable ideal') of intra-party democracy when it is so clearly incompatible with the working of democratic government.

The parties of the democratic left are particularly prone to confusion on this point. The older parties, which in most cases existed in the legislature before they found it necessary to create popular organisations for electioneering purposes after the expansion of the franchise, have usually recognised and insisted that their mass organisations could have no more than 'advisory' functions in policy-making (or alternatively, as in the case of American parties, it becomes recognised that the party's electoral programme drawn up at the quadrennial conventions is in no serious sense binding on the party's presidential candidate should he be elected). But social democratic parties, which in most cases emerged from the world of trade unions, co-operative societies and socialist sects – in which intra-organisational democracy was an article of faith – perhaps understandably assumed that intra-party democracy was a logical concomitant. Typically, therefore, they devised party constitutions which attempted to ensure that the party leaders would be in some sense under the direction and control of the party members. When the party leaders subsequently became members of governments, and in most cases refused to accept either direction or control from the hard core of party activists who tended to control the party organisation outside the legislature, the result among their followers was often disillusionment and despair. One wonders how many democratic socialists – who may never have heard of Michels himself – arrived at conclusions similar to his own about 'the futility of democracy based on a party system'.

The problem of oligarchy in organisations other than parties cannot be examined in detail here. But it must be noted that the problem is different in kind from that discussed above. While the tendency of party leaders to escape the direct control of their followers is essential for the operation of democratic government in a pluralistic society, the comparable tendency towards oligarchy in interest groups and all other voluntary associations raises very difficult problems, especially in situations in which particular interest groups operate in non-competitive situations. It tends to be assumed that the leaders of all organisations must to some degree represent the interests of their members, otherwise they would 'vote with their feet' and leave the organisation. But, as we move towards what Samuel Beer has called a quasi-corporatist society, membership of certain 'voluntary' associations – whether trade unions, professional, or business associations – becomes almost mandatory. Granted that in the great majority of cases these associations have no formally organised and legitimised system of competition for leadership, this is the true context in which the 'iron law of oligarchy' represents a threat to the working of a democratic political system. Oligarchy in political parties helps to preserve for the leaders of a party (when they constitute the government) the necessary freedom of action, in the course of 'attending to the arrangements of the society', to permit them to take into account all other group volitions and demands in that society. But oligarchy within interest groups represents a continual threat to the effective transmission of those volitions and demands. In the interests of efficiency it may be inevitable that governments should, in effect, welcome the establishment of monopoly representation for each principal interest in a society. But much more attention needs to be paid both by social scientists and by governments to the problem of maximising the degree to which interest group leaders reflect the views of their members.

If, as has been argued above, any rigorous form of intra-party democracy is both impossible and unworkable (partly for the reasons elaborated by Michels, but more important, because it would be incompatible with democracy in the polity as a whole) then what criteria must be taken into account when attempting to determine whether a political party is, in any sense, 'democratic'?

(1) It might be suggested that one criteria would be whether party members have an opportunity to take part in the election of the leader of the party (and his principal colleagues?) for fixed terms of office. Thus by a variety of devices the members, or rather the declared adherents, of American parties participate in an indirect election of the party leader as presidential candidate. (And in certain parliamentary systems too – such as that of Canada – the party leaders are also chosen at national conventions which are mainly representative of the party organisations outside the parliament.) But there are many other parties which by common agreement would be considered 'democratic' in which the members of the mass organisation play no formal part whatever in the choice of leaders.

In the case of the British Labour Party, for example, the leader has hitherto been elected by the vote of the Labour MPs who are, of course, elected by the Labour *voters*, not by party members. (In opposition the Labour leader's principal colleagues are also chosen by vote of the Labour MPs although when the party is in office – unlike the Australian Labour Party, which elects the Cabinet – the British Labour Party permits the leader a completely free hand in choosing his ministry; even the formal machinery requiring that the leader should consult certain of his backbench colleagues and the secretary of the party outside Parliament – an arrangement set up after MacDonald's defection in 1931 – has subsequently been ignored by Labour leaders in composing their cabinets).

In the case of the British Conservative Party, until it adopted a new procedure in 1965, the leader was invariably chosen by a process of informal consultation among the leading figures in the party in both Houses of Parliament and in the party organisation outside Parliament. No formal electoral contest for the party leadership was ever held.

The party now provides for a ballot in which its MPs alone take part (the leaders of the extra-parliamentary organisation are no longer given a voice).

If, as I would argue, both the Labour and Conservative parties are 'democratic', then it would follow that it is immaterial whether the members of a democratic political party have a formal voice in choosing the leader of their party (or whether the leader is elected for a fixed or an indefinite term of office.)

(2) Is the existence of a 'mass organisation' of supporters an indispensable prerequisite if a political party is to be considered democratic?

It can be argued that such mass party organisations are desirable in the interests of the good health of the polity. A political party with a fairly large-scale membership outside the legislature is thereby able to spread its financial burden more widely and to avoid excessive financial dependence on a small group of wealthy supporters. In addition, the existence of a large mass party membership may help to involve a larger proportion of the electorate in political activity. The evidence on this point does not suggest conclusively, however, that this consequence follows. The *paper* membership of the mass organisation of British political parties as a proportion of the total electorate is one of the largest in any democracy. Yet the turnout at elections in Britain is one of the lowest among the major European democracies.

An even smaller proportion of the party membership is normally involved in candidate selection or in the choosing and briefing of delegates to the party's annual national conference. So few party members are involved in these conference procedures that there is a continuing risk that an 'unrepresentative' minority may attempt to foist on to the parliamentary party and its leaders policies with which they fundamentally disagree. On most occasions, until the 1960s, this danger was precluded by the working arrangement between the leaders of the parliamentary party and the leaders of a majority of the big unions which usually ensured that the conference endorsed the policies of the parliamentary leaders. When this arrangement has broken down – as in 1960 when Conference rejected the views of the party leaders and adopted a policy of unilateral nuclear disarmament – the parliamentary leaders refused to be bound by Conference decisions with which they disagreed and proceeded to organise the support necessary to secure the reversal of the Conference decision the following year.

On balance it is self-evident (above all when the Labour Party is in office) that both initiative and final authority in decision-making have in the past been in the hands of the leaders of the parliamentary party. But it could be argued that the party's formal commitment to the proposition that the annual conference of the mass party determines party policy has led to perennial intra-party conflicts of a sort which have seriously undermined public confidence in the party and made the Labour Party a less effective contender for power than would otherwise have been the case.

But even if it could be shown that, on balance, the existence of 'mass-parties' of the British type had contributed to the well-being of the polity, it would not seem justified to argue that the existence of extra-parliamentary activity of this sort is an essential prerequisite if political parties are to be judged 'democratic'. Many parties in other polities have either a tiny formal membership or none at all, in which case they usually rely on an *ad hoc* rallying of supporters on the occasion of an election, and make no serious attempt to enrol them on a permanent basis. There is certainly no ground for arguing that such parties must for this reason be classified as 'undemocratic'.

I would therefore argue that neither of the two criteria suggested above – the election of the party leaders by the party members, and the existence of a mass party organisation outside the legislature – can be accepted as an indispensable criterion of 'party democracy'.

(3) A third criterion might be whether the party leaders are both (*a*) *responsible* to the electorate (in the sense of being subject to its arbitrament at periodic intervals) and (*b*) *responsive* to its wishes in the periods between.

The second of these two considerations raises the old argument as to whether democracy means 'government by public opinion'. I would take the view that a political party need not be *responsive* to public opinion to any prescribed degree between elections so long as it remains *responsible* to the electorate, in the sense of abiding by the rules of the game in subjecting itself to electoral judgement and vacating office if it is defeated. In practice, this latter consideration will no doubt tend very strongly to ensure the former (i.e. 'responsiveness' to the presumed wishes of the electorate). But it is none the less a matter for the collective judgement of the party in Parliament and its leaders as to how far they accommodate themselves to public opinion, especially when that opinion is at variance with their own (or expert) opinion on a particular issue. For example, had Churchill become leader of the British Conservatives in the 1930s and decided to defy, rather than accommodate himself to, the mood of appeasement in Britain (which others had used as a justification for a *policy* of appeasement), this would not have made the Conservative Party one whit less democratic, so long as it continued to submit itself to the periodical electoral judgement of the nation.

It could be argued that in a competitive political system the sole criterion on which one can judge whether a party is 'democratic' is whether it abides by the rules for conducting the electoral competition between the parties and the other rules governing the operation of the democratic system. Or, if it proposes to change these rules or institutions, it openly declares its purpose before it is elected to office; for example, if a party proposed to introduce a new electoral system – which might, arguably, work in its own favour. I would, however, automatically classify as 'undemocratic' parties which proposed, if they secured power, to terminate the open competition for political leadership.

To summarise the argument of this chapter: much of the confusion about 'intra-party democracy' arises from a tendency among partisans of the left, in particular, to confuse the functions of interest groups and the voluntary associations with those of political parties. In the former, oligarchical control by leaders is *dysfunctional* for the democratic process; in the case of the latter, the process by which the leaders of political parties escape the control of their party members is *functional* for the working of democracy. If Attlee's (1937) definition of intra-party democracy were rigorously applied, then the Labour Party Conference, 'issuing instructions' to Labour MPs, would, at least when Labour was in office, supersede Parliament as the supreme governing body of the nation.[9]

Notes: Chapter 8

1 *Report on the Labour Party Annual Conference 1980* (London: Labour Party, 1981).
2 C. R. Attlee, *The Labour Party in Perspective* (London: Odham, 1937), p. 93. When he subsequently reflected on his experience in office Attlee took a very different view; see F. Williams, *A Prime Minister Remembers* (London: Heinemann, 1961), p. 91.
3 Quoted in E. Hughes, *Keir Hardie* (London: Allen & Unwin, 1956), p. 208.
4 *The Times*, 12 June 1961.
5 See the exchange of correspondence on this issue with the present writer in the *New Statesman*, 30 June and 7, 14, 21, 28 July 1961.
6 This passage is reproduced from my *British Political Parties*, 2nd edn (London: Heinemann, 1964), p. 626.
7 Beatrice Webb's Diaries, 19 May 1930, folios 53–4.
8 R. H. S. Crossman, foreward to W. Bagehot, *The English Constitution* (London: Fontana, 1963), pp. 41–2.
9 Interestingly enough, Joseph Chamberlain, the principal founder of the mass party in Britain, spoke in 1877 of his plan for 'a truly Liberal Parliament outside the Imperial Legislation' which could formulate party policy and control the actions of Liberal MPs. Quoted in McKenzie, *British Political Parties*, p. 12.

9 Representation in the Labour Party

DENNIS KAVANAGH

The ever-present struggle for power in the Labour Party seems to have reached a new and perhaps decisive stage, with the constitutional reforms voted for at the annual party conference in October 1980 and the special conference in January 1981. The changes – selection of the party leader by an electoral college no longer composed exclusively of MPs, Labour MPs to face a continuous process of re-selection by their constituency parties, and the NEC to draw up the party's election manifesto (passed in October, defeated in January) – are regarded as significant by both advocates and critics. At the time of writing (January 1981) there is no certainty about how the party will resolve its disagreement over these constitutional issues. It is clearly understood by the rival groups that the changes concern the fate of many other policy issues which also divide the party, and the strength of different groups in the PLP. The situation is fluid, and likely to remain so for some time, as defeated groups are tempted to seek to reopen the constitutional questions or leave the party – as defectors to the SDP have done. If the changes are confirmed, some time will have to elapse before the consequences can be properly studied. A new set of traditions and usages, a new 'cake of custom' which colours the working of all constitutions, will not be created overnight.

Demands for constitutional changes in the party are not new. The original draft of the 1918 constitution, for example, stated that it was the task of the NEC, 'prior to every General Election, to define the principal issues for that Election'. Only after protests by the PLP was the constitution amended to allow the PLP a voice in preparing the manifesto. Such demands have been made before, usually in the name of 'reform', or making the party more 'democratic' and 'representative'. The usual object has been to bring the party in Parliament (PLP) and a Labour government more firmly under the control of the movement, or the extra-parliamentary institutions.

What is clear, however, is that as the party's decision-making processes have been opened to public scrutiny, so there has been growing concern at how decisions which purported to be 'democratic' and 'representative' were made. This aspect has been neglected amid speculation about the probable impact of the changes on the policies, the fortunes of personalities and factions, and the likelihood of an exodus of malcontent

MPs. The political left and right have sought to question the democratic credentials of their opponents. They have appropriated and defined differently terms like 'participation', 'democracy', 'grass roots' and 'accountability'. Underlying the dispute is a conflict about the idea of respresentation. Defenders of the independence of the PLP and proponents of Conference supremacy have very different views of 'democracy' and 'representation' in mind. What is remarkable, however, is how the constitutional changes have been achieved without so many other anomalies being touched. For example, it is apparent that Conference, the parliament of the movement, has a curious electoral roll; with its mythical votes, vote-buying by trade unions and local parties, and weighted suffrage, it is redolent of the unreformed British Parliament before 1832.

Before we learn to live with the new institutions and the 'new' Labour Party it is worth exploring in more detail the notion of representation in the 'old' party. There has been a learned and sometimes an acrimonious debate about the location of sovereignty in the Labour Party, as the rival claims of the PLP and Conference were canvassed. The gap between the bolder claims for Conference sovereignty and the actual record, particularly when Labour was in office, has allowed defenders of the PLP to point to traditional practice and usage in resisting reform. The reformers, on the other hand, could point to the 'myth' of Conference supremacy and the idea of intra-party democracy, which are implicit in the party's constitution – never abandoned or decisively flouted – and impose them on the party at large. The tensions and different views on this question are now almost part of the fabric of the party.

In focusing on the different styles of representation in the structure of the Labour Party, this chapter looks, first, at political representation in Britain. It next looks at the NEC, particularly its structure and composition. It then examines the role of the annual conference, particularly the parts played by the unions and the constituency parties, and how the delegates represent their members. Finally, the chapter assesses the likely consequences of recent proposals to make the party organisation more democratic.

I: Political Representation

The Labour Party challenges many features of the British political system. The party has a written constitution and a federal structure, and provides for a sharing of authority between different institutions. The British constitution, on the other hand, is largely uncodified, the system is unitary and formal sovereignty resides in Parliament. The theory and practice of Labour's constitution have given rise to a distinctive style of internal politics arising from its attempts to reconcile the ideal of intra-party democracy with practical aspects of government and traditional British political practices. Recurring themes of Labour politics include: an emphasis on procedural democracy; debates about constitutionalism; frequent overlaps of rival positions on the constitution with left and right factional stands on issues; prolongation of disputes as factions have continued their disagreements across the different organs of the party; and a style of party leadership that places a premium on skills in power-sharing and managing both the parliamentary and extra-parliamentary wings.

An interpretation of the British (or English) attitude to political authority usually takes more note of the Tory emphasis on hierarchy and the independence of government.[1] But the Labour Party's original modest views of leadership as an activity and of the leader as an office-holder are important also. The emphasis on the participation of the membership, respect for majority voting and mandates, the values of anti-elitism and the accountability of leadership to the rank and file pose a contrasting set of values. Although the practice has deviated frequently and sharply from the theory, adherence to these 'founding' values is still widely regarded as the proper code of conduct in the Labour movement.

Some critics of the party's commitment to intra-party democracy have questioned its compatibility with such established British conventions as the autonomy of MPs and the sovereignty of Parliament.[2] Yet the two ideas have so far managed to coexist and, apart from the 1960 conference resolution on unilateral disarmament, the PLP has managed to avoid an outright confrontation with Conference. Coexistence has depended on a general willingness by the different groups to make the constitution work, and the ambiguities, omissions, and room for manoeuvre allowed in the party constitution itself.[3] The Labour Party, more so than most organisations, contains a large element of mythology, one which must not be confronted too openly. As one observer notes, the constitution 'only works when not too many questions are asked about it'.[4]

Such a pragmatic attitude may explain the traditional neglect (even by the recent commission of inquiry) of what representation means in the Labour Party. The questions 'who speaks for the party?' and 'when the party speaks, who does it speak for?' are important and have been neglected. The costs of such neglect have been seen in the confusion about the principles which should guide the reform of the party. Of course, the questions of who is to be represented and how raise many practical difficulties – not least about power in the party – and risk offending entrenched interests, as well as involving scrutiny of many hallowed traditions and procedures. My argument is that attempts at fundamental reform of the party's structure have foundered and will continue to do so because of the unwillingness to grasp this conceptual nettle. The limited impact (as well as the limited nature of the proposals) of inquiries into the party organisation and structure (1955, 1968 and 1980) all illustrate the point. The 1980 commission's proposal of an electoral college to represent the different interests of the party in electing the leader was generally considered to be 'unworkable' when the party confronted the practical aspects of election procedures and how the members of the college could be mandated. At the 1980 annual conference the principle of a broader suffrage was carried by a majority of 98,000 out of more than 7 million votes. Yet the commission ignored such major issues as the structure of the NEC, the block vote of the unions and selection of union delegates to Conference. The reforms proposed in the 1980 party conference and the January 1981 special conference all moved towards 'democratisation', while leaving these questions untouched.

The term 'representation' has acquired different meanings and emphases within the Labour Party as well as within the British political system. A person may, for example, be considered a representative of his constituents as long as he is freely elected and dependent for re-election on them. The term may also refer to a similarity between the representative and those who elect him (e.g. in terms of social characteristics or opinions). Or it may refer to a relationship, for example, that the representative is instructed or mandated, or is in other ways responsive to the views of his constituents. Interestingly, all three major institutions of the party, the PLP, Conference and the NEC, may each lodge a claim to represent the party according to one of the above definitions.

The annual conference, with over a thousand elected delegates voting on behalf of nearly 7 million party members, decides the party's policies and is, in Attlee's words, 'the parliament of the labour movement'. Twenty-seven of the twenty-nine members of the NEC are elected by all or some Conference voters; the executive represents the different sections of the party and is 'subject to the control and directions of the Party Conference, the Administrative Authority of the Party' (Party Constitution, Clause 9, s.1). Finally, there are the MPs who in the 1979 general election were returned by 11·5 million voters. Thus, delegates at Conference may claim to represent the membership of their organisations, the NEC to represent the delegates and, via them, the members, and the PLP to represent the voters. One may discern different forms of representation at work in the Labour Party – functional representation in the trade union section of the NEC, social representation in the women's section of the NEC and representation as a relationship, operating variously through mandates and the direct election of Conference delegates and election of the party leader by MPs.

In looking for clues to the party's ideas about representation it is useful to start with its structure and historical evolution. The original notion of the party as 'an alliance of labour', a coalition of groups with different interests as well as shared goals, has been preserved, even though it has developed from a parliamentary pressure group, speaking for the interest of labour, to a national party of government. The 1918 constitution has remained largely intact, though amendments have been made piecemeal and for particular purposes. The NEC, for example, was originally constituted to represent the interests of different affiliated organisations to the party. The dominant position given to the trade unions was shaped by the political contexts prevailing in 1900 and 1918; the representation on the NEC accorded to the socialist societies and women derives from circumstances which hardly exist today; and the *ex officio* seat on the NEC for the deputy leader was an expedient in 1953 to accommodate Herbert Morrison who had been voted off the constituency section of the executive the previous year. What remains striking in a comparative perspective, perhaps, is the party's continued failure to accord representation to party members as individuals rather than as members of constituent organisations. The importance of the unions as affiliated bodies means that the party is an indirect one. Consequently, it has not embraced the egalitarian principle of 'one man one vote' and left the issue of the 'block vote' untouched.

II: The National Executive Committee

The present structure of the NEC defies any coherent theory of representation. In 1900 the party was organised on federal lines, with members affiliated through the trade unions, Independent Labour Party, Social Democratic Federation and Fabian Society. There were no individual members, though by 1918 there were a few embryonic constituency parties. The NEC at this stage consisted of sixteen members: eleven for the unions, three for the socialist societies, and one for the local trades councils, Labour parties and women's organisations. In accordance with a strict federal principle each section nominated and elected its own representatives to the committee. The party's structure and electoral system allowed the groups to retain their separate identities. In addition (from 1912) there was a treasurer elected by the whole conference. The terms of the Labour alliance were that the ILP muted its demands for socialism in order to retain the money and support of the trade unions.

Those principles were broadly preserved when the new constitution was adopted in 1918. The party opened a scheme of individual membership to local constituency parties so that each constituency had its own party, replacing the local trades councils. The Women's Labour League was converted into women's sections of the new constituency parties. The reformed NEC was enlarged to twenty-three, with thirteen representatives for the nationally affiliated unions and socialist societies, five for the local parties and four for women; the treasurer, as before, was elected separately. But, in a retreat from the pure federal principle, the entire Conference elected members to the executive, though the sections were allowed to make their own nominations. Not till 1937 did the constituency parties regain the power to elect their own representatives.

Sidney Webb and Arthur Henderson had drawn up the constitution over the protests of the ILP. The new structure gave even greater power to the unions who, with five-sixths of the Conference votes, could effectively choose all twenty-three members of the NEC. Henderson's priority was to gain the support of the unions for the new party; he wanted a steep increase in affiliation fees from them and feared that they might break away and form a separate trade union party.[5] Most union leaders were also suspicious of the more prominent ILP leaders, some of whom had opposed the war. Of course, the party also adopted 'socialism', or public ownership, as enshrined in Clause 4 of the new constitution. This was a sop to the ILP. But power was so distributed in the party that any interpretation of the eventual goal would still have a trade union gloss on it. The unions were to provide the ballast against the claims of the 'advanced' socialists in Conference; according to Sidney Webb, 'if the block vote of the trade unions were eliminated it would be impracticable to continue to vest the control of policy in Labour Constituency Parties'.[6]

The composition of the NEC has been modified in the period since 1918 though the basic principles have, except for the 1937 change, remained largely intact. At present it consists of twenty-nine members. The unions elect twelve of their own members, and their votes dominate election of the five women's representatives and the treasurer. The constituency parties elect seven members and seats are reserved for the leader and deputy leader of the PLP. The Young Socialists and the socialist and co-operative societies each elect one member. The trade unions are still in a position to control elections to the NEC, with their votes determining eighteen of the twenty-nine places on the NEC.

What is surprising is that the structure and composition of the NEC have for so long escaped serious scrutiny. The structure was, of course, from the outset a compromise – between the unions and the constituencies and socialist societies. Yet it is difficult today to see the case for each of the separate constituencies to be represented on the NEC. The five representatives for the women's section, for example, are neither nominated nor elected by women members. (Indeed, the party abandoned its separate roll of women members in 1970.) As political figures of national standing they do not confine their interests to exclusively female issues. The section is a hangover from the time when it was feared that women would not be elected by the other sections. But no action was taken on the recommendation of the Simpson Report (1968) that the five women's seats be redistributed among the unions and constituency parties.

The remarkable feature of the constituency section is that it rarely elects local councillors, regional or constituency officials, or other 'grass roots' figures. Indeed, the choices for the women's and constituency sections explain the dominance of MPs on the NEC – the extra-parliamentary body. Since 1945 MPs have supplied between a half and two-thirds of all members of the NEC and over 90 per cent of the women's and constituency sections have been MPs. Yet in no sense are these MPs representative of the PLP. Since 1976 all but one of the five women and all seven of the constituency MPs have been from the left of the party. In annual elections to the twelve-man parliamentary committee – a kind of popularity contest of Labour MPs among colleagues – only a handful of the elected MPs on the NEC also gain election to the parliamentary committee, which is a more right-wing body. In 1980 only Neil Kinnock, who scraped into twelfth place, was also an elected member of the NEC. The MPs appear to be elected by the constituency delegates to Conference on account of their political orientations as well as their national prominence. Paradoxically, while members of Parliament constitute a clear majority of the NEC, MPs as such have no voting rights at Conference and no representation on the NEC. Both in the 1950s, when the Bevanites dominated elections to the constituency section, and in the 1970s, the MPs in this section have been from the minority or left faction in the PLP. Divisions within the PLP have been transferred to the NEC but with an inversion of the political balance. The irony is that the extra-parliamentary arm of the movement often invokes MP members of the NEC against the PLP itself.

A rather different pattern of representation is afforded by the Conservative counterpart to the NEC, the Executive of the National Union. This body is careful to draw representatives from different sections of the grass roots, including the areas, Young Conservatives, women and trade unions. Representatives of these groups sit *ex officio* on account of holding a formal position in the section. The parliamentary party is also represented on the National Union Executive. The Conservative practice of electing representatives because of their formal leadership position in other groups has its counterpart in elections of officials of major unions to the trade union section of the NEC. But Labour makes no provision for territorial representation on the NEC. London, Scotland, or Wales are at least as 'natural' a constituency as women, or the aggregate of CLPs, but they have no vote. As usual, this situation is a product of history, the fears of regional sentiment and interests undermining the party (see Chapter 6 above).

There is little competition for election to the trade union section of the NEC (about twenty candidates for twelve places). A series of 'understandings' and 'traditions' guarantees the major and some middle-sized unions a seat on the NEC almost as of right. The smaller unions contest elections in the hope that, by establishing a 'runner-up' status, they will have an opportunity to claim a seat in the event of a vacancy. The major unions try to keep 'politics' out of the elections. Each large union nominates its own delegate, who by convention is a senior official, though usually he is not the general secretary and does not sit on the TUC General Council. The major unions will vote for each other's candidate, regardless of his politics or personality. They are more concerned to avoid factionalism and to protect good working relationships between the unions on the TUC. Hence the bunching of votes at the top of the trade union elections, as the five largest unions affiliated to the party vote for their own and each other's candidates. In 1979 the top six of the twelve elected trade unionists each gained between 5·3 and 5·9 million votes.

Inertia and a tendency to support the sitting tenant make for a stable membership on the NEC. Over two-fifths of NEC members serve for five years or more.[7] Change usually occurs only when a member dies or withdraws from the NEC. Between 1967 and 1980 no incumbent has been voted off the trade union section, and among the women the only changes in recent years have been Joan Maynard for Lady White in 1972 and Margaret Beckett for Lena Jeger in 1980. Between 1964 and 1974 a right-wing, or 'moderate', majority of 2:1 on the NEC was gradually converted to a left-wing majority, largely through left-wing replacements for vacancies arising from natural wastage. In 1967 when Mr Crossman and Mr Callaghan (who became treasurer) resigned from the constituency section they were replaced by Mrs Lester and Mr Allaun, changes which gave the NEC a leftward tilt. Elections since 1973 of Mr Heffer, Mr Skinner and Mr Kinnock further shifted the balance to this section. The informal rules of the electoral system mean that there is often a time-lag between a change in the mood of a union delegation or Conference and its choice of NEC representatives. The latter has the opportunity to 'catch up' with the change when a vacancy occurs. It was not until after 1970 that the political outlook of the NEC reflected the leftward drift of Conference that had been established by 1967.

A party structure which provides for a separation of powers between different institutions but not a separation of personnel invites a conflict of loyalties. Labour ministers who are also elected members of the NEC are particularly vulnerable to competing loyalties. As ministers they are bound by the convention of collective Cabinet responsibility, yet as elected NEC members they are also responsible to Conference.[8] Historically, the presence of front-bench parliamentarians on the executive helped to keep the parliamentary and extra-parliamentary leaders on the same track and, for the most part, kept the latter subordinate to the former in the initiation of policy. In this situation the voice of the Labour Party coincided with the voice of the Labour parliamentary leadership.

But as the two bodies have moved in different directions and, indeed, have become rival centres of policy – as in the last decade – then problems have arisen. In 1969 Mr Callaghan used his position on the NEC to mobilise resistance to the Cabinet's proposals for trade union reform, *In Place of Strife*, and in 1974 Mr Benn, Mrs Hart and Mrs Lestor openly dissented from government policy on Chile. One solution is to insist that ministers on the NEC adhere to collective Cabinet responsibility in the event of a conflict of loyalty.[9] Another is simply to exclude ministers from membership of the NEC, thus formally recognising the independence of different wings of the movement. At present there is a 'grey area' which allowed a minister like Mr Benn to use his NEC position to promote a variety of policies for 'the party' which were sharply at variance with those pursued by the 1974–9 government. The conflict between the two sides was fully exposed when it came to writing the manifesto for the 1979 election.[10]

Apart from the annual election at Conference there are few mechanisms for establishing the accountability of NEC members. There is no formal provision in the conference timetable for members to report back on the work of their monthly meetings and subcommittees, and the annual conference report provides details only of the attendance and not the votes at meetings. Because the various electoral sections on the NEC do not have homogeneous views on most issues, it is difficult for members to speak for 'their' constituents. Over the years, therefore, much scope has been left for the discretion of individual members, a discretion which, till recently, has been exercised to sustain the position of the parliamentary leadership.[11]

III: Conference

Far-reaching claims are often made on behalf of the party's annual conference. Votes at Conference are distributed according to membership of affiliated organisations. It is largely because the delegates at Conference 'represent' the membership and determine the policy of the party that the party claims to be democratic. But the spectacle at the 1980 conference of union delegations voting on the NEC proposal for an electoral college without any consultation with members raises the question 'in what sense is Conference "representative"?'.

In the first place, it is clear that a large number of party members are either 'ghost' or involuntary members and that the numbers affiliated by local parties and trade unions bear only a rough relationship to the actual membership. Both may and literally do 'buy' votes at Conference, by choosing to affiliate on a higher number than the previous year. At present the constituency parties affiliate (or pay fees for) a minimum of 1,000 members. Recent estimates put the individual membership at about

300,000, an average of 460 per constituency, and for most members the payment of a subscription is the extent of their activity. Many local parties therefore cast a vote at Conference that is probably double the size of the actual membership.

In trade unions affiliated to the party, a political levy is deducted for each union member unless he specifically contracts out. The union then decides how much to transfer from the political fund to the Labour Party. It is open to unions to purchase the number of votes they choose, up to the maximum of their membership. And in so far as the unions' members decide policy position for the party conference, then the opportunity is presented for non-Labour voters or Labour opponents to shape policy. Surveys of the Union of Post Office Workers and Luton car workers found that only a half were aware that they paid the levy.[12] No more than a fifth of the former agreed that the union should affiliate to the Labour Party, and other national surveys have also shown clear majorities of union members and Labour voters wanting the unions to keep clear of party ties.[13] If we link these data with the decline in trade unionists voting Labour (down to 50 per cent in 1979) and the growth of such support for the Conservatives (40 per cent in 1979), then it is reasonable to assume that a good proportion of trade union votes at Conference represent either involuntary members or members who cannot be bothered to contract out. Either way, the so-called membership is grossly inflated. Certainly there is something rather far-fetched about the spectacle of the Transport Workers casting a block of over a million votes, as if this genuinely represented the views of so many people.

A second difficulty concerns the nature of the trade unions' block vote, a long-standing target of reformers seeking to 'democratise' the party. The block vote is so called because at Conference a union is handed a voting card, which bears a number corresponding to the union's affiliated membership. Each organisation is granted one party card for each 1,000 members or part thereof. In practice, the union's general secretary presents a single card which bears the size of his total vote. There is no provision for dividing the vote. The large unions used the system at the TUC conference in 1894 and it was also used at the first party conference in 1900. The procedure is not prescribed in the party's standing orders but has become customary practice. The traditional emphasis on solidarity and on respect for majority decisions in the unions makes the practice understandable. Union leaders prefer to abstain on votes rather than advertise internal divisions over issues.[14] Constituency parties and socialist societies also vote as a block. The system of winner-take-all within organisations has its counterparts both in the first-past-the-post British electoral system which allows a party with a bare majority of seats to assume full power and in the whipped party votes in the House of Commons.

But the major objection to the block vote, as to the British electoral system, is that it may produce a result which is quite unrepresentative of the aggregate votes of the individual electors. Imagine that the delegations of the four largest unions, with a combined vote of over 3 million, were each split 60:40 in favour of a motion. Instead of their votes being split 1·8: 1·2 million votes – a net difference of 600,000 – they will all be cast the same way, a difference of 3 million votes. A change of mind by one delegate in a closely divided delegation can determine the allocation of the whole vote; this is what happened to the 928,000 votes of the AUEW at the 1980 party conference. A change of political mood in a union or a delegation may come about largely through an industrial or other matter. The party's constitution and policy, as Crouch notes (Chapter 7 above) are vulnerable to these unpredictable shifts of mood.

The block vote of the major unions has been a crucial determinant of the exercise of power in Conference. At present the combined votes of the largest five unions exceed the combined votes of the other affiliated 49 unions, 548 constituency parties and 9 other socialist, co-operative and professional organisations. This provides a dual concentration of votes and power at Conference; first, in the hands of 5 out of the 600 odd units at Conference and, secondly, within the majorities of these unions.

There are three consequences of this concentration. First, there is an imbalance between the influence of constituencies and the unions; the combined votes of all the constituency parties, for example, represent only two-thirds of the votes of the Transport and General Workers' Union. Moreover, the imbalance in voting strength between the unions and the constituencies has been growing over time (Table 9.1). A second consequence is that even if the concentration does not make Conference easier to influence, then it at least enhances the opportunities for 'management' by the platform in so far as there are fewer influentials for the NEC or parliamentary leaders to 'square'. In fact, for most of the party's history, the major unions have been staunch allies of the 'platform' and the parliamentary leadership. They have generally supported the non-left side in party debates, proving to be the hammer of 'the fanatics, cranks and extremists' from the constituencies. In the early 1950s the leaders of the three largest unions, the Transport and General, the General Workers and the National Union of Mineworkers, shared a common outlook on many issues coming to Conference, and acted in concert in casting their votes.

Finally, it has made the major union leaders into 'barons' in intra-party politics. The parliamentary leaders have taken care to anticipate or inform themselves about the reactions of the union leaders to new policies and trade policy concessions for the support in Conference of the block vote. In the United States a similar block vote (the so-called 'unit rule') awarded to each state, at quadrennial party conventions to

Table 9.1 *Changes in Conference Voting Strength, 1956–80*

Trade unions	1956	5·630 million
	1980	6·686 million
Constituency parties	1956	1·150 million
	1980	0·686 million

nominate a presidential candidate, enhanced the influence of the large states and state 'bosses'. At the end of the day, the objection to a division of the block vote is not only that it would, overnight, severely limit the influence of individual unions; it might also encourage further political factionalism and organised minorities within the unions. In turn these tendencies might weaken their effectiveness in bargaining over wages and conditions of employment.

Complaints about the representative shortcomings of the system (particularly the block vote) are usually made by those on the receiving end of it; criticisms about the procedures and unrepresentative outcome tend to surface in the group which disagrees with the outcome. Traditionally, the left had cause to complain, as the big unions co-ordinated their votes to frustrate the left and support the right-wing parliamentary leadership. In the early 1950s Aneurin Bevan openly complained about the use of the unions' block vote and questioned whether the union leaders represented their members. By 1960, however, it was Hugh Gaitskell's turn to complain. Claims on behalf of the authority of the 'voice' of Conference and that it represents the voice of the 'rank and file' largely refer to the block vote of the unions. Yet any detailed examination of the mechanics of Conference voting -- regardless of whether the motions favour the left or the right – is rather chastening for those who claim that Conference votes are the voice of the ordinary party member.

IV: Delegates

One may move beyond formal procedures and the reality of membership figures to ask if the views of the delegates are representative of those they claim to speak for. Bagehot long ago noted that political activists were people of 'immoderate' views, that it was their intense concern over issues which caused them to be active in the first place. Critics point to the low participation by rank and file in union and constituency affairs, to dwindling membership of the local Labour parties, and to the different results secret ballots or postal ballots produce in comparison with elections conducted at branch meetings or shows of hands at mass meetings. They may also refer to opinion poll data which frequently show the different preferences between Labour voters or trade union members and those who presume to speak for them.

One procedure for establishing a degree of correspondence between the delegate and member is through the mandate; that is, the delegate is expected to vote in accordance with the policy instructions of the people who elect him. Most constituency parties do instruct their delegates to the annual conference on the major issues and provide an opportunity for the delegate to report back after the conference.[15] But there is no uniformity in the procedures of choosing delegates – some parties call special meetings for the purpose, others choose at the local party's AGM – and the whole process is usually informal.

The wording of the resolutions and the timing of the conferences of the affiliated trade unions – which occur between April and June before the party conference – allow some discretion for the union delegations to the party conference. As Minkin observes of the union conferences, 'some subjects were covered, some partially covered, some not covered at all'.[16] Because some union conferences meet at intervals of longer than a year the original mandate may be quite out of date when the party conference assembles. And the compositing process which produces the final resolutions for the conference may mean that only some parts of a resolution are compatible and other parts incompatible with the delegate's original mandate. There have also been occasions when a union has flatly disregarded its mandate (e.g. the action of the Woodworkers' Union in breaking its mandate on the issue of the rearmament of Germany in 1954, or the Boilermakers in voting for an electoral college for electing the leader and control of the manifesto in 1980). For both the special party conference in January 1981 and the election for the deputy leader the unions relied on various methods of ascertaining the members' views. Some held ballots or conferences, some left it to local officials and others left it to the union leaders to decide how to cast the block vote. The lack of uniformity and, in some cases, the flimsy attempt to consult prompted many observers to call for a set of guidelines or model rules.

Circumstances sometimes mean that the voice of the grass roots, when uttered, is less than faithfully represented at Conference. Yet the system can be defended. It remains the case that where the mandate is clear and the composited conference resolutions present a clear choice, then the union delegations vote according to the mandate. To objections that the votes should not be committed so far in advance of the conference debate, one may point out that whipped members of Parliament and councillors, as well as union delegations, have to cope with such pressures. Defenders may claim that the question about representativeness poses a non-problem, that it is the role of active party members – simply because they are committed, informed and concerned – to shape public opinion, and that to be out of step with public opinion at one time does not preclude the possibility of other people being converted in time. It might also be added that one can hardly complain about the procedures as long as membership of the party is open to the public, members are able to participate in decisions and delegates are freely elected. If people do not participate then they can hardly expect their views to be represented.

V: Social Representation

Occasionally demands are voiced that the party's leadership be more socially 'representative' of the rank and file. Social attributes, it is assumed, colour political orientations. A typical complaint about the PLP's social unrepresentativeness (particularly the lack of manual workers and large proportion of middle-class members) of the general electorate or of Labour voters is: 'The composition of the party and its representative groups in Parliament and town halls should broadly reflect the class, race and sex of those we claim to represent.'[17] We have seen in Chapter 4 that there is ample evidence of a similar middle-class bias in the composition of the NEC and local party activists. Some members of the Campaign for Labour Party Democracy have recommended the mandatory inclusion of at least one woman and manual worker on any selection shortlist of candidates. But the pursuit of social representation alone may produce unrepresentativeness on other dimensions. In the USA the McGovern–Fraser reforms produced a more socially representative Democratic convention in 1972, in terms of delegates who were young, or female, or from minority racial groups. But in terms of their attitudes and policy preferences they were poles apart from Democratic voters.[18] Their preferred candidate, McGovern, was duly crushed in the presidential election.

The continuing debate about the mandatory re-selection of Labour MPs illustrates a number of these problems. One complaint is about 'entryism' or the takeover by unrepresentative groups (i.e. in terms of policy preferences) in small decaying local parties. The general management committee, the local party's ruling body, consists of some sixty delegates from the affiliated organisations in the constituency and such subsidiary units within the party as ward committees and the women's section. Objections to the power of general management committees to dismiss MPs centre on whether such a small group should have this power. One remedy is to open the selection process to all, or at least more, party members. The thinking appears to be: more selectors = more participation = more representative outcomes. But proposals to open the selection to the membership at large (460 on average!) fall foul of the great 'untouchable', a change in the structure of the party which affects the position of the unions as affiliated bodies in local parties. A proposal to open the selection meeting was rejected in 1974 by the NEC, on the grounds that the system of delegates from affiliated bodies was essential to protecting the interests of the unions.

Parties in the USA and Belgium have used primaries for selecting candidates. In Belgium participation is more strictly confined to party members than in the USA.[19] But the British Labour Party, because of its adherence to delegatory democracy, has to reject the principle of one man one vote. Greater accountability of MPs to the constituency party means, effectively, accountability to the GMCs rather than the membership at large.

VI: Democratisation and Representation

'Democratisation' of the party or, more properly, party reform has come to the Labour Party quite suddenly. It is part of a wider impatience with our political institutions, many of which have been subject to reform in recent years. Both the Liberal and Conservative Parties have done something to broaden participation in the selection of candidates and leaders. In the USA there has been an orgy of major reforms designed to democratise the operations of the political parties.

A more straightforward reason why the party's 'cake of custom' has been cracked lies in the activists' perceptions of and reactions to the record of Labour governments since 1964. There was disappointment with many policies and a widespread sense of resentment and frustration at the way Conference decisions had been ignored. By 1970 the authority of Conference seemed feeble. A new generation of activists, in local parties and union branches, soon proved to be more assertive and reasserted the goal of intra-party democracy. Constitutional changes which would institutionalise the authority of the extra-parliamentary movement were seen as the means of binding the PLP to Conference.

There is also a practical reason behind the impetus for reform in the Labour Party. As the sense of shared political purpose in the movement has waned, so the separation of powers and federal structure has come under strain. It is the decline of shared agreement on political values and policies between left and right that has spilled over to affect the party's structure and established rules of the game. When majorities in the parliamentary and extra-parliamentary parties are speaking with different voices on so many issues – as was frequently the case after 1966 – then questions of representation, accountability and authority in the party assume a new urgency for both bodies.

Reforms which move in the direction of more direct democracy and accountability of leaders to rank and file are in accord with many of the party's earliest values. One view of political authority (by the Campaign for Labour Democracy) is that 'it is delegated, or vested in a representative only when it cannot be directly exercised and then only by election . . . on the understanding that the delegate is directly responsible to the rank and file.'[20] There are two key steps in this doctrine of intra-party democracy. The first, why the rank and file should control the leadership, has been well ventilated. But the second, how representative the rank and file is of the Labour electorate, is hardly ever discussed. The active minority amounts, at most, to about 100,000 out of 11·5 million Labour voters. Numbers alone are not decisive; but more important are the many signs of a growing 'gap' between the two groups. There is the loss of party members (which may mean that the remainder are even less representative), the long-term loss of Labour votes, the issue disagreements between a number of party policies and Labour voters (see Chapter 1 above), and the dominance of left-wing MPs in NEC elections.

This situation gives rise to two paradoxes. One is that greater participation may mean less representativeness, that is, participation by activists, many of whose views diverge from those of Labour voters. If the party becomes more 'purist' in the sense of absolute commitment to issue positions, regardless of electoral popularity, then it risks losing elections. In a dominant two-party system, with the parties evenly matched in popular support, and the electorate rather 'centrist' in its policy preferences, then a party which wants to gain votes has to be a 'catch-all' one. It has to accommodate and adjust to different interests, and even dilute its ideology in a seach for votes. Such a strategy is rejected by many activists. An organisation, particularly a voluntary one like the Labour Party, has to reach both voters and activists. Labour's problem is that its constitution is now giving a greater role to the members/activists, when they are a diminishing, and probably unrepresentative, number.

Any organisation or movement has to strike a balance between commitment to its principles and to effectiveness, whether the latter be measured in internal unity, votes, making profits, or maintaining public support. The 'principled' view of the activists sees the party's goal as bearing witness to the truth, to socialism, and leaving it to people outside the party to respond. According to Crossman: 'Those who assert that their sole object, or even the main object, of the Labour Party today should be to regain office seem to me to misconceive not merely the nature of British socialism, but the workings of British democracy.'[21] The other strand emphasises the complexity of problems, the need to compromise with different points of view, to attract support outside the ranks of the already committed and, accordingly, to 'dilute' the principles in the interests of organisational effectiveness.

There is little doubt that the recent reforms will radically shift power from the MPs (elected by voters) to the trade union and constituency activists. Conversely, it seems apparent that 'pure' or 'intra-party' democracy will suffer in the search for votes and the willingness to accommodate a coalition of interests and views.[22] In Austria the Socialist Party has opened policy-making to supporters who are not members. The change was made to appeal to liberal 'floaters' and has weakened the ideological elements in the party.[23] Labour's new participatory politics will reward the activists who, by definition, will have the time, energy, ability and concern about issues to get involved. Hence the position that as the party has become more participatory, so it has been less representative of ordinary Labour voters. And whether constitutional changes will enhance or weaken a party's ability to win elections is not an unimportant consideration.

The second paradox is common to most organisations. Notwithstanding the party's formally democratic procedures, the active minority has relative freedom to set the party's goals. This is due in large measure to the quiescence of Labour voters and most members. Yet the qualities of apathy and indifference among voters limit the ability of the activists to socialise or mobilise members into acceptance of their goals. Many voters and members will vote Labour at elections and still disagree with party policies, just as members will support their trade unions in strikes while rejecting many of the union's political aims. Where an organisation's goals require relatively low levels of commitment, for example, voting or paying a levy, then apathy presents few problems to the organisation. But it may limit the effectiveness of the organisation when it tries to mobilise its followers or latent supporters for more demanding tasks or sacrifices.[24]

It is to Michels that we owe so many of our insights, as well as some of our confusions, about democracy in party organisations and its relationship to democracy in society. Michels pointed to the oligarchical tendencies in organisations, notwithstanding the best efforts of activists to retain democracy (i.e. rank-and-file control of the leader). He was aware that such pressures as electoral competition with other parties, the desire of leaders for office, and claims, made in the name of representative democracy, that the party should be representative of and accountable to the electorate, would all weaken democracy in the party. Michels wanted party leaders to be accountable to the members rather than the voters; the influence of the latter was that of 'outsiders', the 'non-elect', as it were, and would inevitably strengthen the tendencies to oligarchy and dilution of ideology.

It is interesting that so many nuances of the present debate about the party's constitution are captured in Michels's discussion. One group of reformers wants to take intra-party democracy literally and the effective implementation of the reforms would give the extra-parliamentary arm of the movement much greater control over the parliamentary arm. They are more concerned to assert socialist principles in policies, and to control the MPs regardless of the electorate. Theirs is a 'democracy of the committed', as Ian Mikardo claimed at the 1977 party conference. Spokesmen for the MPs are more concerned with winning elections, with representing the voters, and with the administrative feasibility and political acceptability of policies. These goals, in turn, require that MPs have flexibility and discretion. The former invoke the activists on their behalf, the latter invoke the electorate, and both proceed to offer different views of party democracy and 'correct' policies. So far the left has successfully exploited the theme of 'participatory democracy' and 'representation' to advance 'socialism' in the party. More control of the election manifesto, election of the party leader, also subject to recall, by an electoral college composed largely of members outside the House of Commons, and mandatory re-selection of MPs in the lifetime of each parliament, all amount to a fundamental redistribution of power to the activists.

Procedural and constitutional changes do matter. Yet it is also the case that the political left and right in the party have promoted and resisted schemes of constitutional reforms as a means of advancing their own positions and ideologies. In this sense constitutional issues may be given more prominence than their 'true' significance merits. One suspects that, given the current ideological divisions in the party, no constitution would work well. Conversely, if the diverse elements in the party united on policy and strategy, it is likely that *any* constitution would be acceptable to the different groups.

This chapter has analysed the different principles of representation at work in the Labour Party. Members of the party have held sharply different views of what 'Labour democracy' entails. To date, the various views have managed to coexist, however uneasily. Yet the constitution, in spite of the contrasting interpretations placed on it by Labour ministers and Labour activists, was unsatisfactory to both groups. The activists, in the course of the last decade, have seized the initiative to remake the party in line with their own goals, and in line with what they regarded as the party's original values. The reforms voted for in 1980–1 primarily concern the power relationships between the party organs and organisations: Conference, NEC, PLP and constituency parties. Many other aspects of democracy – concerning 'real' members, territorial representation and equal weighting of each individual vote – have been ignored. The reforms, however significant for the distribution of power in the party and the eventual working of the British constitution, have been limited and flawed, when examined against the criterion of making the party more representative of voters or members.

Appendix

At the January 1981 special party conference delegates were asked to choose in a ballot between five different methods of selecting future leaders. These were:

	Votes
Electoral college at party conference	6,283,000
Postal electoral college	434,000
Separate electoral college	11,000
Ballot of individual members	431,000
Miscellaneous	6,000

With the principle of an electoral college accepted, delegates were asked to choose between seven different proposals.

Option one NEC plan for 33 per cent MPs, 33 per cent constituencies, 33 per cent unions, 1 per cent socialist societies: 1,763,000.
Option two 38 per cent MPs, 30 per cent constituencies, 30 per cent unions, 2 per cent socialist societies: 192,000.
Option three 30 per cent MPs, 30 per cent constituencies, 40 per cent unions: 59,000.
Option four Union of Shop Distributive and Allied Workers' plan for 30 per cent MPs, 30 per cent constituencies, 40 per cent unions and socialist societies: 1,763,000.
Option five 33⅓ per cent MPs, 33⅓ per cent constituencies, 33⅓ per cent unions and socialist societies: 24,000.
Option six General and Municipal Workers' Union plan for 50 per cent MPs, 25 per cent constituencies, 25 per cent unions and socialist societies: 2,386,000.
Option seven Engineering union plan for 75 per cent MPs, 10 per cent constituencies, 10 per cent unions, 5 per cent socialist societies: 992,000.

The four least popular selections were then eliminated and a second ballot called. The outcome was: option one (NEC), 1,757,000; option four (USDAW), 1,813,000; option six (GMWU), 2,685,000.

The NEC's formula was then, in its turn, eliminated and a final choice made between the USDAW plan giving the unions 40 per cent and the GMWU plan giving MPs 50 per cent. Its result was: USDAW plan (30/30/40), 3,375,000; GMWU plan (50/25/25), 2,865,000.

The successful formula was then put, after consequential constitutional amendments had been passed on a show of hands, to a card vote for ratification. The conference voted formally to adopt the USDAW plan by 5,252,000 to 1,868,000 – a majority of 3,384,000.

Notes: Chapter 9

1 S. Beer, *Modern British Politics* (London: Faber, 1969).
2 R. T. McKenzie, *British Political Parties* (London: Heinemann, 1964).
3 For example, the constitution has no guidance as to what happens when the NEC and parliamentary leadership disagree on the contents of the manifesto. And the provision that the PLP decides, 'the method and timing' of implementing policies in the party programme provides ample room for manoeuvre by the parliamentary leadership.
4 P. Jenkins, *The Battle of Downing Street* (London: Charles Knight, 1970), p. 76.
5 R. McKibbin, *The Evolution of the Labour Party 1910–1924* (London: Oxford University Press, 1974).
6 McKenzie, op. cit., p. 508.
7 ibid., p. 520.
8 Except for the leader and deputy leader of the PLP, who are *ex officio* members of the NEC.
9 For the texts of Mr Wilson's statements on the collective responsibility of ministers in all circumstances, see his *The Governance of Britain* (London: Weidenfeld & Nicolson, 1976), pp. 232–4.
10 D. Butler and D. Kavanagh, *The British General Election of 1979* (London: Macmillan, 1980), ch. 4.
11 L. Minkin, *The Labour Party Conference* (London: Allen Lane, 1978).
12 M. Moran, *The Union of Post Office Workers* (London: Macmillan, 1974).
13 J. Goldthorpe, D. Lockwood, F. Bechhofer and J. Platt, *The Affluent Worker in the Class Structure* (Cambridge: Cambridge University Press, 1968).
14 The unions have usually been careful to distinguish their political and industrial roles at Conference. Their main concern has been to maintain free collective bargaining, while leaving policy initiatives in the hands of the parliamentary leadership. See M. Harrison, *Trade Unions and the Labour Party since 1945* (London: Allen & Unwin, 1960). Between 1956 and 1970 the unions submitted an average of twenty-six resolutions to each conference. The average for the constituency parties was 389. See Minkin, op. cit., pp. 38–41.
15 E. Janosik, *Constituency Labour Parties in Britain* (New York: Praeger, 1968).
16 Minkin, op. cit., p. 164.
17 F. Morrell and B. Sedgemore, 'Setting Labour on the long road to democracy', *Guardian*, 26 November 1979.
18 J. Kirkpatrick, 'Representation in the American national conventions: the case of 1972', *British Journal of Political Science*, vol. 5, pt. 3 (July 1975), pp. 265–322.
19 J. Obler, 'Intraparty democracy and the selection of parliamentary candidates: the Belgian case', *British Journal of Political Science*, vol. 4, pt. 2 (April 1974), pp. 163–86.
20 Morrell and Sedgemore, op. cit.

21 R. Crossman, *Labour in the Affluent Society*, Fabian Society Tract No. 325 (London: Fabian Society, 1960).

22 On this, see E. Wellhofer and T. Spencer, 'Models of political party organisation and strategy: some analytical approaches to oligarchy', in I. Crewe *et al*., *British Political Sociology Yearbook*, Vol. I (London: Croom Helm, 1972).

23 M. Sully, 'The Socialist Party of Austria', in W. Patterson and A. Thomas (eds), *Social Democratic Parties in Western Europe* (London: Croom Helm, 1977).

24 Moran, op. cit., pp. 136–7.

Index

ASTMS (Association of Technical and Managerial Staff) 108
AUEW (Amalgamated Union of Engineering Workers) 60, 180-1, 212, 220
Abrams, Mark 9-10, 45
Alt, James 14
Amalgamated Union of Engineering Workers 60, 180-1, 212, 220
Ashley, Jack, MP 80
Asia 75-6
Attlee, Earl
- Bevin's support of 55-6
- Conference, on 192-3, 201
- criticism of 62
- dependence on Cripps and Bevin 56
- government of 62, 100
- leadership of 3, 55
- minister, as 55
- Morrison's chances damaged by 56
- Morrison's services to 61
- party factions under 55-6
- party organisation, on 192, 201
- personal character of 55
- social class of 100
- succession to 55

Australian Labour Party 103, 164, 177, 198

BBC (British Broadcasting Corporation) 14, 42
Bank of England 76
Beckett, Mrs Margaret 209
Belgium 13, 175, 216
Benn, Rt Hon Anthony Wedgwood, MP,
- candidacy for leadership 60, 105
- Conference (1980), at 191
- de-centralisation favoured by 144
- detachment from colleagues 61, 66, 210
- franchise for leadership election widened by 191
- government, in 59, 61, 66, 89, 144, 210
- left-winger, as 60-1, 89, 191
- NEC membership 54, 62, 66, 210
- parliamentary leadership challenged by 62-3
- rebuked by Callaghan 66
- re-selection of MP's achieved by 191
- social class of 100, 105
- technocrat, as 59
- union wage policy, on 187
- workers' control pressed by 144

Bernstein, B 123
Berrington, Professor Hugh 4, 105
Bevan, Rt Hon Aneurin, MP 54-7, 61, 64, 66, 100, 213
Bevanites 56, 59, 71, 208
Bevin, Rt Hon Ernest, MP 55-6, 152
Bogdanor, Vernon 165
British Election Study 14, 20, 26, 38, 42
British Political Parties 7
Bullock Report 148, 185-7
Butler, David 12, 70, 74
Butskellism 132

CBI (Confederation of British Industry) 186
CFTC (Confédération Française des Travailleurs Chrétiens) 174
CLP's *See* constituency parties
CND (Campaign for Nuclear Disarmament) 57, 105, 125
Callaghan, Rt Hon James, MP,
- Benn, rebuked by 66
- Benn's assault 62-3
- career of 61
- devaluation and 59
- followers disappointed by 62
- government of 61-2
- leadership and 3, 54, 57, 60-2
- NEC membership and 54, 209-10
- party faction under 61
- popularity of 11
- revolt against Wilson 59, 66
- services to Wilson 61
- social class of 100
- succession to 55

Cambridge Economic Policy Group 186
Campaign for Labour Party Democracy 215, 217
Cant, Bob, MP 80
Castle, Rt Hon Mrs Barbara 54, 64, 88, 101
Chamberlain, Rt Hon Neville, MP 153
Chile 210
Churchill, Lord Randolph 54
Churchill, Rt Hon Sir Winston, MP 200
Clause 4 (of the Labour Party's Constitution) 96, 119-20, 207
Clay Cross 161
Cole, Professor G. D. H. 103, 152
Common Market. *See* EEC
communism 60, 181
Conference (Labour Party)
- Attlee on 192-3
- constituency parties and 210-12

delegate survey at 114
electoral college and 220
faction fighting at 111
Gaitskell defeated at 57, 193-4, 199, 213
Labour Government uncontrolled by 120, 191, 193-4, 216
left's victories at 90
leftward drift of 209
NEC elections and 205
NEC instructed by 192, 210
Parliament of Labour movement 192, 205
party constitution and 203, 216
PLP instructed by 192-4, 199
policy-making by 120, 140, 192-4, 199, 203-7
questionable democracy of 111, 177, 203, 210, 213
rank and file's part at 164, 213
representation at 205, 210
responsibility of Labour ministers to 209
reverse at hands of PLP 193, 199
selection of leader by 90
special (1981) 220
trade union dominance over 176-81, 194, 205, 207, 211-13
unilateralism and 193, 199
voting rights of MP's at 208

Conservative Goverment
collective responsibility of 59
consensus and 62
criticised by Labour left 76
electoral gap under 45
local authorities and 5, 159
planning by 63
tax-cutting by 41
temporary unpopularity of 38
trade union dealings with 173

Conservative Party
class and 19, 37
conferences of 192
Executive of 208
Labour voters and 14
leadership of 51, 198
left and right in 70
loyalty in 51
membership of 176
representative of electorate 28, 37
supporters of 26-7

Conservative policies 11, 26, 140

constituency parties
block voting by 211
decision-making 179
delegates to Conference 114-15, 132, 179, 210-14
election of party leader 164
factions in 85
general management committee of 215
ideology 85, 87, 179
left wing 87, 179-80
Liberal 164
membership of 206, 211-13
NEC and 208
Sidney Webb on 194
unilateralism 179
unrepresentative 215

Constitution for the Socialist Commonwealth of Great Britain, A 153

Constitution of the Labour Party 96, 205

Co-operative Development Agency 144

Co-operative store 162

Council for Social Democracy 191

Cousins, Rt Hon Frank 57-8, 61, 180

Crewe, Ivor 2-3, 5, 106, 108, 129-30

Cripps, Rt Hon Sir Stafford, MP 54-6, 66, 100, 103

Crosland, Rt Hon Anthony MP 2

Crossman, Rt Hon Richard, MP
Bevan's ally 57
career of 66, 193, 209
Conference, on 193-4
NEC chairman, as 193
party constitution, on 6, 193-4
party object, on 217
questionable democracy, on 194
social class of 100, 145

Crouch, Colin 6, 212

Crown Proceedings Act (1947) 157

Crowther-Hunt 147

Curtice, John 139

Dalton, Baron 100, 103

Danish Social Democrats 13, 140

Deakin, Arthur 180

Dell, Rt Hon Edmund 187

Democratic Party 105, 174, 215

Devolution Acts 143-4

Diaries of a Cabinet Minister, The 168

Distressed Areas Act (1934) 142

Donoghue, Bernard 150

Dunwoody, Hon Mrs G. P., MP 103

EDM's (Early Day Motions) 4, 72-6, 91-2

EEC (European Economic Community)
Gaitskell opposed to 57

Labour Government's application to enter 58
Labour left's hostility to 2, 27-8, 60, 71
Labour MP's advocate increase in powers of 147
Labour Party divided on 2, 27-8, 37, 62, 91
Labour policy on 2, 27-8, 42
Labour voters reject 2
Early Day Motions 4, 72-6, 91-2
Ecology Party 41
elections (parliamentary)
by-elections 14
capacity of Labour to win 175
defeat of Labour in 2, 10, 57, 59, 191
falling support for Labour at 10, 14, 17, 19, 41, 111, 129
Labour majority in (1945) 154
left-wing gains at 4
Wilson returned in 60
See also British Election Study
English Constitution, The 194
Epstein, Leon 71
Europe, political parties in
left divided 3
membership 176
Netherlands 174
professional class 103-4
right-wing 51
social democrats 12-13, 140, 174, 176, 185
social divisions 18
socialists 140, 175-6, 218
state aid 176
trade unions 174-5
European Economic Community. *See* EEC

Fabians 96, 103, 162, 206
Finer, S. E. 99
First World War 152
Foot, Rt Hon Michael, MP
elected deputy leader 60-1
elected leader 67, 71, 91
NEC membership of 54
seeming indifference to office 66
social class of 105
trade union dominance accepted by 63
Forrester, T. 121
French Socialist Party 104, 131, 140, 175-6
Future of Socialism, The 2

GLC (Greater London Council) 14
GMWU (General and Municipal Workers Union) 212, 220-1
Gaitskell, Rt Hon Hugh, MP
Bevan's support of 61
career of 12, 56, 193-4
complaint about unions' block vote 213
Conference and 57, 193-4, 213
death of 55
defeat at Conference (1960) 57
elected leader 56
followers disappointed by 62
grateful for union presence 179
leadership of 3, 56-7
nationalisation and 57
NEC membership 54
opposition to EEC 57
party faction under 57, 65, 193-4
social class of 100
unilateralism and 193
General Strike, the 152
George-Brown, Lord 57, 100
Germany 53, 71, 147, 174, 185
Golding, John, MP 80
Gordon, I. 123
Gordon-Walker, Baron 100
Greater London Council 14
Greece 76
Greenwood, Rt Hon Arthur, MP 103, 153
Guttsman, W. L. 103, 105
Gyford, John 144

Halsey, A. H. 162
Hanby, V. 102
Hardie, Keir, MP 192-3
Hart, Rt Hon Dame Judith, MP 210
Hattersley, Rt Hon Roy, MP 101
Healey, Rt Hon Denis, MP 54, 67, 101
Heath, Rt Hon Edward, MP 60, 142, 147, 159
Heffer, Eric, MP 54, 209
Henderson, Rt Hon Arthur, MP 61, 96, 103, 207
Hindess, B. 121
Hindon, Rita 9
Hirschman, A. O. 122
Holland, S. 122
Houghton Report (Report of the Committee on Financial Aid to Political Parties) 115-16, 178
House of Commons Expenditure Committee 142
House of Lords 26, 59, 62, 165
Housing Finance Act (1972) 140, 161

ILP (Independent Labour Party) 55, 206-7
In Place of Strife 210
Independent Labour Party. *See* ILP
Industrial Common Ownership Act 144
Industrial Democracy 185-6
Industrial Relations Bill (1969) 178

International Monetary Fund 60
Ireland, Republic of 13

Janner, Hon G. E., MP 103
Jay, Rt Hon Douglas, MP 100
Jeger, Baroness 209
Jenkins, Rt Hon Hugh 60, 101, 103, 191
Jones, G. W. 150
Jones, Jack 61, 180-1

Kavanagh, Professor Dennis 4, 7
Keith-Lucas, Bryan 154
Kilbrandon Report 141
Kinnock, Neil, MP 208-9

LSE (London School of Economics) 103
Labour and the Nation 153
Lansbury, Rt Hon George MP 55
Layfield Committee 156, 159
Legal Aid and Advice Act (1949) 157
Lestor, Miss Joan 210
Liberals
  absence of breakthrough by 15
  changing loyalties of 11, 67
  election of leader 164, 216
  rising vote of 130
Local Government Act (1958) 140
Local Government Act (1972) 147
Local Government and Planning Act (1979) 140, 144
London 5, 135-6, 139, 145
London School of Economics 103
Luard, Evan 147

MacDonald, Rt Hon J. Ramsay, MP 52-5, 61, 100, 103, 198
Mackenzie, Robert 6-7
Mackenzie, W. J. M. 136, 160, 162-3, 179
Mackintosh John 147
McKenzie, Robert 6-7
McKibbin, R. 96, 151
manifesto 40, 191, 202, 219
Maynard, Miss Joan, MP 209
Michels, Robert 106-7, 194-6, 198, 218
Mikardo, Ian, MP 219
Minkin, L. 116, 145, 214
Morrison, Lord (Herbert)
  Attlee at odds with 56
  Attlee's rival, as 55
  local government and 55, 66, 158
  London Labour Party led by 152 158
  NEC membership of 206
  party leadership and 56, 66, 158
  services to Attlee 61
  social class of 103

Mosley, Sir Oswald 55
Moyle, Rt Hon R. D., MP 103
Must Labour Lose? 9

NALGO (National and Local Government Officers Association) 108
NATO (North Atlantic Treaty Organization) 63, 77
NEC (National Executive Committee)
  Benn and 62
  Bevanites on 56
  Callaghan and 59
  class and 4, 95, 102, 121, 215
  Conference and 192
  constituency parties and 55
  electoral college plan 220
  election manifesto and 90 191, 202, 210
  election to 164, 181, 205, 208
  Gaitskell and 57
  Labour Government and 4, 191, 210
  left-wing domination 186, 209, 217
  MP's dominance on 208
  PLP and 4
  parliamentary leadership and 62
  policy-making by 140, 163
  structure of 205-9
  trade union domination of 6, 176, 179, 206-7
NHS (National Health Service) 155
NUM (National Union of Mineworkers) 212
NUPE (National Union of Public Employees) 108
NUT (National Union of Teachers) 108
National Executive Committee. *See* NEC
National Government 142
National Plan 148, 154, 184
Nationalists 15, 41, 139, 143-4
New Towns Act (1959) 156
Noel-Baker, Hon Francis E., MP 103
North Atlantic Treaty Organization. *See* NATO
North Sea oil 41, 185
Northern Ireland 61, 139, 141, 143, 149
Norway 140

Olson, M 116-17, 120, 122
Ombudsman (Parliamentary Commissioner for Administration) 157, 160
Owen, Rt Hon Dr David, MP 100, 144, 147, 155, 191

PLP (Parliamentary Labour Party)
  autonomy of 4, 202-4
  Conference and 203-4, 208
  dominated by the right 3, 90-1
  ideological make-up of 70, 78, 82, 87-9

leadership of 71, 202, 205
left versus right in 3-4, 69-71, 80-1, 88-91
manifesto and 202
membership of 69, 78, 81
NEC and 208
party organisation and 6
powers of 69
progress of left in 69-71, 78, 82, 91-2
representation of voters by 205
re-selection of MP's 90, 202
social composition of 4, 102-4
Parliamentary Commissioner for Administration (Ombudsman) 157, 160
Parliamentary Labour Party. *See* PLP
Parti Socialiste (French Socialist Party) 104, 131, 140, 175-6
Passfield, Lord. *See* Sidney Webb
Political Change in Britain 11
Poplarism 151-3
Popular Front 55
Powell, Rt Hon Enoch, MP 11, 54
Price, Christopher 140

Radice, Giles 147
Rallings, C. 108
Rees, Rt Hon Merlyn, MP 101
Regional Development Incentives: Report (House of Commons Expenditure Committee) 142
Report of the Committee of Inquiry into Local Government Finance (Layfield Committee) 156, 159
Report of the Committee of Inquiry on Industrial Democracy (Bullock Report) 148, 185-7
Report of the Committee on Financial Aid to Political Parties 115-16, 178
Report of the Royal Commission on the Constitution (Kilbrandon Report) 141
Rhodesia 58, 76
Richards, Peter G. 154
Rodgers, Rt Hon W. T., MP 144, 147, 191
Rose, Richard 9
Rowett, J. S. 152, 154

SDP (Social Democratic Party) 1, 202
SNP (Scottish Nationalist Party) 143
SPD (Sozialdemokratische Partei Deutschlands) 13, 174, 176, 178
Scanlon, Lord 180
Scotland
conflicts of interest in 46
Conservative plans for 142
devolution for 61
economic decline of 142
electoral swing in 87
Labour Government expenditure in 141, 143
Labour popularity in 116
Labour rivalry with SNP 143
Labour seats in 5, 139
National Government expenditure in 142
nationalist party in 142-3
Secretary of State for 149
Seyd, P. 116
Sharpe, L. J. 5-6
Simpson Report 207
Shinwell, Baron 66
Shore, Rt Hon Peter, MP 101
Silkin, Rt Hon John, MP 103, 105
Silkin, Rt Hon S., MP 103
Skinner, D. E., MP 209
Slater, Harriet 80
Smith, Ellis, MP 80
Snowden, Lord 103
Social Democracy, Council for 191
Social Democratic Federation 96, 206
Social Democratic Party 1, 202
Social Democrats (Germany) 13, 174, 176, 178
socialism
advanced by left wing 216
ambiguity of 65
Continental 40
effect of Commons service on 70, 88
enshrined in Clause 4 207
imposition from above 146
local road to 153-4
'menace of bureaucracy' 164
nature of Labour Party's 40
Party membership and 117, 120-1
Social Democratic Federation and 96
threat to individual liberty from 157
Webbs on 153
winning electorate to 40-1
Socialist League, the 55
South Africa, Union of 76
Southend East 14
Stansgate, Lord. *See* Anthony Wedgwood Benn
Stead, Michael 139
Stokes, Donald 12, 70, 74
Summerskill, Hon Mrs S., MP 103
Sweden 147
Swingler, Stephen MP 80
Switzerland 13

TGWU (Transport and General Workers Union) 57, 60, 175, 180, 212
TUC (Trades Union Congress)
conference of 211
Labour government and 6
NEC and 209

objections to legislation by 59, 64-5
party-union collaboration 182
strikes and 184
wage limit sponsored by 61
TUG (Trade Union Group) 178
Taff Vale 172
Thatcher, Rt Hon Mrs Margaret 11, 62, 84, 140, 146
Third World 76, 105
Times, The 136, 145, 193
trade unions
affiliation to the Party 171-82, 206-7, 211
block vote of 7, 177, 180, 194, 207, 211-13
Cabinet representatives 64, 100
centralisation 6, 147-8, 151-3, 171, 182-4
Conference, at 199, 210-14
defence policy 64-5
democracy 162, 177, 185-6
electoral college 191, 220-1
entry into politics 103, 172
extension of rights 2, 182
growth of 6, 20, 108, 171, 181
income restraint 60, 172, 181-2, 186-7
influence on the Party 65, 151-2, 175, 178-9, 182, 212
law relating to 37, 45
leadership of 64, 151, 180-1, 185-7, 212
left-wing 59-60, 179-80, 187
militancy of 23, 187-8
NEC and 164, 176, 178-81, 205-9
Party bargains with 3
Party dependence on 6, 96, 171, 175
Poplarism 151-3
power of 37, 45, 65, 171, 178, 183-4, 187-8
right-wing 179, 187, 213
sponsorship of MP's by 97, 178
'social contract' with 60
solidarity 65
Trade Unions Bill 59
wage bargaining by 5-6, 45, 181-2, 187, 213
workers represented by 65, 152, 185
See also TUC
Trades Union Congress. *See* TUC
Transport and General Workers Union. *See* TGWU
Tribune Group 4, 72-3, 83-4, 90, 186
Trotskyists 60

USA (United States of America)
block vote of unions in 212-13
election of party leader in 198
fragmentation of government in 164-5
middle-class in Democratic Party in 105
right-wing party in 51
selection of candidates in 216
social representation in 215
unions and political party in 64, 174, 212-13
Vietnam policies of 120
USDAW (Union of Shop, Distributive and Allied Workers) 220-1
Union of Post Office Workers 211
United Front 55

Vietnam 58, 120

Wales
devolution for 61
economic decline of 143
Labour seats in 5, 86-7
popularity of Labour in 116
Secretary of State for 149
Webb, Beatrice (Lady Passfield) 194
Webb, Sidney (Lord Passfield)
belief in meritocracy 96
Conference on 194
constituency parties on 194
Fabian, as 96, 103
left-wing meetings held by 103
party constitution drawn up by 207
right-wing on 179
trade union vote, on 194
Wertheimer, Egon 52-3, 62, 65
White, Baroness 209
Whiteley, P 4-5, 123
Williams, Philip 3
Williams, Raymond 136
Williams, Rt Hon Mrs Shirley, MP 144, 147, 187, 191
Wilson, Rt Hon Sir Harold, MP
ally of Bevan 57
Callaghan's services to 61
conservatism of 58
devaluation under 58-9
EEC and 58, 60
election victories of 10, 12, 60
electoral defeat of 55
followers disappointed by 62, 65-6
House of Lords and 59
leadership of 53, 57-60
NEC membership of 54
party factions under 58-9, 65-6
resignation of 56, 60
social class of 100-101
Trade Union Bill and 59
Women's Labour League 206

Young Socialists 207